CCCC STUDIES IN WRITING & RHETORIC

Edited by Steve Parks, University of Virginia

The aim of the CCCC Studies in Writing & Rhetoric (SWR) Series is to influence how we think about language in action and especially how writing gets taught at the college level. The methods of studies vary from the critical to historical to linguistic to ethnographic, and their authors draw on work in various fields that inform composition—including rhetoric, communication, education, discourse analysis, psychology, cultural studies, and literature. Their focuses are similarly diverse—ranging from individual writers and teachers, to work on classrooms and communities and curricula, to analyses of the social, political, and material contexts of writing and its teaching.

SWR was one of the first scholarly book series to focus on the teaching of writing. It was established in 1980 by the Conference on College Composition and Communication (CCCC) in order to promote research in the emerging field of writing studies. As our field has grown, the research sponsored by SWR has continued to articulate the commitment of CCCC to supporting the work of writing teachers as reflective practitioners and intellectuals.

We are eager to identify influential work in writing and rhetoric as it emerges. We thus ask authors to send us project proposals that clearly situate their work in the field and show how they aim to redirect our ongoing conversations about writing and its teaching. Proposals should include an overview of the project, a brief annotated table of contents, and a sample chapter. They should not exceed 10,000 words.

To submit a proposal, register as an author at www.editorialmanager.com/nctebp. Once registered, follow the steps to submit a proposal (be sure to choose SWR Book Proposal from the drop-down list of article submission types).

WORKER WRITERS
COMMUNITY ARCHIVING
IN ACTION

Jessica Pauszek

Boston College

Conference on College
Composition and
Communication

NCTE

National Council of
Teachers of English

National Council of Teachers of English
1 E. Main St., #260, Champaign, Illinois, 61820
www.ncte.org

Staff Editor: Cynthia Gomez
Manuscript Editor: Michael Ryan
Series Editor: Steve Parks
Interior Design: Mary Rohrer
Cover Design: Pat Mayer
Cover Image: Melanie Hubbard

ISBN 978-0-8141-0245-9 (paperback); ISBN 978-0-8141-0246-6 (EPUB);
ISBN 978-0-8141-0247-3 (PDF)

It is the policy of NCTE in its journals and other publications to provide a forum for
the open discussion of ideas concerning the content and the teaching of English and the
language arts. Publicity accorded to any particular point of view does not imply endorsement
by the Executive Committee, the Board of Directors, or the membership at large, except in
announcements of policy, where such endorsement is clearly specified.

NCTE provides equal employment opportunity (EEO) to all staff members and applicants
for employment without regard to race, color, religion, sex, national origin, age, physical,
mental or perceived handicap/disability, sexual orientation including gender identity
or expression, ancestry, genetic information, marital status, military status, unfavorable
discharge from military service, pregnancy, citizenship status, personal appearance,
matriculation or political affiliation, or any other protected status under applicable federal,
state, and local laws.

Every effort has been made to provide current URLs and email addresses, but because of the
rapidly changing nature of the web, some sites and addresses may no longer be accessible.

Library of Congress Control Number: 2025934628

CONTENTS

For Bushia

LIST OF ILLUSTRATIONS

NOTES ABOUT TERMINOLOGY/ABBREVIATIONS

FWWCP: Federation of Worker Writers and Community Publishers. FWWCP refers explicitly to the 1976–2007 organization and members who were part of this group within this time frame.

FWWCP/FED refers to the network before 2007 (FWWCP) as well as after 2007 (FED) through their ongoing connections.

TheFED and FED indicate the post 2008 group only. Somewhat confusingly, the FWWCP often referred to themselves as "the fed" in their early days, so the style difference of capitalized letters in TheFED is important for distinguishing the two.

TUC refers to the Trades Union Congress. While there are multiple TUC locations throughout England, I will specifically be referencing the Trades Union Congress Library Collections at London Metropolitan University.

Whenever possible, quotations are kept in the spelling and punctuation of the quoted authors and speakers. Therefore, quotations will include a mixture of Englishes, dialects, and variations on spelling.

ACKNOWLEDGMENTS

I AM OVERWHELMED BY THE number of people who have invested their energy, love, attention, time, and knowledge into this project.

The ideas for this book began at Syracuse University, where I was supported through the Composition and Cultural Rhetoric program as well as the Humanities Center Dissertation Fellowship Program. I would like to thank Lois Agnew, Patrick Berry, Collin Brooke, Kevin Browne, Marcelle Haddix, Krista Kennedy, Rebecca Moore Howard, Brice Nordquist, Eileen Schell, and Tony Scott for the many conversations and unwavering support that allowed me to develop this project. I could not have completed this work without the support from other institutions and colleagues as well. Neal Lerner and Chris Gallagher have been key mentors and advocates of my archival work for many years, and I'm grateful for their ongoing support. I thank CCCC for their support in the form of an emerging researcher grant. To my Texas colleagues and friends who helped me brainstorm early ideas, thank you: Shannon Carter, Ashanka Kumari, and Nicole Farris.

I am indebted to the support I've received at Boston College, including research leave, grants, and stellar mentoring. My incredibly gracious colleagues in the English department have pushed and encouraged me. Thank you especially to Paula Mathieu, Carlo Rotella, and Aeron Hunt, who each read versions and offered such generous and guiding feedback. Aeron Hunt reinvigorated my revisions through her masterful editorial work. Jean Franzino, Rhonda Frederick, Rebekah Mitsein, Tina Klein, Jim Smith, and Min Song provided many needed conversations, words of advice, and moments of support. To my writing partners Christy Potroff, Jovonna Jones, and Eddie Bonilla: Thank you all for your feedback, for motivation, and for your friendship. Thank you to Melanie Hubbard, Dave Thomas, and Ashlyn Stewart, in the digital studio, who have guided me on many questions about metadata and preservation. A fantastic team of graduate collaborators have enhanced my archival work: Noël Ingram, Mike Lyons, Angie Muir, Hannah Clay, Emily Beckler, Justin Brown-Ramsey, Lauren Crockett-Girard, Chase Hockema, and Jo Mikula. And to the undergraduate crew that has embarked on this work through every glitch, new platform, and eye-straining amounts of metadata, thank you: Emma Janda, Hannah Bell, Ellie Strahorn, Madison Schatzman, and Molly Missonis.

To the SWR team: Thanks to Ellen Cushman for her generous and enthusiastic editorial guidance on the proposal and early manuscript; to the proposal and manuscript reviewers who provided such helpful and incisive feedback; to Cynthia Gomez for leading a transparent and efficient production process; to Michael Ryan for such gracious feedback and careful copyediting; and to Kurt Austin: I appreciate your work in making this a smooth publishing process.

This project could never have existed without the support from Jeff Howarth at the TUC Library Collections at London Metropolitan University and Nick Pollard. Between Nick's intuition for saving the FWWCP documents and Nick and Jeff's advocacy for preserving these working-class histories, they have enabled me to be part of this extraordinary history. I am so grateful to both of you for the essential work you have done to give the FWWCP Collection a home and for our continued collaborations.

Each piece of this project is infused with Steve Parks's guidance and collaboration. Steve embodies what it means to be an incredible mentor, collaborator, and human. The energy and time he puts in to support other scholars' work is unparalleled and has taught me so much about community building, particularly in the way he uses resources to strive for more democratic and humane futures.

Thank you to the FWWCP, TheFED, and Pecket members who have brought me into their community. From sharing your stories, teaching me hidden histories, and for making me feel at home in England, thank you. My life has been enriched because of your friendship and perspectives. Especially, thank you to Sally Flood, Dave Chambers, John Malcolmson, Roy Birch, Lucia Birch, Louise Glascoe, Ashley Jordan, Roger Mills, Roger Drury, Tom Woodin, John Sheehy, Florence Agbah, Billy Cryer, Corrine John, and Pol Nugent, as well as to the Stevenage Survivors and Newham Writers groups. I am incredibly grateful to Pol for showing me such friendship, providing a constant home base, and always encouraging conversations about class identity. We have been together through each stage of this project (from archives to post offices to explorations for the best scones), laughing and learning. She has given hours and hours of support and has made the history of Pecket come alive for me.

Friendship continues to deeply impact my work. Dana Powers inspired my love of writing and teaching and gave me the confidence that I could make both parts of my life. Megan O'Neill introduced me to composition and rhetoric, and I've never been able to look back, thanks to her outstanding mentoring and friendship. Erin Frymire has read many drafts, given such valuable feedback, and has constantly cheered me on. Charlie Lesh continues to be a wonderful writing partner and friend who shares my sense of home and working-class values.

No combination of words can ever fully articulate how much this book is imbued with the love, support, and memories of my family. My family shows love through action: cooking me meals, sending homemade care packages, texting and calling with encouragement. Through them, I see firsthand the meanings of hard work and generosity. It is no wonder that I'm drawn to writing about communities when I have been surrounded by one like this my whole life. I could not have imagined more loving grandparents than my Bushia and Dzia Dzia (Annie and Ray) and grandma and grandpa (Paula and Tim)—their memories have motivated me to highlight stories from working-class people, and their love continues to sustain me. Cha Cha Juli and Uncle David are always looking out for me, and I'm immensely grateful for their encouragement, love, and support. Amanda, Georgie, Aurora, and Mila don't let me take myself too seriously and constantly make me laugh. Yet I know they are always rooting for me. Ryan Adamczak and Steph Wisniewski embody all the best things about home and the ways that friendship lasts across states and time, jobs, and life changes. Barb, my mom #2, has listened and offered advice or support across decades, and she grounds me in reminders to live life fully. To Timmy Pauszek, I am so glad to share conversations on this journey, in coffee shops or car rides, at home or across the globe. Vincent Portillo challenges my thinking and makes me laugh every day. From encouraging me to go birding and take breaks (with Goldie) to brainstorming ideas or processing archival documents for days on end with me in London, these moments embody constant support and care—and they mean everything to me.

And finally, thank you so very much to my mom and dad. They are two of the most selfless, generous, and loving people I know. They have always done whatever they could to help our family have a good life, and they have given up many things for me to have opportunities that paved the way for my education. My mother has taught me tenacity through the way she lives her life and has shown me how to advocate for myself and others. My father has shown me unmatched work ethic and strength. I hope that seeing this in writing will somehow convey my immense gratitude and love for everything that you've done for our family.

PERMISSION ACKNOWLEDGMENTS
A version of Chapter 3: Biscit Politics was previously published in *College Composition and Communication* as "'Biscit' Politics: Building Working-Class Educational Spaces from the Ground Up" in vol. 68, no. 4 (June 2017), pp. 655–83.

Some pieces from Chapter 2 and Chapter 4 appear in "Writing From 'The Wrong Class': Archiving Labor in the Context of Precarity" published by *Community Literacy Journal,* vol. 13, no. 2, 2019, pp. 48–68, and in "Preserving Hope: Reanimating Working-Class Writing through (Digital) Archival Co-Creation" in vol. 18 of *Across the Disciplines.*

Cover photo credit: Melanie Hubbard.

All materials featured in the cover collage were originally created by members within the Federation of Worker Writers and Community Publishers or TheFED: A Network of Writing and Community Publishers between the years 1976 to 2014. The ethos of the Federation was to "make writing accessible to all," and many members played an important role in the creation of these documents. The layouts and editing for *Federation Magazines* were done by Pat Smart and Nick Pollard. The preservation of these documents is owed to Nick Pollard and his donation of these materials to the Trades Union Congress Library at London Metropolitan University in 2014.

Archival photos from the FWWCP Collection are used with permission from the TUC Library Collections, at London Metropolitan University.

Archival materials from Pecket Well College are used with permission from Pecket Learning Community.

When I talk about class, I am talking about power. Power at work, and power in the larger society. Economic power, and also political and cultural power

—Michael Zweig, *The Working Class Majority: America's Best Kept Secret*

Class is always in some sense present: whether in our refusal to accept it, our inclination to acknowledge it or insist on it or, as in some cases, our being privileged enough not to have even noticed it.

—John Kirk, *Twentieth-Century Writing and the British Working Class*

WHERE I'M FROM

"Jessie, don't be dumb like me. Be smart, okay? You go to school and keep learning." My bushia[1] (grandma Annie) would say this to me frequently while I was growing up in the predominantly Polish first ward of Dunkirk, New York.

I never doubted how smart Bushia was. Bushia always seemed to have the answer when I needed it. She knew the best secrets to cooking and gardening and healing. She could identify different types of birds and tell you how things worked. She was a voracious reader of religious texts, herbal remedies, how-to manuals, and more. At one point, she mentioned to me how much she wanted to read *Gone with the Wind* because she knew it was popular in her youth. But she didn't think she would be able to. She had heard how big the book was and thought she "wouldn't be smart enough for that." When I brought home a copy of the one thousand-plus-page tome, she stayed up day and night to finish it within the week, noting passages she wanted to discuss with me, questions about characters, opinions about the plot, and words she would look up in a dictionary.

When Bushia died, I cleaned out her room, finding reassurance of how much she valued learning: throughout every text—from anatomy books to mechanical manuals, sewing kits, cooking magazines, scriptures, and bird books—she wrote notes, underlined key phrases, asked questions, and made connections. I can't imagine a moment when she wasn't writing down ideas or findings. However, as much as my memories about her connect to learning, reading, and writing, these moments were only after she had lived many years focused on work: on the farm, tying grapes; in the factory, as a cleaner, as a cook; raising not only her own six children but also me as her grandchild and helping with many of my cousins.

My Bushia was born in 1928 and grew up first speaking Polish on the family's 60 acres of farmland in the village of Arkwright, New York, which sits about an hour west of Buffalo. This was the first piece of land her family owned in America. Bushia called it "the birthplace" because she and her siblings were born in the house there. Her family was poor, living without electricity or indoor plumbing, working long days to sustain whatever they could during the Great Depression. When Bushia attended the one-room school building nearby, she learned English with the mediating help of her classmates, many of whom also spoke Polish. But this learning wasn't easy. Remembering these experiences, Bushia would tell me how, when the teacher asked them to name the picture of a duck, Bushia spoke up and said "kaczka" (duck, in Polish). After all, it *was* a *kaczka*. But the teacher wanted the English word. After being reprimanded and laughed at for the use of Polish or her pronunciation in various moments throughout her youth, Bushia internalized that she was dumb. *Kaczka*, Bushia learned, was not for "smart" students.

While she always enjoyed learning, Bushia never felt "good at it." She never completed high school because her father died unexpectedly after walking home from work in a snowstorm. At only sixteen, Bushia took on her role as the eldest child and went to work at the company her father had worked for—the American

Locomotive Company (or ALCO), since her mother, Katarzyna, had six younger children to care for at home and spoke only Polish. At ALCO, Bushia printed blueprints for items to be manufactured. ALCO was also where she eventually met my Dzia Dzia (grandpa) Ray, who worked there when he returned home from World War II. He was salutatorian of Industrial High School but was drafted into the army and never got to go to college.

Figure 1: American Locomotive Company ID, Annie Schilling (Pauszek). Artifact scan courtesy of Kathleen Pauszek.

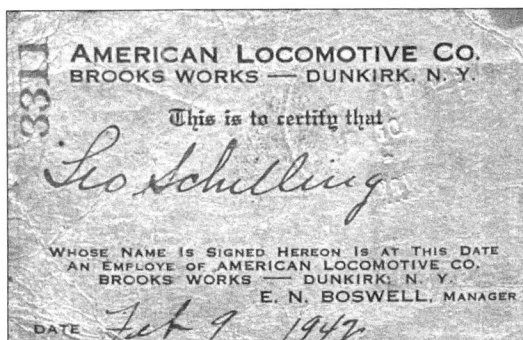

Figure 2: American Locomotive Company employee card, Leo Schilling.

Figure 3: American Locomotive Company
ID, Raymond Pauszek. Artifact scan
courtesy of Kathleen Pauszek.

Despite all the things Bushia knew—two languages, how to
drive and fix cars, how to make blueprints, how to recognize birds
and bones, how to cook, bake, can, and garden, how to make and
mend clothing—she always told me she was dumb. After all, she
"didn't have proper schooling." But I never believed her; I never
will. I don't know when I really absorbed the term "working
class," but once I did, it gave me a framework through which to
understand how she saw herself in terms of class deficits—how
forcefully her socioeconomic experiences influenced her to believe
she was lacking intelligence. I wish I could have explained to her the
various literacy practices she was skilled in through her knowledge
of manufacturing and printing. That her ability to speak, read,
and write in two languages was an asset. I wish that I could have
explained to her what I now know about literacy and language,
about the ways her literacies represent more than what some people
only associated with her class identity, her first language, her lack of
educational degrees, or her family's immigrant history.

The way my Bushia identified as a worker—rather than as a learner or as a writer—is common throughout my family. My uncle Ray, the third of six children, always joked that his generation wasn't smart enough but that my cousins and I had the brains to make up for their lack. He would say, "All the smarts in this family skipped us, but luckily they went to you." I never believed him either. "Smarts" were never the issue; money and opportunities were. So, my family worked in the factories and did janitorial work. They worked manual labor jobs and saved their money so that the next generation could go to college. And we did go to college because of their sacrifices and encouragement—they pushed us, overworked to provide for us, and forcefully reminded us, "You don't want to spend your life in the factories."

My dad is Bushia's youngest child. At eighteen, he started working in a local printshop. For over forty years, he worked in printshops occupied by copiers and Heidelberg presses, machines with buttons and levers at every level. These are machines that make you get your hands dirty, that make you move large loads of paper on them before you step up to check your ink and walk alongside the massive machine on a platform throughout your print run. When I was a kid, my dad would take me into the paper room at work, where a rainbow emerged along the walls with reams separated into color-coded categories. He'd let me pick out sheets of paper to write and draw on. I remember coveting those colorful sheets, feeling I was so special to get them. I remember the pristine color-coding separating my favorite blues from the brightness of red and orange. The precision and splendor of the rainbow paper room was juxtaposed with the loud churning of the machines that loomed over me in the next room—where the black and gray of the machines blended into the dimness of the factory.

During all these moments, I didn't know that I was working class. But I remember that my dad's hands were always stained. No matter how much he washed them, black ink seeped into the crevices of his calloused palms. Black ink circled the sides of his nails and outlined each crease of his skin. Sometimes, people would ask: Why are they so "dirty"? And, until then, I would forget that having ink-stained hands made my dad identifiable in some way. Sometimes, in his few breaks from work, we would look to see if his hands got "cleaner," noting the faded lines and lightened patches. These breaks were never long enough for us to see the full effect.

My family's history is full of literacies embodied through their work beyond classrooms and traditional educational spaces. But as I've reflected on these moments, I've noticed that no matter how much knowledge my family has shared with me, that hasn't changed the fact they have all felt unintelligent because of their educational backgrounds and daily work. Bushia was always reading and writing for herself, and thankfully she would share letters and drawings with me, but she never saw herself *as a writer*. My uncle worked in a factory and spent his life manufacturing printing ink, but he never felt that his knowledge and expertise were significant. My dad was responsible for printing the words and images of others on a daily basis, in a commercial printshop, which allowed for the circulation of writing in various forms. And yet none of them felt part of a writing community.

I always knew that my family's stories were connected to labor, but I've since been able to consider how these are also stories of literacy, about how my family never saw themselves as having permission, intelligence, or knowledge to write and publish their stories—despite making the ink for publishing, printing the words and images of other people, or writing every single day.

CLASS LABORING AND COMMUNITY SOLIDARITY

My family has always instilled the value of hard work in me—but working-class life often fails to bring luxury or even comfort sometimes. It is precarious: too often one rough patch away from disaster. My parents married when they were nineteen years old. When Mom was pregnant with me, she fell and broke her pelvis. When she was twenty-six, the age I was when I wrote my dissertation, doctors told my mom she'd never walk again. Medical debt piled up, and I went to live with Bushia and Dzia Dzia as an infant while my older sister went to our other grandparents, so Mom could attempt to gain mobility and learn about life in a wheelchair. Other people might have said my mom was "disabled," like the doctors did, but even in my earliest memories, I remember us talking about something being "Kathy friendly" or not. This wasn't a euphemism to shy away from bodily decline or pain or anything else—we all knew and lived with the medical realities every day, my mom more than everyone. But it was a way for her and our family to translate and internalize needs in our lives; what was accessible or friendly for her wasn't just about physical mobility but also included attention to costs, transportation access, food restrictions, desires, familial needs, and more. How we functioned as a family included my mom's specific context and multifaceted needs, not about a disability or a disabled person in general. Still, the impacts—financial, mental, emotional, and physical—of disability were there every day.

Because of these circumstances, my dad needed supplemental employment. He worked additional jobs at another printshop, a local supermarket, and doing all the "fix-it" tasks he could around town. Too often, he was working eighty hours a week. But I never seemed to notice the negative side of that because we were always surrounded by our community of friends and family. I didn't know then that he was supporting our family of four on less money per year than I made in graduate school as a writing instructor earning just $16,000. Inflation or not, it shocked me to hear that we lived on so little. But I didn't equate not having those "cool" channels like Nickelodeon and MTV with not being able to afford them. I didn't know that going out to eat regularly was typical for some families because our family cooked at home. I didn't know that hand-me-downs weren't the standard for "new" clothing because each time an aunt or cousin gave me a garbage bag full of clothes, I looked forward to finding what treasures might be there.

One of the proudest memories I have of my dad is him being named Employee of the Month and Employee of the Year so many times that the company decided to name an award after him. But, of course, this isn't the norm. There are many hard-working people who never get awards named after them or any recognition of their labor. I was grateful to see my father get this because we saw how hard he worked every day; however, this award and the pride that came with it didn't prevent my father from being in a precarious position when he got pneumonia and suddenly went into kidney failure. This award—and the twenty-two years and three months of labor he put into this specific printshop—didn't exclude him from living paycheck to paycheck with new medical debt that added to the long-term medical bills for my family. This recognition didn't save him from precarity when COVID-19 caused the company to downsize. Acknowledgment of high-quality work didn't equate to security.

Each of these moments defined my family and the community of my youth, a community that understood economic hardship but also identified with each other and experienced solidarity through shared laboring. So many people in our city lived like us and shared similar values of work, community, and education. Many fathers and mothers worked at Niagara Mohawk moving coal from the freight trains or at Carriage House packaging jelly and peanut butter. Others worked making ink at CPS, manufacturing shovels at True Temper, bottling juice at COTT, or producing dog food at Purina. These factories employed my family and shaped the working-class life we lived. But within these factories, many people were also laid off, like my Dzia Dzia, when ALCO and the Al Tech Steel plants closed. These were the same people you'd see at the Polish clubs in each part of town and share a laugh or a beer with. They were the people who, despite having little of their own, continued to give, baking dozens of coffee cakes at holidays, shoveling and snow-blowing sidewalks for anyone who might not be able to, sharing food from the garden and homemade canned items each summer. Anyone was welcome for dinner without question. In these moments, work wasn't the focus because community ethos and support were. This sense of identification with each other on a human level, combined with the understanding that work was about livelihood and survival, not choice or desire, continues to influence how I see myself in spaces where I live and work.

Deindustrial Impacts

My sense of identity was deeply impacted growing up during what Sherry Lee Linkon calls the "half-life of deindustrialization," specifically in a location "where people live every day with the tangible evidence of the past, in buildings where people once worked and in empty lots where neighbors' homes once stood" (4). As I look back now, it is quite clear how much my sense of identity emerged from living in a small Polish neighborhood in the Rust Belt amid the ongoing aftermath of deindustrialization. I was born at a hospital named for Horatio G. Brooks, of Brooks Locomotive Works Company. Brooks was responsible for bringing the first locomotive to my hometown in the 1850s, and his company later merged to create the same American Locomotive Company (ALCO) where my great-grandfather, my Bushia, and my Dzia Dzia worked. And then ALCO closed. After the closure in the 1960s, the surrounding area became home to other factories such as Roblin Steel and Alumax Extrusions and took on the name Progress Park Industrial Complex (Eck). The restoration of this area was made possible through a donation from local citizens and the Kosciuszko Polish Home Association, which sponsored our hometown monument to Polish war hero Tadeusz Kosciuszko and hosted gatherings for both celebrations and funerals (Ławicki II and Gołębiowski). Unfortunately, the name Progress Park felt like a cruel joke, as I looked at the boarded-up factories where my family members and so many others had lost their jobs. Instead of progress and hope, the half-life continues to inflict deindustrial havoc, according to the New York State Department of Environmental Conservation, with at least one factory maintaining its status as a Class 2 Superfund hazardous waste site, meaning it is a "significant threat to public health or the environment" (Al Tech Update). These hazardous remnants sit just yards away from the local high school where my best friend teaches—a reminder of what used to be and a stark preface for the next generation of graduates.

My hometown is a mixture of Polish pride and factories that closed, each time taking a piece of the city's soul. I lived with daily reminders of deindustrialization, but I was in graduate school before I could articulate how deeply they impacted my own community and so many communities across the world. My own lived experiences have shown me that my class, combined with

Figure 4: Abandoned factory buildings, Dunkirk, New York. Photo by Jessica Pauszek.

my Polish ethnicity, and my understandings of disability affect the things I know as typical. They impact the way I interact with people around me and how I understand myself. These stories illustrate intimate moments of community building that filled each part of my childhood and represent the values and experiences that I bring to my own work.

I didn't know growing up that we were working class. That wasn't a term we used. But these moments of gathering and sharing, of scrimping and making do, were typical for us. They represent the ever-present nature of class that cultural studies scholar John Kirk explains in his book *Twentieth-Century Writing and the British Working Class*. Kirk argues that, on a daily basis, we embody class through both the choices we make and those we do not: "Class, more generally, is implicated in all manner of lived experience: shopping, going on holiday, playing and watching sport; class is what we eat and the way we eat it, where we live, how we work, or not, how we fall in love, how we die" (1). In this way, Kirk notes that class manifests not in a singular and easily definable way but rather "in a plural sense—as *identities*" constantly changing through economic structures and cultural understandings of ourselves in relation to others (28). My identities most forcefully emerged from the languages and customs we shared, where we lived, the work we did, and varying abilities that impacted my family. Of course, however, these parts of my identity intersect with my whiteness, gender, educational background, and more. And throughout this book, I attempt to account for many intersections with class.

LOCAL MEANINGS AND GLOBAL COLLABORATIONS

Although working class, as a term and identity, means different things for everyone, it gives me an entry point for why I care about the projects I describe in this book, focused on working-class communities who speak up against their marginalization and work to preserve their histories. Without these personal narratives here and the stories I'm able to share as part of my research, my family's story would not be preserved or "archived" in many ways. This provides a crucial lens for my commitment to such archival work and the necessity of preservation. And I'm grateful to work by William DeGenaro ("The New Deal"), Daphne Desser ("Reading and Writing the Family"), and Candace Epps-Robertson (*Resisting Brown*) for reminders that family narratives are also valuable for their theoretical insights.

At its core, this book is about inscribing a space for working-class literacies to be preserved—for humanizing, highlighting, and valuing working-class histories, writing, and people. Michael Zweig writes that class involves economic, political, and cultural power (4); this book articulates and celebrates the cultural power that is created when communities can preserve their own stories. Power, in these examples, comes from solidarity through "shared experience, rooted in daily interaction and collaborative labor" (Linkon 3). When I was in graduate school, I learned of a network called the Federation of Worker Writers and Community Publishers that illustrated this sense of community and cultural power through their writing and publishing. The history of this network was something I first learned through reading, but this book has been possible because of meeting the members and learning from them—from their willingness to accept me into their community.

The Federation of Worker Writers and Community Publishers, or FWWCP, was a network of working-class writing groups and publishers that existed throughout England from 1976 to 2007. It also spread transnationally during this time and later evolved into an offshoot organization that has been in existence from 2008 to the present called TheFED: A Network of Community Writers and Publishers. A note about naming: while the FWWCP refers explicitly to the 1976–2007 organization and members from this time period, I use FWWCP/FED to refer to the network before and after 2007 through their ongoing connections. TheFED indicates the post-2008 group only.[2] In 2013, I met members from the FWWCP and TheFED, and this meeting turned into a decade-long (and ongoing) collaboration that has since shaped not only my research but also my personal understandings of class. In our early meeting, I recognized a community that felt familiar to me. But in their writing and through our conversations in the years since, they put words to the feelings of working-class life, of deindustrialization, of struggle and loss, as well as of happiness and accomplishment, that I hadn't read before. Working with this network has afforded me the chance to see how my personal identity can also be a part of the academy, and it has shown me how writing in community can inspire solidarity and social action. How writing can bring us together, heal, and provide an avenue for hope.

Ultimately, this book describes some of the history, processes, and lessons that came out of these collaborations, which I will refer to as the FWWCP Archival Project. This project includes the building of a print and digital collection alongside FWWCP and FED members. It is a project committed to valuing and archiving the labor, history, and testimony of writers and publishers who have been bricklayers and miners, bartenders and chimney sweepers, seamstresses and activists—about those who put their body on the line each day to be able to survive. About people who are imperfect. About those who are often framed as "dumb" or "uneducated" by themselves or others because they have been conditioned to believe that working-class life is a lesser, and under-educated, life. Within this group, I have come to understand more about myself, my life, and the widespread impacts of working-class conditions on physical, mental, emotional, economic, social, and linguistic pieces of our identities. Working-class identity is not just about struggle and loss, though. It is also about community solidarity, friendship, social action, and compassion. There is no singular working-class identity, but there are ways to connect with or differentiate ourselves alongside a multiplicity of class experiences. To be sure, working with a group of British working-class writers who are generations older than I am is not identical to my own experience in America growing up in the deindustrial remnants of a city. But I'm struck by the ways that class identity in these disparate moments and countries has been a unifying force. We have all come to this project understanding the importance of preserving a multiplicity of working-class voices and experiences through writing. Of course, I'm not claiming that all working-class people or working-class ways of life are wholly good or moral, but we start from the premise that these experiences are important and should not be rooted in deficit thinking. Working-class identity is complex and nuanced.

My own identity currently feels like one of being in between. As I type now, I know that the laboring I do—I hesitate to call it that from time to time—is different from the life on the farm and from work at the steel mill, the locomotive manufacturer, the shovel factory, the food production plant, and the print and ink shops ingrained in my family's history. The discursive spaces that I read and write about now differ from the physical spaces where I grew up and the discourses from home. They also differ from the visible and embodied reminders or "class and cultural markers" (1) that working-class studies scholar Janet Zandy describes as the observable reminders that leave an "imprint of work on the body" (4), such as my father's hands, my great-grandfather's missing fingers, and more. Without these memories or these understandings about education and work, about labor and the value of inquiry, about costs of living and the affordances of a community, this book would not exist. It is this understanding of working-class precarity that helped me identify with the community writers and publishers in England and beyond. But meeting and learning from the FWWCP/FED has allowed me to write this book and forced me to navigate the unexpected collision of personal and academic work, research and friendships, working-class life and a now white-collar profession.

I enter this discussion with a humbling knowledge of the bodies that have labored for me to have this opportunity and so many others throughout my life and of the people who have endured both the visible ink-stains, like my father, and the invisible markings of laboring for themselves and for others. Everything that has led me to "be smart," as Bushia told me, and to succeed in my "proper" education is because of them. Through them, I learned about the value of hard work, regardless of reward. I learned the value of inquiry that transcends traditional learning sites and formal instruction. And I saw the value of being part of a community that is connected through our experiences rather than simply defined by a class category.

I wish my Bushia were alive to see that this book embodies what she taught me and all the knowledge she shared. I wish she knew this book would not be possible without the ink my uncle, her son, produced and the printing another son, my father, did. Knowledge and skills like theirs enable this book as much as my own. But it was their labor and sacrifices that made my education possible and helped make this book a reality.

As much as this is about reclaiming and preserving the pasts of working-class people, I also hope this book finds others needing to hear that their lives and literacies are meaningful today.

Chapter 1

Becoming a Worker Writer

I'D LIKE YOU TO IMAGINE that you're an embroidery machinist in East London during the 1970s—the daughter of a Russian Jewish immigrant. You've already raised a family at home, and your swollen hands ache with the repetition of daily factory work. Or imagine you're a janitor in an old industrial town in West Yorkshire—after leaving behind your home country of Ghana, the only community you've ever known—unable to speak much British English or even read and write in your native language. Or imagine you're a dropout from school, looking for work at the local job center in London. You're working class, maybe even without work right now, and for most of your life you've felt stigmatized because of this class identity. Of course, alongside these feelings about class, you're also acutely aware of the educational differences between you and middle-class or posh people—even the way some people look at you when you speak. You see and feel these differences intensely, even though plenty of others do not. But what can you do about it anyway? Then, one day, you see a flyer on the bus or hear something in the local pub about working-class people like you gathering to share and even write stories about working-class life. You want to share your thoughts, but you're not a writer. Still, you're tempted to see what this group does. So, you decide to attend one of these writing and publishing groups in the local community hall.

At your first writing group, you meet people who value your experiences, and they make you realize you have something to say, too. This group gives you confidence and encouragement week after week. With support from this community, you soon begin writing your own life story, some poetry, and even contribute to an

1

anthology connected to memories from home. This network enables you to become a *worker writer,* eventually publishing your life story and collaborating with others in magazines, community history books, and more. Similar to many members, this is the first time that you've felt your life experiences and literacies are meaningful. Feeling the impact of this camaraderie, you bring along others to join—and they bring along their mum, a brother, a friend, or even their children. An entire group of worker writers gather week after week, year after year, inviting new people to share their stories.

This is not solely an exercise of imagination. These experiences represent those of real people—whom I describe throughout *Worker Writers*—who became part of their local writing and publishing groups and eventually founded or joined the Federation of Worker Writers and Community Publishers (FWWCP). The FWWCP began in 1976, when eight writing groups gathered in East London at Centerprise, a combined coffeehouse, tutoring center, and bookshop. Drafting a constitution for their newly formed organization, the FWWCP would later describe their goal as "making writing accessible to all" (Federation, "Constitution"). Within its first two years, the FWWCP developed an executive committee and a membership base across England, revised their constitution, and advertised to new groups to increase working-class involvement in writing and circulating their own histories. In 1978, they also published their first anthology, *Writing,* which included poems, short stories, photographs, drawings, and comic strips. The FWWCP developed from a collective belief that, locally and nationally, working-class people needed a space to express their ideas and be heard in a supportive setting: "The purpose of the Federation shall be to further the cause of working class writing and community publishing, by all means possible" (Federation, "Constitution"). Despite the support from FWWCP members, promoting working-class writing was a precarious endeavor that involved financial instability, as well as humiliating and hostile dismissals on local and national levels from people in positions of power. Given these challenges, the likely story would be that the FWWCP disbanded shortly after its creation.

That didn't happen. Instead of meeting a quick demise, the FWWCP remained an active network for over three decades—from 1976 until 2007. Across the years and amid challenges, the FWWCP expanded to include over 120 member groups and associate groups and thousands of individual members across the globe, including Australia, Canada, France, Germany, Mauritius, New Zealand, Northern Ireland, the Republic of Ireland, Scotland, South Africa, Spain, Sweden, the United States, and Wales. Each group developed a substantial set of works, including self-published booklets or chapbooks, poetry collections, newsletters, magazines, anthologies, and more—a particularly significant feat if you remember most of this community building happened prior to the widespread use of computers, the internet, and mobile phones. FWWCP members have documented some of this history in various anthologies throughout the years (see Federation, *Once I Was a Washing Machine*; Federation, *Writing*; Maguire et al.). However, it's unlikely that most people reading this book will know these texts or how to access them.

Much of the reason that few people (both within academia and beyond) know about the FWWCP is, I believe, connected to the underrepresentation and even forceful dismissal of working-class voices and the resulting lack of a sustainable means of preserving these publications. Most of this history was circulated through ephemeral community channels using low-cost chapbook publications or small print runs available for local distribution. Moreover, without a structure for preservation, these materials were in disarray. As time went on, FWWCP publications were often hidden in people's homes, saved for personal use and remembrance but without a chance of being accessed widely. In effect, a public archive of these materials was missing.

This created a dilemma: The FWWCP developed an extensive, multifaceted, transnational corpus of self-published, working-class writing in the twentieth century, yet few people knew this history or could access these publications because no archival structure existed. This problem, and the subsequent formation of a proper FWWCP archive, is the main topic of exploration here. The process of archival construction, which I will refer to as the FWWCP Archival Project, has required transforming ideas of preservation and circulation into a tangible collection of materials that can be used. This hopeful archival endeavor was contending with very material constraints of space, time, labor, and money, as well as often precarious circumstances of the writers within the FWWCP.

Worker Writers describes the physical process of gathering, curating, archiving, and cataloging thousands of FWWCP materials, which has enabled this network to be preserved for future generations and even to come alive again through print and digital collections. When I mention the FWWCP Archival Project and the work *we* have accomplished, this "we" typically refers to a core group of the FED executive committee[4] (Roy Birch, Lucia Birch, Dave Chambers, Sally Flood, Louise Glascoe, Ashley Jordan, John Malcolmson, and Roger Mills), Nick Pollard (FWWCP/ FED member), Steve Parks (scholar and FWWCP/FED affiliate), Jeff Howarth (Academic Liaison Librarian), and me who were the main group planning and enacting the strategic and logistic work at the foundational stages of the project. While the FED officially formed after the collapse of the FWWCP, many of the executive committee members listed here were involved in both iterations of the organization for varying time frames between the 1976 to 2007 FWWCP and 2008 to present FED. Beyond this core group who motivated and sustained the FWWCP Archival Project, this work has also grown to involve a fluctuating team, which I'll mention in specific moments.

A goal with the FWWCP Archival Project and my goal with this book is to highlight the valuable work done by the FWWCP/ FED and the collaborative process we navigated through moments of precarity, to foreground community values, community representation, and archival access for working-class communities. In doing so, I seek to theorize a model of community partnership and archival work that is attentive to class-based structures such as labor, finances, and materiality. This community-based process helps us uncover new ideas of working-class writing and collaborative archival work, but it also informs pedagogical values that come from communities beyond traditional classroom spaces.

Wanting an archive and creating one are very different things, and I had no experience in developing one before. I started with questions about how conversations of class and labor connect with community writing and archives: Where are working-class writers and writing represented? Where is working-class, community writing stored, preserved, perhaps even taught? As I read scholarship within the disciplines of writing studies and working-class studies, and as I spoke with people doing archival work, I kept coming back to the same points: While many people work with archival materials, few scholars build archives *with* communities, enacting the methods of archival creation and curation. There were also few examples of working-class archives featuring writing *by* community members. Emma Penney and Sophie Meehan's brilliant work creating the Working-Class Writing Archive in Ireland is the most similar project seeking to preserve writing that "has never been catalogued, preserved, or archived before" ("About").

Reasons for a lack of archival building with community members or lack of working-class writing in archives vary. Sometimes, of course, people represented in archives are no longer alive and cannot participate in archival creation. Other times, institutional structures do not invite or value collaboration from nonacademic communities. Moreover, many collections that might include documents on topics connected to working-class life and labor often do not include publications written by workers or are not focused on the processes and products of writing so much as the histories of labor, social movements, and industrial organizing.[5] In creating an FWWCP archive, we were faced with a different task because living FWWCP members actively wanted to archive their network's materials and the writing they created, without the resources to do so.

Material conditions remain a key factor for FWWCP members' writing, as well as impact the FWWCP Archival Project's status. By this, I mean that FWWCP writers often explicitly described the material conditions surrounding them including the presence (or lack) of money, food, housing, jobs, transportation, clothing, health insurance or medical needs, pensions, access to education, and technology for home or school. But these conditions also shaped the precarious circumstances within the FWWCP Archival Project—a project that often had fluctuating material resources. Therefore, I have remained interested in how community partnership work is impacted by (sometimes even stalled by) material circumstances, challenging the economic structure of collaborative projects. At each stage of this archival creation, our work has been affected by the laboring of bodies, influx of finances, access to transportation, physical conditions of the people involved, and changing social conditions.

In making visible the methods of archiving with working-class community members, this book seeks to reenvision writing studies to consider the people, writings, and resources often overlooked in the material processes of preservation, and to instead highlight and learn from them. In effect, this book considers how we might change *where* we look when we think about community writing, literacy, and archives, *who* makes these decisions, and *how* we move through the processing of archival documents.

"YOU'RE ONE OF US":
CLASS SOLIDARITY AND ARCHIVAL HOPE

Before I explain the technicalities of how the archive came into existence, I want to recount a moment that shaped my positionality within this work. A common question academics ask me is how and why did I (an American scholar) end up archiving working-class writing in London? The short story is that in 2013 I traveled to England as a graduate student[6] with the goal of researching working-class community writers. It was the first time during my graduate education that I had seen similarities to my own upbringing. Reading about the FWWCP gave me a community I hadn't found on private college campuses, language I hadn't read in most academic articles, and complex feelings of class that I couldn't always articulate but felt each time I made the three-hour trip from the prestigious university on the hill to my deteriorating hometown. After corresponding with some still-active FWWCP/ FED writers, they invited me to attend their writing groups and their yearly FEDFest (a daylong writing festival) in London.

I applied for internal university grants of around \$300–\$500, a privilege of my R1 institution, and worked to pull together money for a five-day trip. I was a researcher traveling to a new community where I suspected I might be the American outsider.

From the beginning of our interactions, though, FWWCP/FED members didn't treat me like an outsider. This fundamentally shifted our collaboration. Rather than have me stay in a hotel, members opened their homes to me. They offered me tea and baked me homemade Victoria sponge cake. They cooked me proper Yorkshire pudding and roast leg of lamb. They invited me to join their local poetry readings and pub nights. The first instance of this happened when I was introduced to Pol Nugent via email. I hadn't met her before, but she graciously offered to house me while I met with FWWCP/FED members and attended the FEDFest. At this time, she was the Archive Project Director for Pecket Learning Community (otherwise known as Pecket), a long time FWWCP/FED member group. Pol offered to bring me to Pecket's location in Halifax, West Yorkshire, so I could meet some founding members. But our correspondence wasn't only about the technicalities of this meeting or the organization. Instead, it included what foods I wanted to eat, if there were places I wanted to visit, what items I might need for comfort. We shared experiences of caring for elderly family members since this was shaping both of our lives at that moment. These personal interactions impacted my research before I even landed in England.

The moment I arrived, I felt at home. Pol greeted me with a hug as if we were already friends, and we exited the train station as she began explaining the area's history. Driving around, we saw reminders of the city's industrial activity, from the signs for textile mills to the long-lasting canal system. The area was known for its coal mining, woolen mills, and particularly for its quarries of Yorkshire sandstone—the materials that made up almost every building around us. These remnants of working life were juxtaposed with intense greenery of the moors. This reminded me of my hometown, where the natural beauty of Lake Erie was offset by a view of smokestacks from Niagara Mohawk, the coal-fired power plant that sat as a fixture on the horizon—the factory that was a source of air pollution, acid rain, and forever chemicals in the water.

During the drive, Pol and I connected over the importance of labor and the ways that education impacted us. Pol still didn't know my interest in the FWWCP/FED was anything other than academic, but she asked what sort of work my family did. I shared my family's history of factory work and told her about home. I told her about my grandmother's hope for me to get the education that she didn't have. That evening, I met Pol's mum as we ate our dinner and talked at the house. Later that night, Pol explained to me that they had been wondering what an American scholar from a private university might be doing researching British working-class writing from decades ago.

And, then, she said to me, "Ah, Jess, I'm made up.[7] You're one of us."

This moment of identification represents the heart of this project and its emphasis on solidarity. Even across the ocean, I was one of "us": not an outsider or a scholar but a working-class person who fit in with this group. The most significant moments of learning for me with the FWWCP/FED have occurred while drinking tea, sitting across a kitchen table or couch from someone, sharing a pint in a pub, shopping in local markets, or exploring the city with them. Describing these moments allows me to present what members themselves shared with me—in their own words and interactions, now alongside analysis of documents from an archive we have curated together. Being welcomed into someone's home, sharing meals, and including personal details changes your relationship to research. I call this the kitchen-table ethos of the FWWCP Archival Project, which allows me to grapple with blurring the boundaries of personal, community, and academic life.

Without these embodied moments of community solidarity and identification—across generations, location, lifestyle, and class—this project does not exist. These connections have reaffirmed how my piece of deindustrial America echoes FWWCP/FED narratives and have allowed me to see my home discourses as connected to a larger project about preserving the work and testimony of community writers/publishers, many of whom put their bodies on the line to survive as machinists and miners, seamstresses and steel workers. FWWCP/FED members have provided me access points to their network's histories, and they have often shaped the material aspects of how and why the physical collection of documents looks as it does today. They have accepted me as one of their own. Each of these experiences reinforce to me that the working class can form a dynamic, global community, rooted in solidarity—distinctive in multiple ways but still capable of traversing nationalities and races, languages and geographic borders, generations and experiences. These experiences are also how I learned about and gained access to documents that explain the origins of the FWWCP and later TheFED.

THE ORIGINS AND CONTEXT
OF THE FWWCP AND THE FED

By the time the FWWCP officially formed in 1976, it was clear to many working-class people that they needed a space of solidarity. FWWCP members Dave Morley and Ken Worpole describe tensions building in the 1960s and the response as such:

> Groups of working class people, finding that no formal structure dealt adequately with needs and issues as they felt them, began to represent themselves. They took direct action in the form of rent-strikes, the playgroup and nursery movement, squatting, housing and tenants' co-ops, free schools, the creation of local and accessible print and resource centres. (Maguire et al. 11)

Self-representation and organization by working-class writers also began to take off, particularly in the early 1970s, through groups such as Centerprise, one of the first alternative community bookshops in London; QueenSpark Books, which was committed to recording local histories in Brighton; and smaller writing groups such as the Basement Writers in London and Scotty Roads in Liverpool. Tom Woodin, an education scholar and long-time FWWCP member, in *Working-Class Writing and Publishing in the*

Late Twentieth Century, provides a stellar history of working-class writing and publishing movements that shaped the FWWCP, as well as the network's origins and impacts.

The FWWCP developed within and was responding to these contexts, hoping to create an inclusive space for working-class writing when the working class was systematically marginalized. Growing out of this environment, the FWWCP thus became, as member Nick Pollard notes, a "political organisation" that "sought to represent marginalised cultures, specifically the culture of the working classes" (Maguire et al. 179–80). In fact, the FWWCP developed publishing platforms to highlight the experiences of worker writers across England and beyond. Woodin describes the FWWCP as "a historical reaction . . . by those 'left behind' in the wake of publicised cases of upward mobility during the 1960s" (*Working-Class Writing* 8). Building upon these feelings, the FWWCP became a community-based network for working-class people to share their experiences with others who also felt dismissed, discounted, or marginalized in some way, and to act with hope to change limiting and demeaning views of working-class people. Members understood that working-class life and people are full of complexity, and they sought to portray this through writing. Ultimately, through their inclusive publishing practices, the FWWCP was able to represent an array of working-class voices and perspectives in order to push against monolithic ideas of working-class life.

This process wasn't easy. The FWWCP believed in its early days that they might receive support from institutions around them looking to highlight the arts. In fact, the Arts Council of Great Britain gave the FWWCP some money for the printing of their first anthology, *Writing*, in 1978. As described by Greg Wilkinson in the foreword, this publication came about from "a belief that writing and publishing are too important to be left to any minority class," meaning the so-called elite (Federation, *Writing* 3). Fourteen working-class writing groups contributed to *Writing* and provided information they hoped would encourage readers to join future groups. The FWWCP felt excited to gain financial support from local and national grants organizations to create a publication appreciating and valuing working-class writing. Some hoped this would allow the FWWCP to break into mainstream publishing avenues. In 1979, the FWWCP received support from the Gulbenkian Foundation, a charity with private funding for community projects in the arts, science, education, and more. This money allowed FWWCP members to gather with each other for meetings and even allowed them to pay a coordinator who could help organize the expanding national network (Maguire et al. 25). However, this financial support ran out after two years.

Depleted funding caused some of the first moments of struggle in the FWWCP, but it didn't take long until the FWWCP found itself navigating financial woes alongside class stigmas and feelings of dismissal by those in power. In fact, around the same time of the Gulbenkian grant submission, the FWWCP also submitted a grant application to the Arts Council, hoping to secure money again for a paid worker. Without incoming funding, the FWWCP would be limited in their ability to structurally support the network with publishing costs and travel expenses for executive committee members to gather for meetings, the cost of hosting their annual festival, and more. The Arts Council had funded the FWWCP before, so the executive committee was hopeful for continued support, especially after the publication of their anthology. However, the Arts Council's reply to their request issued a devastating emotional and financial blow to the network. The committee indicated that, "No recommendation for grant-aid from the Literature budget can be forthcoming. The members [of the Arts Council] were in one voice in judging the examples of literature submitted: they considered the whole corpus of *little, if any, solid literary merit . . .*" (qtd. in Maguire et al. 149; emphasis added).

Underlying this dismissal was not only the Arts Council's evaluation of what writing was considered "literary" but also an ideology of who was to be considered a writer. In additional correspondence, the Arts Council emphatically reminded the FWWCP that they were not "real writers":

It may seem unfair to you that some people are more talented than others, and indeed it is unfair; however, it remains a fact that talent in the arts has not been handed out equally by some impeccable heavenly democrat. You are right to think that the Arts Council views itself as a patron of the arts. This is, indeed, our function. It is important that we do all we can to increase audiences for today's writers, *not that we increase the number of writers*. There are already too many writers chasing too few readers. Although the real writer will always emerge without coaxing, it is not so easy to encourage new readers into existence! (qtd. in Maguire et al. 153)

The Arts Council's gatekeeping rhetorics—"talent . . . has not been handed out equally"—stood in stark opposition to the FWWCP's belief that everyone can be a writer and that writing should be community based (qtd. in Maguire et al. 153). While it is entirely understandable that the Arts Council could not fund every grant application they received, this response went beyond a standard, respectful rejection and instead positioned the request for funding as almost preposterous. Many FWWCP members felt as if the Arts Council was saying that working-class people didn't have talent as writers or deserve a voice or platform for publishing. These injurious statements serve as reminders of the ways working-class people are often haunted by how others with economic, social, or educational power label them as deficient. Such negative labeling also seemed quite contradictory to the fact that the Arts Council had funded the FWWCP just a few years prior.

The Arts Council's response is not only telling about the ideologies circulating as to who could actually create capital-L Literature but also representative of the diminished governmental support of the arts more broadly. Around the time the FWWCP formed and began publishing, the UK was undergoing a radical shift in collective institutions, and this became particularly detrimental to working-class people. In *Chavs: The Demonization of the Working Class*, Owen Jones describes the economic and social policies that negatively affected the working class in the UK, particularly under Prime Minister Margaret Thatcher's administration from 1979 to 1990, as "the legacy of a very British class war" (10). Jones further argues that Thatcher's

> assumption of power . . . marked the beginning of an all-out assault on the pillars of working-class Britain. Its institutions, like trade unions and council housing, were dismantled; its industries, from manufacturing to mining, were trashed; its communities were, in some cases, shattered, never to recover; and its values, like solidarity and collective aspiration, were swept away in favour of rugged individualism. Stripped of their power and no longer seen as a proud identity, the working class was increasingly sneered at, belittled and scapegoated. (10)

As Jones suggests, Thatcher's administration and its neoliberal economic and social policies proved disastrous for the working class. In fact, after Margaret Thatcher's move from Secretary of State for Education and Science to Prime Minister, the Arts Council budget was cut by 4.8 percent and arts funding was increasingly privatized (Billington). In its first few years of existence, then, the FWWCP was fighting not only classist ideologies about who could produce valuable writing but also the slashing of governmental support and moves toward privatization.

While the Arts Council's rejection could have been the proverbial nail in the coffin, the FWWCP remained determined not to let the statement define their network or prevent its continuation. Instead, the network persisted for over three decades. These were times when working-class people felt the impacts of unemployment reaching close to three million, the 1984–85 miners' strike signaling to many the defeat of the trades unions, and the increased privatization of previously public services—changes that systematically stripped away the working class's collective rights and institutions they relied on. British labor economist Guy Standing describes the years 1975–2008 as the "globalisation era" in which "commodification

[was] extended to every aspect of life—the family, education system, firm, labour institutions, social protection policy, unemployment, disability, occupational communities and politics" (43–44). In other words, during the decades the FWWCP existed, commodification and deindustrialization propelled the British economy and emphasized the value of individuality and entrepreneurism. In the national political establishment, working-class agency and solidarity were dismissed and demeaned rather than championed and valued. The FWWCP's response to this negativity was to build a communal writing and publishing network.

Because the FWWCP lasted for decades, the network also became a space for writers to grapple with ongoing impacts of globalization and deindustrialization, sometimes explicitly through writing about it and other times by disconnecting from these realities. Working-class studies scholars John Russo and Sherry Lee Linkon explain the long term impacts of deindustrialization, noting that its "social costs . . . persist over decades and generations. Jobs lost in the late 1970s continue to affect communities and individuals today" ("The Social Costs" 185)—often through "a complicated set of factors including globalization, offshoring, deregulation, downsizing and technological change" (186). Indeed, deindustrialization has lingered across generations coping with downsizing, economic loss, and the move away from human labor. Deindustrialization and its impacts are imbued in the history of the FWWCP and its unexpected survival. When working-class people in the FWWCP felt diminished by a lack of humanity in the economy, they were able to find community with their local groups. Or, as one publication states, "The FWWCP grew out of a great need for working-class writers to be united and acknowledged . . . The Federation is our collective, national voice" (Federation, "Development Report November 1989").

Intentional community building became key to the FWWCP's perseverance. Building community was an active process, which took the form of writing groups, oral history groups, the collaborative production of working-class publications, community performances, poetry readings in support or protest of various events, workshops, and festivals. Gathering and organizing together, the FWWCP sustained itself against negative social attitudes about the working class and the circulation of rhetorics of individual responsibility. One early member group, named the Liverpool 8 Writers' Workshop, noted that the "best working class writing not only reflects in some ways the experience and struggles of working class people" but can even "directly or indirectly enhanc[e] solidarity" ("Socialist or Working Class?" 4). Moreover, the network also understood the importance of cross-generational collaboration, developing anthologies by and for children, such as *It's Our World As Well: Poetry and Prose by Children of the Federation of Worker Writers and Community Publishers* or *Stories for Children,* as well as including local students as artists in some publications. In later chapters, I will explore the FWWCP's community in more detail, but for now I want to provide a sense of the range of ways the FWWCP moved forward even after being rejected for the Arts Council grant. These examples also point to the scope of what we've worked to preserve as part of the FWWCP Archival Project.

Writing Groups and Membership: Between 1976 and 2007, the FWWCP expanded to include at least 120 groups, amassing thousands of members through its tenure. Because the number of writing groups and members was constantly fluctuating, and each group's identity was malleable, it is impossible to describe them in any singular way. In fact, in *The Republic of Letters,* FWWCP members write, "No two groups are alike, for all have different histories and origins" (Maguire et al. 21). However, at the foundation of these groups was a commitment to gather consistently (some groups met weekly while others met biweekly or monthly) to write together or share writing and provide supportive feedback, often with tea and biscuits. Some groups would also host performance events, produce newsletters or broadsheets or pamphlets, publish individual chapbooks or group anthologies, design and attend peer-taught writing workshops, and hold poetry readings.

Each member group had to apply to the Federation to be sure that they aligned with the FWWCP Constitution, but the ways that each group functioned and the types of writing they produced

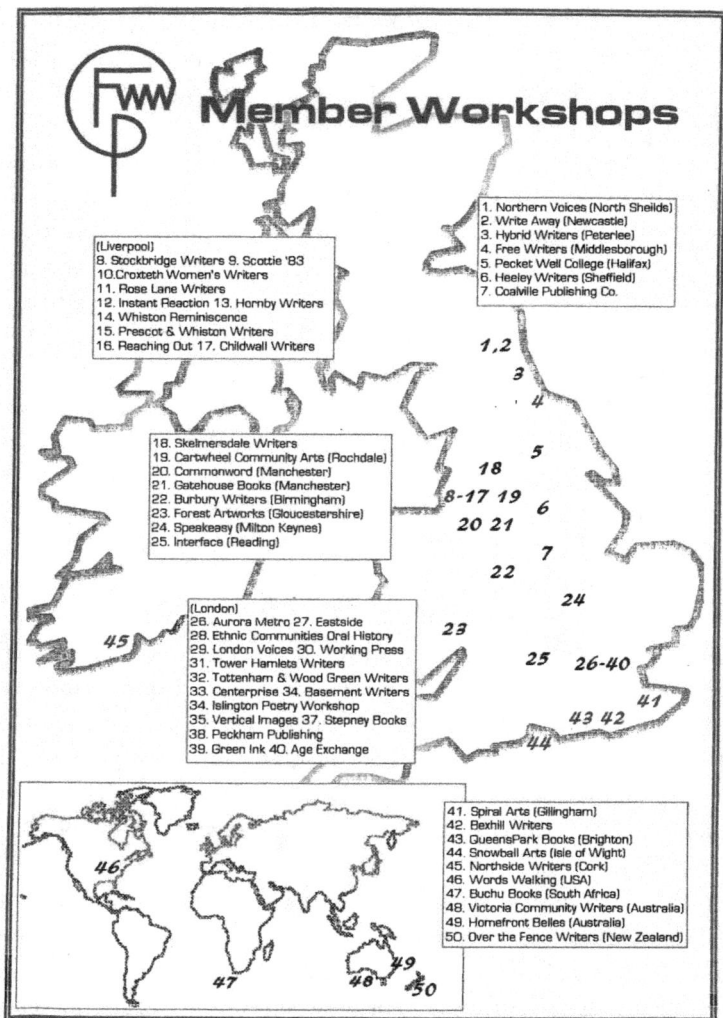

Figure 5: FWWCP Member Groups Archival document, circa 1990s.

varied by topics, genres, dialects, languages, and more. Here is a partial list of some member groups and a brief overview of some types of publications they created:

- The Basement Writers: Began in 1973 in East London and included school children and adults who would publish small booklets of poetry and prose and perform their work through public readings.
- Bristol Broadsides: Published stories about living in Bristol (South West England) and the types of jobs there, including coal mining, rail work, and farming.
- Centerprise Publishing: A cooperative bookshop, youth club, café, and community center in London, committed to supporting adult literacy and publishing through autobiography, history, and poetry.
- Commonword: Located in Manchester, Commonword was considered an "umbrella group" because it included multiple writing groups within the larger Commonword community. Some of these groups focused on stories of sexuality, including the creation of gay and lesbian writing groups, such as Northern Gay Writers, or writing from Black writers and women writers.
- Ethnic Communities Oral History Project: Based in West London, this group published testimony (often multilingual) about the immigrant journey and life upon coming to England.
- GROW (Grass Roots Open Writers): A group from East Sussex, focused on providing "a safe and supportive environment, that helps our members to build their social skills, confidence and self-esteem" ("GROW Constitution").
- Pecket Well College (Pecket): A user-led college for adult basic education in West Yorkshire, which published stories documenting the struggles of adult learners and peer teaching models for basic education.

- QueenSpark: Started as a local Brighton newspaper in 1972 and then developed into QueenSpark Books where members would often publish autobiographical stories that included subjects of childhood, family, going to work, war, and more.
- Stepney Books: Focused on stories about living in the East End of London.
- Stevenage Survivors: Highlighted poetry or stories written about or by survivors of mental distress in the East of England region.

These groups illustrate some of the breadth of the network's content. In addition to the common themes represented within these groups, individual writers took up topics such as industrial labor, food and memories from home, learning struggles, and gendered and racial identity. Local groups also had opportunities to connect to the larger national (and later international) Federation through publications and other collaborations.

Publishing in community with other groups allowed the FWWCP to showcase their capacious national and international membership. Alongside individual or local group publications, the FWWCP published national anthologies featuring writing across the UK, as well as newsletters such as *Fed News* and magazines such as *Voices* and *Federation Magazine* that discussed the organization's international membership and events (such as FWWCP trips to Ireland, France, the US, and more). Each of these publications provided a chance to build community across written text as they shared ideas through the circulation of these publications. While most groups were based in England, many writers identified with other ethnic, regional, or national communities. Beyond its vast geographic scope, the network also brought together writing groups across languages and cultures to establish an inclusive sense of working-class identity.

Working-class identity was the primary focus of the FWWCP, and some of the most meaningful work members did was to expand emergent ideas of working-class identity through both written and in-person discussions and debates. Many members took on such topics as social stigmas that disparaged working-class jobs or unemployment, lack of traditional educational experiences, and varying physical and mental abilities. These became topics of solidarity. Some of this work happened during regional or national events such as writing workshops and performances. The largest event every year was the FEDFest, or the Festival of Writing, usually held over a weekend where members would attend workshops, write, and perform celebratory readings. Bookstalls became a way to sell and exchange published work. These occasions provided members the chance to see what was happening in other regions and allowed them to bring other working-class publications back to their local communities.

Publications Scope: Publishing is a key piece of the FWWCP's legacy because it represents the community-based methods they engaged as well as the diversity of genres and topics covered in FWWCP writing. In the early years, members would publish various types of writing often in chapbooks, duplicated through a mimeograph and held together with staples, relying on collaborative, low-cost forms of publishing. Sometimes groups would gather to cut, paste, and staple, collectively producing a zine-like format. Most distribution and circulation of these publications happened in the streets, at festivals, and within local communities, which further highlighted how the FWWCP enacted alternative literacy practices similar to other countercultural movements. Eventually, some groups were able to publish perfect-bound booklets with an ISBN or ISSN. These are now more easily trackable—but are often out of print or inaccessible.

In their scope, diversity, content, and authorship, the FWWCP publications represent a rich history of working-class testimony in the twentieth and twenty-first centuries that spans generations, geopolitical boundaries, genres and themes, languages and vocations. Indeed, as the network grew through geographical dispersion of members, so did the perspectives on working-class experience that were published. Topics shifted and included key issues such as (but not limited to) migration, women's writing, adult basic education, mental health and wellbeing, family, sexuality, language, politics, food, war, and specific vocations such as dock work, machining, and coal mining. Genres and styles were just as expansive, featuring community-based histories about specific locations, writing groups, and trades in forms such as memoirs, life stories, poetry, recipe books, oral history, and more. Writers used genres that they hoped would keep their history alive for themselves and their families. As a corpus, the FWWCP's publications comprise geographically, ethnically, and racially diverse narratives, which sometimes included multi- or translingual writing, moving between dialects and languages. The content showcased experiences across genders and sexual identities, education and work, as well as various embodied experiences. In other words, working-class identity within this network—as within global working-class populations—was neither homogeneous nor static. A sense of working-class identity and culture, as experienced through the FWWCP, shifted as members aligned, critiqued, and envisioned their own roles and experiences alongside others. The FWWCP, therefore, is an example from which to learn about how working-class individuals and groups came together, as part of a federation, to develop their own literacy practices to push against social and political structures that marginalized their experiences— and in so doing, articulated, developed, and revised rich frameworks of class politics.

COLLAPSE: THE VANISHING ARCHIVE

If we consider the sheer volume and expansiveness of the FWWCP network, alongside the community of writers who supported each other across decades, it represents a significant working-class history. But as I've suggested before, few people today know anything about the FWWCP unless they were a part of it or connected to a member. Without an archive, the texts they created were often ephemeral, changing hands but never fully coalescing to document the FWWCP's history.

Members worked toward developing an archive of FWWCP publications on multiple occasions to showcase for themselves and future generations what they had accomplished together. At one point, an FWWCP worker was able to store publications in a rented office. But saving boxes of publications was much different than the systematic work of processing and building an archive. Over the years, the membership aged, and the FWWCP failed to make many long-standing connections with younger generations. Then, in 2007–08, the struggling membership base faced further problems with the organization's bankruptcy and a global financial crisis.

Without an archive, the FWWCP's legacy was dependent on word of mouth or a chance encounter with a publication in a local shop or family home. After what seemed to be a complete collapse, the FWWCP rebounded slightly in 2008 with an offshoot organization called TheFED: A Network of Community Writers and Publishers the community that welcomed me. But TheFED was a labor of love, grounded in belief in the community, without resources to sustain it. Still, the mission of the new organization picked up on the FWWCP's goal of making writing accessible: "TheFED aims to encourage and promote writing done by ordinary, working-class people and people who may struggle to get their ideas down on paper" (TheFED). TheFED flailed for a bit after its creation, but continues today in a small capacity, including some FWWCP founding members as well as new members with no connection to the original organization.

An archive of working-class writing for the FWWCP/FED would be a statement that this writing was indeed worthy of preservation. The mission and imperative of TheFED became the creation of such an archive. After being told they weren't "literary" enough, or weren't talented enough writers, an archive would reinforce the Federation's value. Yet extensive economic, material, physical, and epistemological constraints prevented this project from being realized in any sustainable way for decades. Without adequate funding, labor, and resources, FWWCP materials mostly ended up in boxes, hidden away, in some instances perhaps never to be recovered. Fortunately, this is not how the FWWCP/FED story ends. Between 2012 and today, a new collaborative structure formed that has enabled the creation of print and digital collections for the FWWCP/FED's documents and publications.

DOCUMENTING THE FWWCP ARCHIVAL
PROJECT/THEORIZING COMMUNITY ARCHIVES

The FWWCP Archival Project has evolved across decades, but I'd like to highlight some of its contours. This includes a multi-year community collaboration focused on archiving publications and other important artifacts from the FWWCP/FED's tenure. The main archival process has taken place across countries—the United States and England—and has involved the intellectual input of dozens of FWWCP/FED members, faculty from multiple universities,[8] special collections librarians, community and university archivists, oral historians, and many graduate and undergraduate students. Through this collaboration, we have officially created the Federation of Worker Writers and Community Publishers Collection (FWWCP Collection, for short), which is housed at the TUC Library Collections at London Metropolitan University (hereafter, TUC Library Collections at LMU).

The FWWCP Collection now amasses over 2,350 FWWCP/FED publications and thousands more administrative archival documents, such as constitutional papers, membership files, meeting minutes, annual reports, correspondence, flyers, workshop descriptions and much more. These documents fill over ninety acid-free, clamshell archival boxes and represent thousands of writers across groups. Indeed, the FWWCP Collection at the TUC Library Collections at LMU is the largest formalized preservation of the entire network's publication history, administrative legacy, and membership.[9] The physical formation of this collection also represents an intellectual and historical commitment to increasing access to working-class writing. In other words, for an institution and group of people to take this on, it has also allowed us to now emphasize the collection's invaluable contribution to preserving working-class writing.

Since 2013, I have led the physical efforts to document, sort, move, and create an inventory of the donated materials for this collection. Before that, Nick Pollard and Jeff Howarth managed the necessary setup and donation of the materials, which took months given that they had to be gathered, packed into a van, and driven from Sheffield to London. From there, Steve Parks and I developed study-abroad summer classes that would allow students from the US to collaborate on processing the collection and to learn from FED members. A few years later, Vincent Portillo joined this core group, and between the pair of us, we have now physically moved, touched, boxed, indexed, or rechecked nearly every single document in this collection in England to get them into their current (and hopefully permanent) storage. These moments of tactile labor have enabled the collection to be used by other researchers, teachers, students, community members, FWWCP/FED members, and their families, as well as created possibilities for future use.

Preserving the network's history and publications has been paramount for all of us from the beginning. But *how* to accomplish this was less certain. And while I am the mouthpiece here, writing about my interpretations, this work is possible only through the collaborative efforts of people involved in the FWWCP/FED. Therefore, I rely on members themselves, as well as their descriptions, memories, writings, and archival documents from the network. These writers let me into their community and made me a member of their network; they trust me to share their stories and be part of preserving their histories. And they continually provide me access to stories that otherwise might be lost. Together, we have experienced moments of happiness and fear, loss and new life, confusion and joy. We have navigated moments of personal struggle and organizational uncertainty (almost to the point of complete disintegration) amid larger socioeconomic and political upheaval: Brexit; the Trump and Biden presidencies; a barrage of prime ministers in May, Johnson, Truss, Sunak, and Starmer; and a pandemic. Given all these moments of community building/breaking, our partnership has developed into an intimate community that traverses geographic spaces and discursive identities.

Of course, this type of community project has been informed by disciplinary voices as well. Preservation, particularly in the form of archives and archival documents, has been a popular topic of research in writing studies for decades now, with plenty of articles, edited collections (Graban and Hayden; Kirsch et al.

Unsettling Archival Research; Kirsch and Rohan; Ramsey et al.) and special issues (Kirsch et al. "Unsettling the Archives") devoted to the topic. The field has produced numerous examples of scholars traveling somewhere to explore archives, hoping to unearth records or stories that others haven't seen or know little about. Within writing studies, a rich history of archival scholarship has informed my thinking on conducting archival research in connection with community literacy practices (Douglas; Epps-Robertson; Schneider); developing oral history and/or archival materials with communities (Carter and Conrad; Mutnick); understanding our embodied presence with archives (M. Powell, "Dreaming"; K. Powell); developing methodologies and historiography (Glenn and Enoch; Gold); discussing archival methods (L'Eplattenier; Ramsey et al.); and finally considering connections to the digital humanities (Enoch, "Coalition"; Enoch and Gold; Rawson, "The Rhetorical Power"; VanHaitsma). These works have grounded my thinking and inspired new possibilities in my understanding of archival work. However, as I began work on the FWWCP Archival Project, I struggled to find disciplinary models to guide a path for the labor involved in actually building the FWWCP Collection.

Few examples focus on the material practice and labor involved in constructing, maintaining, and promoting the use of archives. Here, I mean the minutia of metadata, realities of funding and storage, and the distribution of often-unpaid labor to do the work of moving and accessioning documents, creating finding aids and exhibits, digitizing, and more. And when we began the FWWCP Archival Project, even fewer examples existed. My own experience with not knowing where to turn to for these answers is likely connected to what Michelle Caswell called in 2016 an important "gendered and classed failure" (par. 5) where "almost none of the humanistic inquiry at 'the archival turn' . . . has acknowledged the intellectual contribution of archival studies as a field of theory and praxis in its own right" (par. 4). Indeed, when we began, I had almost no idea of archival studies as a discipline nor how it would connect to writing studies. Since then, Gesa E. Kirsch et al. followed up on Caswell's claim in a special issue called "Unsettling the Archives," but the main curatorial work for the FWWCP Collection was largely completed at this point. Moreover, writing studies had not yet developed a rich theory of community-based archives, which our project demanded. In more recent years, Ellen Cushman ("Wampum"), Janice W. Fernheimer et al. ("Sustainable Stewardship"), and Terese Guinsatao Monberg ("Ownership") have written about communities shaping the content and creation of archives. This dynamic changes the possibilities of archival creation and community partnerships. For instance, when I began this work, writing studies' archival methods were not easily inclusive of the FWWCP/FED's own sense of how the network should be archived, as they were often premised on an economic comfort and institutional support not shared by most FWWCP/FED members. I'd like to build on these discussions with a particular emphasis on creating archives *with* community members based on *their* expertise and embodied experiences.

When we began this work, scholarship rarely mentioned how to negotiate sponsorship between academics and non-scholarly communities, educational institutions and community-run organizations, privatized education and working-class people— all of which also involved a negotiation across geographic borders and material barriers. But that is the work of community-based projects. Take, for example, the question of communicating: Some FWWCP/FED members do not have daily access to computers, internet, or mobile phones. Therefore, checking in via email was not an inclusive or instant form of communication nor were international phone calls across time zones. There was no road map for developing an archive beginning with structural instability. But the exigency for preservation required a reflexive understanding of the community's ethos and goals. In the absence of a scholarly framework and guaranteed institutional support, our methods grew out of precarity and community-driven methodological choices. Therefore, explaining *how* and *why* the FWWCP Archival Project was able to achieve our goal of collaboratively developing an archive provides something quite new to the field. To explore this, I focus on the material negotiations and rhetorical actions our community partnership undertook to *construct* both a print and a digital collection of working-class community writing.[10]

When I say construct, I intentionally mean to focus on the physicality of labor that archival construction requires. This book is not metaphorically about archives,[11] and the material conditions it discusses are not abstractions. Rather, this book is about archival construction made possible through the material movement of people and thousands of documents across cities and countries transported on buses, tube transit, cars, planes, trains, ferries, and more. Movement for some people required wheelchairs and canes; other times, myself and others, as impromptu archivists, walked miles with heavy backpacks. This book is about bodies in motion—about the sorting, boxing, and reboxing of publications and the physical labor it takes to make a working-class collection usable. It is about the purposeful choices we made, and the lifting, touching, reading, filing, and keystrokes needed to process materials into folders and boxes and spreadsheets while developing metadata for print and digital collections. These moments are entangled with the ebbs and flows of life across a decade, including the inconsistent exchange of money and information and the negotiation of changing bodies and minds. However, just as much as this book is about the physicality of labor, it is also deeply ingrained with relationships and communication. From emails, calls, text messages and WhatsApp, social media messages, and handwritten letters across the world, we managed time differences and various access to technologies. Archival construction also involves group discussions, focus groups, workshops about archival strategy and next steps, design brainstorming, and many conversations in kitchens and pubs. It has required laborious grant writing for a glimmer of an opportunity as well as grappling with bits of money pulled together, countless hours of unpaid and invisible labor, and extensive work in the hope that it would amount to something.

Given all of these pieces of uncertainty, this book is also about what happens when forward motion is disrupted—how do we proceed when we meet obstacles in our bodies, minds, funding, and more? Community building is time consuming and unpredictable, but we can learn from and adapt to this process at every stage, if we allow ourselves that uncertainty. Our labor has taken years and is ongoing. But this process has ultimately allowed for the construction of a community archive, which has relied on working-class solidarity and flexible thinking to make a dream become a reality. I have become an unexpected archivist, not formally trained in the work of accessioning and processing but learning it because there was no one else. Sometimes this meant fumbling around, unsure of what came next—revising, reformatting, reindexing, and reboxing as the collection expanded, new information appeared, or we realized new potential uses for the materials. But one thing remained clear to me and to others involved: If we didn't archive the FWWCP/FED's history soon, it was certain no one ever would (or could, given the possibility of loss and deterioration of documents).

My goal here is not to provide a singular model or process to replicate. Just as many of us value writing as a series of processes and revisions, I view archival work in this way: The FWWCP Archival Project continues to be a recursive process of construction and revision, as well as an effort to produce material outputs. Therefore, I discuss key moments (often uncertain and precarious) along our way that contributed to us reshaping our methods. In accounting for the circumstances that shaped our process, we can make visible structures of class that are often left undiscussed or uninterrogated. In effect, I want to provide an example of what happened when we attempted to build an archive that not only documented working-class life but also began from the structural precarity of inadequate financial, spatial, and labor resources. This attention to process offers an opportunity to reframe disciplinary histories as well as accounts of partnership work and archival methods.

I want to push against community partnerships and community archival methods that might assume middle-class stability and values and, in doing so, attempt to shift the focus of such work to the precarity often experienced by working-class (as well as welfare-class and working-poor[12]) communities—the communities most often the site of such partnerships. I want to be clear that I am not suggesting archival projects or community projects that fail to discuss class or precarity are wrong, or that this project somehow avoids all middle-class assumptions and privileges. But my hope is that we can continue to expand disciplinary discussions to be inclusive of class-based discourses as we strive for equitable and ethical community literacy and engagement practices. Documenting embodied stories of class, labor, and materiality allows us to make visible the often invisible labor, decision-making, and experiences that go into community partnership work, particularly with working-class communities. As a subfield of writing studies, community literacy or community engagement scholarship has largely elided discussions explicitly focused on working-class identity and economic precarity. In particular, I aim to focus attention on the representation of literacy practices by working-class community writers who partner with us. If we do not discuss and document these processes, we risk negating realities of class differences and nuances within community projects and institutions, as well as among community members and researchers. We need to explore and discuss precarious conditions, articulate the material importance of varying resources, and reflect openly on how these pieces impact our positionalities within the projects we do. This connects to the materiality of archival preservation and the documentation of history in ways that can also reshape the methods/methodologies we use in community partnerships. As Michael Zweig explains, "Because class is a question of power, understanding class can add to the power of working people" (5). Building on this idea and hope for expanding the "power of working people," I aim in this book to reenvision how we understand class and power in community partnerships. Throughout the FWWCP Archival Project, we have continuously revised our methods, motivated by the centering of community choice and the acknowledgment of power in all stages of archival development.

WHAT THIS BOOK DOES AND WHAT WE CAN LEARN
Throughout this book, I am committed to representing a multiplicity of processes and products as part of the FWWCP Archival Project because there is not just one singular story. I rely on

tactile archival documents from past decades and stories, feelings, discussions, situations, and emotions that emerged during our ongoing curation efforts. For instance, I explore class identity historically within the FWWCP/FED artifacts and how class identity informed the development of the FWWCP Archival Project. I find myself in the middle of pulling together archival documents while being guided by conversations with some members who still survive. In this way, I sometimes rely on Jacqueline Jones Royster's idea of "critical imagination" as a crucial tool for researchers "in questioning a viewpoint, an experience, an event . . . and in remaking interpretive frameworks based on that questioning" with the recovery of past experience (83), when I connect pieces of history and stories through letters, meeting minutes, and publications. Other times, FWWCP/FED members guide and nuance my connections through their perspectives of the documents, events, or moments I discuss. Multiple chapters grow out of moments of dialogue or stories by FWWCP/FED members, most often through our conversations rather than what might be considered a formal interview. The goal with this approach is to further highlight the embodiment of community-based knowledge and collaboration, to give voice to moments that fundamentally shaped this project, especially when they do not fit neatly into university-based methodological frameworks. I hope it allows us to see the humanity of the person and their insights alongside the writing, an affordance not often given when working-class people are dismissed intellectually or viewed only for their labor.

An explicit focus on class and labor is an ethical necessity right now as we consider community literacy and partnership work. But it is also a pedagogical entry point through which to talk about, learn from, and consider working-class writers. Most writing studies scholarship explicitly about class is nearly fifteen years old and has often not been focused on community partnerships. Thus, while historically important (and crucial in my own scholarly development), this scholarship provides neither a current class-based discussion nor an emphasis on community partnerships with working-class communities as the FWWCP Archival Project can do. Rather, writing studies scholarship has focused on working-class students within the composition classroom (Carter and Thelin, although published in 2017; Dunbar-Odom); on how class has been elided within our disciplinary movements and histories (Parks, *Class*); and on how working-class people construct identity outside of the academy, such as in a bar (Lindquist) and in popular culture (DeGenaro, *Who Says?*). Nancy Welch considers "the silence surrounding the rich history of in-the-street working-class rhetorical action against both the interests of capital and the state forces in place to protect capitalist interests" (90), which has informed my own work. But her focus remains more specifically on the composition classroom and on teaching public writing.

I align *Worker Writers* with these projects and am indebted to their legacies, but my focus on community partnerships, such as the FWWCP Archival Project, articulates something different, particularly exemplifying how working-class communities self-organize to build their own inclusive movements, using writing, literacy, and rhetorical acts to achieve these goals. *Worker Writers* quite adamantly centers the literacies of FWWCP/FED members, those who might be described as "factory workers, the unemployed, immigrants, the poor, the homeless, the urban underclass" or the "others" that John Trimbur notes when we tend to think about class in writing studies[13] ("Review" 390). These descriptors of course represent people—writers, learners, workers—community members who, in my experience, are both within academic spaces and outside of academia. What might we learn from an explicit focus on class and labor when we explore and archive the writing and histories of factory workers? What if we restructured community partnerships, classrooms, and university spaces to allow for more of these working-class voices to be preserved and heard?

I believe that seeing, reading, and interacting with texts written by working-class people can signal to students and scholars (working class or not) how class operates in our educational settings and within non-university communities, and this work has implications for how we build partnerships, how we understand the power embedded in archival methods, and how we teach writing and community literacy. Too much of working-class history is relegated to remnants and margins—but what if we feature it? In *The Mind at Work*, Mike Rose writes, "One thing I've learned . . . is the powerful effect our assumptions about intelligence have on the way people are defined and treated in the classroom, the workplace, and the public sphere" (xxxix). Rose's statement here parallels assumptions about intelligence that FWWCP/FED members felt, that my family felt, and that still impact many community members and students. Therefore, I want to dispel these deficit views and instead advocate for explicit attention to working-class voices. This builds on William DeGenaro's call to make the struggles of class inclusivity known: "Rhetoricians can expose scholarly audiences to working-class voices—voices that have much to say about literacy, culture, identity, equality, and democracy. In short, class-conscious rhetorical scholarship can allow working-class voices to participate in important conversations" (*Who Says?* 8). Eighteen years after DeGenaro's invitation, though, writing studies still needs to catch up and particularly needs to explore what it means for working-class people to *participate* in these discussions about literacy, culture, and identity.

Recent years have returned an important focus to precarity and labor *within* the university or within historical examples of work. I want to build on and extend this shift to specifically talk about how we understand class and approach community partnership work, with the writing and words from working-class members informing this discussion. For example, conversations about gendered labor (Enoch, *Domestic Occupations*; Gold and Enoch; Schell) and academic labor involving contingent workers within university settings (Kahn et al.; Kannan et al.; Riedner) have been significant in expanding a focus on work and labor. More recently, student loan debt, particularly for first-generation and working-class students, has also gained renewed attention (Daniel, "Freshman Composition"). Similarly, classroom practice has come into focus, for instance in Christina V. Cedillo and Phil Bratta's suggestion that teachers might "take up positionality stories as one way to engage social class frankly in classroom discussions, to expose the myth that everyone in college is middle class, and to spark conversations about poverty, access, and social justice" (220). Tamera Marko et al. powerfully detail how differently maintenance workers at Emerson College were treated from students at the university, both attending the same translingual English Language Learning class ("Proyecto Carrito"). These pieces are crucial to discussions of economic precarity within and beyond our university structures. This scholarship exemplifies the valuable storytelling and writing that happens when we include workers' experiences in our discussions. But the university community is a key focus for this important work. The FWWCP Archival Project focuses explicitly on working-class writers and class-based discussions that most often are *not* considered part of the university, gleaning insight *from worker writers* who are actively part of historicizing their own archival documents outside of a strictly academic setting. The creation and use of the physical and digital collections have focused on FWWCP/FED members and scholars alike.

In listening to worker writers through the FWWCP Archival Project, I've learned many lessons about how working-class communities negotiate their own understandings of class, literacy, and writing. I am constantly reminded of the importance of sharing embodied moments of class and labor and making visible the conditions that shape our work. In other words, I hope readers here experience a book that focuses both on the archival products we curated together and the process of construction. This dual focus allows us to respect working-class documents and honor the stories that enabled their creation. It also allows us to see how working-class people write about their lives, giving worker writers the chance to contextualize and influence how others may experience their writing now and into the future. To be sure, the tangible creation of the FWWCP Collection in London remains an incredible source of pride and achievement for all of us involved; it is the manifestation of a decades-old hope. For me, this collection is a physical representation of the work I did—something that appeals to me on a deep level. I haven't worked in factories like my family, and that often bothers me. However, alongside these complex personal emotions about work and labor, our collaboration recognizes that workers and their value are much more than simply their production. When we focus on the processes of creating an archive, we see how the hopes, failures, stall-outs, revisions, and successes consistently influenced our partnership and project. We see how the FWWCP Collection is not a product abstracted from people but also richly informed by the processes, networks, relationships, and materiality of the FWWCP Archival Project.

LESSONS LEARNED

As I reflect on what I've learned from my work with community members, a few lessons feel particularly relevant not only to this project but also to others interested in community partnerships or archival work.

Lesson 1: Make Visible the Impacts of Precarity

The FWWCP Archival Project pushes us to consider which voices and histories we preserve and how being attentive to material conditions and their precarity might allow us to do more ethical community and archival work. This means talking about false starts, failures, minor successes, and the process of rebuilding alongside successful products. It also means talking transparently about the labor involved—who does it, why, and with what resources. Rather than gloss over these elements, I've made them part of these chapters.

Worker writers' experiences continue to be relevant not only historically but also currently as we continue to think about global precarity and class today. Within writing studies, discussions of precarity have intensified in recent years (see Daniel, *Anti-Capitalist Composition*; Hesford et al.). Hesford et al. argue that "precarity has become a key concept in scholarly work devoted to the study of the affective, relational, and material conditions and structuring logics of inequality" extending from labor, war, environmental impacts, and more (2). And Daniel suggests that capitalism can be taken up within composition classrooms, considering the destructive impacts of student debt, precarity, and workplace inequality (*Anti-Capitalist*

Composition). These frameworks provide a lens for writing studies scholars to theorize material conditions that impact the world around us, as well as how we labor.

I extend this focus to the materiality of community projects, archival methods, and the histories and writing we in/exclude within the field—thinking particularly about how layers of precarity might impact steps along the way. In the FWWCP Archival Project, precarity has effects on multiple levels, from the material precarity of thousands of publications and administrative documents scattered across England to the ideological and affective sense of whose histories are worthy of preservation. FWWCP/FED materials were held in boxes under beds or inside attics and garages, tucked within desk drawers or among bookshelves—sometimes literally rotting away without proper storage. The condition of these publications—boxed away, hidden in personal archival spaces, and sometimes physically deteriorating—is also an apt material example of working-class narratives. These publications were written by a group of people not readily accepted as writers, who have felt that they and their histories have been neglected, underappreciated, marginalized, hidden, or forgotten.

As we planned our archival processes, the feelings of writers and the physical conditions of the materials developed into new concerns about precarity that we are still navigating on both practical and ideological levels. For instance, depending on uncertain monetary support, mostly volunteer labor, and resources for storage space, archival boxes, and labels, makes it harder to sustain an archive. Most authors still alive at the beginning of the project were older, many with health limitations that would inhibit their ability to network and travel in the ways needed to preserve their publications. Beyond these practical concerns, we faced choices about how to select and categorize texts. Typically, archivists, librarians, or scholars are the decision-makers and knowledge-creators in this work. At times, this threatens to make project management inaccessible or exclusive in ways that privilege professional discourse rather than community insights. In other words, precarity affects who gets to be archived, how, and with what resources. As working-class writers faced economic and social precarity, such as inadequate working conditions and personal feelings of uncertainty, these experiences formed both the backdrop of the materials and the content of the publications.

Exploring FWWCP texts today also allows us to see them within a renewed context of socioeconomic uncertainty, deindustrialization, and globalization. In *The Half-Life of Deindustrialization*, Linkon writes powerfully about the ongoing social and psychological impacts on working-class communities:

> Like toxic waste, the persistent and dangerous residue from the production of nuclear power and weapons, deindustrialization has a half-life . . . [which] generates psychological and social forms of disease, as individuals and communities struggle with questions about their identities and their place in a global economy that has devalued workers and their labor. (2)

While Linkon focuses on American-based literary examples, her framing helps make sense of deindustrialization's harrowing effects—economic, social, psychological, health, and more—on working-class lives more broadly, including writers in the FWWCP. We are still feeling the impacts of neoliberal principles perpetuated by the Thatcher administration in the UK (and Reaganomics in the US) that undermined collective institutions such as trades unions and dismantled once-powerful manufacturing industries. The FWWCP/FED responded to such attacks by providing working-class people a space to reflect and write collaboratively about their occupational knowledges and class experiences. Because most of these publications were written during deindustrialization or its half-life, they often explore social, educational, and political marginalization in writers' lives and the emotional and psychological ramifications of the process. Indeed, many of these writers have witnessed the deterioration or collapse of their own economic, physical, emotional lives and the workplace structures around them. These experiences of job loss and the shift away from manufacturing work continue to resonate in conversations about class identity, the rise of neoliberalism, and the impacts of deindustrialization.

Most of the archival materials and examples that I discuss represent experiences of inequality from laboring to writing to publishing and beyond in the 1970s and into the early 2000s. These worker writers in the FWWCP/FED mostly belonged to the proletariat population of that time. However, as much as this project looks backward at history, it also offers current and future-looking possibilities for students and scholars today thinking about deindustrialization's half-life and the changing social and educational structures around us. As Guy Standing explains, "a profoundly different global class structure is taking shape" with a new class of workers called "the precariat" ("The Precariat and Class Struggle" 4). What if we use these past examples of working-class formations to engage students today, to consider our own class identities and material needs, and to make visible current structures of inequality?

Lesson 2: Methods/Methodology Informed by Community Solidarity
Perhaps the most significant thing I've learned from working with the FWWCP/FED is the power of collaborative work that is informed by the complex hope and action of building solidarity. While I will showcase how the FWWCP/FED built solidarity in other chapters, this has been at the forefront of the process and values of the FWWCP Archival Project, and it has fundamentally shaped the methods and methodologies we've used moving forward in archival curation and construction. In this way, acknowledging precarity doesn't mean focusing only on negative aspects but rather including the possibilities that emerge when people identify across experiences.

Harnessing this power of solidarity and collaboration meant being flexible and open to community members informing, changing, as well as developing their own methods of archival work. Developing a deeply collaborative partnership has enabled us to make embodied stories of class visible through methodological choices. These choices also model the writing pedagogies and practices that the FWWCP/FED built throughout its tenure, including developing community-based, democratic, and inclusive forms of publishing. In this way, the FWWCP/FED provides a community-based approach to writing that can inform our work within and beyond academic/higher education spaces.

Collaborating with FWWCP/FED members has changed, invigorated, and redefined the methods and methodologies within this project in tangible ways. By relying on insights and stories from FWWCP/FED members, our roles within the FWWCP Archival Project are constantly toggling between experts and learners, storytellers and listeners, to collaboratively create a project as a diverse and complex *community*. Listening and valuing community members' knowledge was more than just a methodology, however; the stories they shared were not only significant theoretically but also shaped the tasks at hand and the methods by which we completed them.

The FWWCP Archival Project thus stands as a testament to the possibility of taking what Malea Powell, Aja Y. Martinez, and others have proposed: stories as theory (Powell, "2012 CCCC"; Martinez). Expanding on their insight in connection to the FWWCP/FED texts reinforces the power of community stories as a valuable framework and allows us to reshape archival methods to account for community stories, knowledges, and insights. This approach shaped my orientation to the community I was working with. For me, solidarity was rooted not only in the valuing of literacy practices and writing but also in deeply connected personal friendships— something not typically accounted for in academic work. My Rust Belt beginnings enabled me to identify with FWWCP/FED writers in ways that I didn't account for, and research is no longer something that I can easily demarcate from personal experiences. Jessica Restaino has usefully described the way "intimacy" and "blurred boundaries" or "collapsed walls between the personal, the academic, and the analytic" (9) may push against the division of "friendship and work, between love and research, between the private and the public" (10). Ultimately, Restaino suggests that we might learn something in those moments of possibility that "teach us to become *new* writers, researchers, friends" (13). This blurring feels similar to the community-building that occurred within the

FWWCP Archival Project. While some archival research came from documents and artifacts, most research for this book emerged during moments of being, listening, sharing, eating, drinking, and experiencing.

Lesson 3: Understanding Class Itself as Changing and Contextual
Working-class literacies and working-class identity are at the forefront of this book for the purposes of solidarity, uniting, and acting on commonalities. However, class is not a stable concept with a simple definition or representation, and it cannot be reified into a monolithic category. Indeed, while my moments of identification with FWWCP/FED members in England and beyond were important for collaboration, not all working-class people experience class similarly. Instead, class is complexly interwoven with multiple pieces of our identity, stalling some possibilities while enriching others. Even within the collective of the FWWCP/FED, neither class position nor class culture was uniform. The network never intended it to be, which is why the FWWCP/FED serves as a valuable example of solidarity across positionalities. As we consider how class might shape literacies, we must continually remember that these experiences are contextual and contingent moments reflecting various identities and cultures.

In the 2016 inaugural issue of the *Journal of Working-Class Studies*, Sherry Lee Linkon and John Russo reflect on the nuances of class-based representations: "[W]hat we mean by class changes depending on the situation in which we are using it . . . class involves relations of power, based in economic positions that shape individuals, culture, history, and interests" ("Twenty Years" 5). Such an understanding of class opens interpretations that Linkon and Russo describe as often taking two routes. The first perspective is that "class is a position, a relationship, a social force" (5). The second understands class as "a social category and a culture, which we study by identifying the shared values and practices of working-class culture and by tracing how people express or enact that culture through actions and expressions" (5). In these examples, the circumstances that place a group of people within a class position based on connections to capitalism do not mean that all in that group also share the same values. No matter how we think about class, working-class culture and experience are not homogeneous. Working-class people, similarly, cannot and should not be essentialized as a single group.

While I attempt to tell a story of a collective, a federation, the FWWCP/FED comprises various individual members, groups, histories, and values. Therefore, I discuss working-class identity in ways that account for diverse circumstances. Sometimes, the main group I discuss will, indeed, include a majority of white, British, working-class members; however, even within this group, we find combinations of English, Scottish, and Welsh nationalities as well as Irish—including Northern Irish and Irish national (i.e., not British) identities. These include varying regional, gendered, ethnic, and linguistic backgrounds. During some moments, instances of whiteness, gendered oppression, and racism appear, which I describe with as much transparency as archival documents will allow. Other times, the group I discuss will include transnational community members from the backgrounds already mentioned as well as participants who are American, Australian, Bangladeshi, Canadian, French, German, Ghanaian, Greek, Iranian, Jewish, Polish, South African, Spanish, and more. In other words, the working-class communities I describe are complex, global, multiethnic, and heterogeneous.

This book acknowledges the humanity of the working-class people within the FWWCP/FED—people who, like all of us, are fallible. The FWWCP/FED was not a static entity; it shifted with its membership through moments of insight, learning, argument, love, and even failure. I neither want to gloss over the contentious issues nor allow them to prevent deeper engagement, because looking at these moments, we see how a working-class network defined and redefined itself based on evolving understandings of what it means to be working class. Indeed, the FWWCP/FED network provides us an entry point for conversations about transnational community literacy connected to what sociologist Satnam Virdee describes as "multiethnic coalitions of class solidarity" ("On Race"). This begins with an acknowledgment that there are indeed class differences, that class is experienced differently and even named differently among working and non-working people, but that there are still values about class identity that can allow people to identify with each other across experiences.

Representation of class and class differences—specifically through the voices of the working class—is crucial to this project. Many people within the FWWCP/FED saw class identity as multifaceted—something that was necessarily inclusive of gendered experience, racial identity, and heritage. Therefore, I show how some members grappled with class alongside other identities. At the same time, cautious reflection on how groups function remains crucial, and a true representation of the working class must also include moments of extreme disagreement. I hope that these examples of collaboration and conflict from the FWWCP Collection can nuance future discussions of class identity. Ultimately, the FWWCP/FED history provides a story of solidarity and collective efforts by working-class people, as well as a story about a complex fracturing of working-class communities.

In other words, I am not suggesting that the FWWCP/FED was idyllic or without fault: We must fully acknowledge that some working-class people both within and beyond the FWWCP/FED engage in racist, sexist, xenophobic, or homophobic language and behavior. However, we must not take those attitudes to represent the whole group or class. Instead, what the FWWCP/FED history shows is how a group that was racially, ethnically, and linguistically diverse, as well as differently abled and with various economic backgrounds, navigated understandings of identity and reshaped their rhetorical spaces to suit the needs of members. This group created rhetorical spaces (writing workshops, open forums in publications, and meetings) to specifically make room for debate and for reassessment of objectives and values.

Adapting to changing contexts became a key marker (and point of contention) of the FWWCP/FED network as it sought to expand working-class writing and publishing. Therefore, I trace a shifting understanding of class identity, work, and labor impacted by intense moments of political instability from roughly the late 1960s to the present, across geographical spaces. The FWWCP/FED's history is enmeshed in broader social and political moments: the Vietnam War, the Iranian Revolution, the Women's Rights Movement, the 1984–1985 Miners' Strike, the Falklands War, the Troubles in Ireland, the global financial crisis of 2007–08, and more. Moreover, some members in the early years of the FWWCP write about their own lives, incorporating stories about women's suffrage movements (1910s), the Blitz (1940–41), and memories from World War I and World War II. The purpose of this book is not to cover all these moments but rather to explore how worker writers respond through writing across changing social conditions.

Today, the global representation of class remains significant, as it connects to an increasingly transnational world following a pandemic that has left working-class people in precarious positions worldwide, disproportionately affecting working-class people of color. We can use the FWWCP/FED to see multiple representations of class amid such precarity and acknowledge the everyday literacies that have been overlooked for too long. Class-based discussions within writing studies and across disciplines must continue to think across boundaries, especially considering local and global impacts.

Class—whether it is represented in the FWWCP/FED, a discipline, or in our everyday practices—resists simplistic definitions. It must. Class is not definable in one way, and all of us are so much more than just our class identity. But the FWWCP/FED offers points through which to enter class-based discussions: within writing studies and across disciplines; between recovering literacy and rhetorical histories of the past and practicing ideas for future archival preservation; and in connection with communities, activists, and people interested in the possibilities of writing for social change. The FWWCP/FED also presents a model of collaboration that foregrounds community agency through working-class voices. It is a model that, while flawed in some moments, celebrates working-class culture through shared experiences, actions, and often values about the possibilities of writing in a community. Such possibilities include the belief that writing can indeed impact lives, materially and socially. As teachers and researchers of writing and literacy, I hope we can all be part of such a community.

STRUCTURE OF THE BOOK
AND CHAPTER BREAKDOWNS

Within the history just detailed, *Worker Writers* continues to explore these questions: What happens when we construct archives with community members and consider issues of materiality and class? And what might a methodological framework that is attentive to embodiment and precarity add to archival and community-partnership work? I offer some possibilities throughout this book with a historization of the FWWCP/FED as well as an account of the creation of a physical archive that manifests the value statement that these working-class histories and literacies are indeed worthy of preservation. The examples within this book would not be possible to share in this way without community-member input and access to these archival documents. Therefore, I interweave stories about the FWWCP/FED from archival documents and from the retelling of members themselves to illustrate a dynamic interplay of class-based identity, labor histories, and literacies, which challenge conventional understandings of literacy, archives, and histories within writing studies. Indeed, possibilities for class solidarity can emerge through community literacy and writing networks, which is why I argue that community archival projects must account for lived and embodied experiences as frameworks through which to build community-partnership efforts.

Chapter 2 presents the origins of the FWWCP and the process of becoming a national organization. This chapter begins with Sally Flood, a working-class writer and founding FWWCP member in East London, who became a key access point for me in the FWWCP's history. This chapter considers the material circumstances of where, how, and under what conditions working-class writing has been preserved by Sally and other members of the FWWCP. I describe how the FWWCP developed a kitchen-table ethos that foregrounds community insights and expertise. Such work, I argue, can also transform our disciplinary histories and methods.

I then move, in Chapter 3, from the creation of the national organization to focus on a local manifestation of an FWWCP member group: Pecket Well College (Pecket), a residential college created by working-class people with reading and writing difficulties. This chapter describes how precarity impacted the community organizing, sustainability, and preservation of Pecket as a learning community. Pecket's self-directed model of literacy challenges notions of expertise, redefines intellectual and knowledge-creation work, and reenvisions pedagogical tools based on community abilities. Specifically, I argue that Pecket's agency and literacy practices provide our field with new examples of vernacular, pedagogical, and organizational literacies that we can use to reshape our research methods and especially our community partnership work.

Chapter 4 turns to describing the embodied processes of constructing the FWWCP Collection and showing how our disciplinary methods might be (re)shaped when working with/archiving the literacy practices of disenfranchised populations. Our methods included sorting and accessioning materials, developing metadata, and creating products such as finding aids, reading guides, collaborative publications, and more. Here, I show how the FWWCP/FED members contributed to the FWWCP Collection in tangible ways and the products we created through this collaboration.

The historical and theoretical work of Chapter 5 could only emerge because of the FWWCP Collection's creation. Focusing on the FWWCP/FED's mission and values, I trace key moments concerning how the group maintained a working-class ethos within a changing political landscape, ultimately arguing that the FWWCP/FED created an expansive notion of working-class identity that complexly dealt with intersectional identity politics. To construct this history, I examine central FWWCP/FED organizational documents—which are now archival material—including minutes, publications, and membership reports that show how the group understood, composed, and enacted their ideas of class solidarity. Without the archival process, the documents would not have been available.

The conclusion juxtaposes the history of the FWWCP/FED with the 1966 Dartmouth Seminar, a key event in writing studies history, where over fifty teachers in the US and UK gathered to discuss the teaching of English. Examining these histories side by side, I consider the types of working-class voices that were left out of our field during and after this foundational disciplinary event. I suggest how the material conditions of the Dartmouth Seminar differed from those of the FWWCP as a way of arguing for how the FWWCP Archival Project can help us reshape the ways we see literacy, writing, and writers in complex ways. I offer this as a reimagining of writing studies to attend to the ways in which working-class writers, writings, and histories have struggled to enter the field in tangible ways. Similarly, I argue that we must consciously work toward building community partnerships that are transparent about precarity and inclusive of community members. Only such work, I believe, will make space for inclusive partnerships that highlight and value working-class literacy practices.

Chapter 2

Building a Federation

"WOULD YOU LIKE TO HEAR IT from the beginning?" FWWCP/
FED member Sally Flood asked with a lilt in her voice, not really
a question but an invitation for me to hear her story. The first time
I met Sally[14] was in London, England, at the 2013 FED Writing
Festival (FEDFest). This event was meant to be a chance to discuss
preserving the FWWCP/FED's legacy and how a team might
go about creating an archive. We had planned group discussions
and individual interviews to get insight from members. But time,
money, and geography were not on our side. Many members had
been unable to attend the FEDFest for some years because of their
health, the difficulties of traveling, and the rising costs. We worried
that this might be the last FEDFest. The moment felt urgent. If
something didn't happen then, maybe nothing ever would. So,
when Sally asked me if I wanted to hear her story, I listened. It was
clear from the beginning of our interaction that this was not going
to be the question-and-answer exchange for which most academic
research methods prepared me.

Sally Flood, born in 1925, was an eighty-seven-year-old,
working-class woman from the East End of London.[15] She sat in
her wheelchair, with wrist braces supporting her arthritic arms, and
offered to tell me about how she went from being an embroidery
machinist to sitting with me at a community writing festival, a
proud, working-class mother and published writer. I sat on the edge
of my seat, opening my computer to record us, as well as my phone,
just in case. Over fifty working-class writers, between the ages of
twenty-five and ninety, had come to London for a day of writing,
reading, and, most importantly, community. Sally spoke with such

excitement in her East End accent, known even today as a working-class accent—what some members might say was "not posh like the queen"—while the bustle of the festival surrounded us.

Sally handed me a book of poetry and directed the conversation again, asking if I'd like to hear one of her poems. Of course, I said yes. During her years of embroidery work, Sally would steal bits of time to write poems about her life, only to rip up the scrap poems before her boss came by. In 1979, she published the collection *Paper Talk* through the FWWCP; it sold for 45 pence a copy (roughly 95 cents USD) then. As I listened to her read, I was struck by the starkness of her poem, "Time to Think":

My mind is as grey
As the surrounding streets
And the drizzle repeats itself
In my brain
Too quiet, the factory stands
With empty machines
And crates
Waiting to be moved
Into another overcrowded factory.

Ghosts whisper in my ears
Of other years
Of laughter and voices
Competing against
The deafening roar
Of machinery.

But now, the deathly silence
Sits upon me
And in that silence
Generations of the exploited
Are coming alive
And whispering
Their dreams
And their fears. (Flood, *Paper Talk*)

Sally's writing describes the precarity experienced by many workers—shaped by overcrowding, exploitation, as well as unstable working conditions. While this poem provoked different emotions than the joy I felt being at the FEDFest, it was a stark reminder about what sparked the FWWCP's creation and of what was at stake in our preservation project. It was also a testament to those who began the network and continued advocating for working-class writing for thirty-seven years leading to this moment in London.

My experience listening and being guided by Sally's memories and writing is an example of the community-based methods that have shaped the FWWCP Archival Project. I argue that member-led storytelling and a collaborative ethos motivated the archive's formation and have been essential to enacting archival preservation that is deeply and essentially community based. In fact, situations of storytelling provided key information to guide how we would later gather and even recover some materials. Sally's storytelling allowed me access to knowledge of where the FWWCP/FED writers wrote, how place impacted them, and insider information about the group. She gave me a copy of *Paper Talk* during our encounter to contribute to an archive—crucially, before we even had an archival location established and before we had archival documents sorted and organized. In this way, Sally and others took on the role of archivists in the collection's earliest moments, taking the first steps toward developing and assembling a physical collection of materials, including giving access to their own physical documents that would later become archival materials.

For me, zooming ahead to recount the physical creation of the archive without telling these stories would not only overlook the time and labor involved in this long-term partnership, but it would also risk minimizing the immense contributions that FWWCP/FED members made. They articulated and curated the histories they want preserved, despite their own material and authorial precarity. Therefore, this chapter argues for the central importance of community stories to archival methodology, valuing community literacies by enacting methods that prioritize them, and collaborating with worker writers. In this way, archival methods intertwine with embodied practices of community engagement to the point where the community is an active part of the intellectual and physical development of their own archives. Without their stories and literacies, no archive would exist.

Of course, no one story can (or should) represent the entirety of an expansive network, but I begin with Sally because she has been a key access point for me in understanding the FWWCP/FED community. Even more, Sally embodies the soul and ethos of the network: She was one of the founding members, a longtime fixture on the executive committee, active in publishing anthologies and newsletters, and one of the longest active members in the FWWCP/FED's history through her involvement in groups such as the Basement Writers, Age Exchange, Newham Writers, and more. She continued to write into her nineties. Here, I weave together stories that Sally and others shared with me, as well as insights I've gleaned from their writing, as evidence to consider what the stories of people, writing, and networks in the FWWCP/FED can bring to community literacy, archival studies, and working-class studies. The FWWCP Archival Project challenges how we frame the value of community-generated literacy projects and how we engage the materiality of *where* these writers are writing, *why* their writing emerged, and *how* and by *whom* these writings and histories are being archived. However, this requires a shift in how we engage not only ideologically but also materially with such communities. With the help of Sally's retellings and the archival structures/practices and documents that these called forth, we can begin to account for the precariousness of working-class writing experiences, as well as explore the possibilities of the FWWCP/FED's literacy practices.

LISTENING TO COMMUNITY STORIES AND LITERACIES

The official FWWCP Collection (the boxes creating over ninety linear feet of material) in London began with individual community members cherishing their own collections, which were tucked away in their homes. How did these individual people and collections come together into an archive? In the initial absence of an official brick-and-mortar space, storytelling was a crucial means of connection because it became a way for those in precarious positions to circulate their memories. Scholars of writing and rhetoric have long understood storytelling as a complex practice that is both deeply theoretical and active. Candace Epps-Robertson, for instance, notes that for her grandmother, "stories were not just talk" but "a tapestry of lessons and histories, and often a catalyst for action. . . . Stories have the ability to incite paradigm shifts in our collective histories" (xiii). Just as Epps-Robertson relies on her grandmother's understanding, I have relied on community members to inform my understanding of partnership work through the FWWCP Archival Project. What I learned through this storytelling altered not only how we moved forward with archival choices but also shaped the ethos of the project by creating embodied moments of conversation and action rooted in the desires of the community rather than disciplinary frameworks.

Learning community stories also means being attentive and responsible to the people who share them. Rachel C. Jackson and Dorothy Whitehorse DeLaune, a Kiowa Elder, describe the importance of "community listening": a practice that asks scholars not simply to take stories apart but "instead to put them together by bringing what we know . . . in order to engage and participate in the story, to share in making the narrative rather than taking control of it" (41). While Jackson and DeLaune focus on decolonial storytelling, the communal work of "building [stories] into larger narratives that connect us in relationship with each other" (52) has been a critical component of my time with the FWWCP/FED. The FWWCP/FED enacted and valued this type of community listening as they shared their stories in person during performances and gatherings, as well through newsletters, publications, and writing groups. Each FEDFest was meant to build these relationships and continue the expansion of these stories. And I learned these stories as I was welcomed into members' homes, sat at their kitchen tables, met at community centers, shared car rides, and talked in their local pubs.

As much as the FWWCP/FED valued their stories and welcomed the chance to share them with me and others, they feared what might happen when this circulation stopped. Coming together has become difficult (sometimes impossible) for many FWWCP/FED members, so the priority of the FWWCP Archival Project has been to protect these moments from being forgotten. The archival process would not be complete if only the publications were collected—the embodied process itself is an intrinsic part of the community archive that needs to be preserved for the archive's historical power to be fulfilled. As a testament to the power of community listening, I'd like to continue with a story from Sally Flood that illustrates the powerful circulation of working-class voices, in effect flipping the script to show how the FWWCP/FED members have been teachers, experts, and self-curators of their histories.

ACCESSING FWWCP/FED HISTORIES
AND GATHERING MATERIALS

After my initial meeting with Sally at the FEDFest, she invited me to her home to talk. The next time I was in town, I made my way to East London, taking the bus line toward Whitechapel, in the Tower Hamlets borough. It was pouring rain as I tried to find my way to Sally's street. From the bus and during my hurried running adventure, the sights and sounds of the East End combined multiple languages and cultures: from Bangladeshi to Pakistani restaurants, from the mosque to the Whitechapel Gallery, from fish and chips shops to Jewish bakeries. This was my first time being able to step foot near the places Sally wrote about in her poetry and see the community Sally lived in.

When I got to Sally's house, she answered the door and told me she had been living in this row of Georgian, terraced houses for decades. We entered at ground level, where a staircase with a chairlift allowed Sally to get back to the main living area on the next floor. As we ascended the staircase, Sally pointed me into the kitchen while she moved from her chairlift to her walker and said we would start in there. She already had assembled a collection of photographs, newspaper clippings, and publications for me—personal documents, archived in the private spaces of her home but largely unknown beyond this space. I wondered about the precarious conditions of these documents in front of me: How old were these artifacts? Were there other copies? What would happen to them when Sally could no longer show these writings and tell these stories? Where would they be stored?

My thoughts quickly returned to the present because Sally was talking, and I hadn't set up my computer or phone to record our conversation. "I've made us some tea. Do you 'ave suga' in your tea? I mustn't 'ave it. [. . .] But I've got some biscuits here for us," Sally said, as she looked down at the table and motioned for me to look at her arrangement of FWWCP community publications. I took a biscuit, and she started talking as if in the middle of a story already brought on by the memory of the publication: "You know, I'm still in touch with a few of 'em [FWWCP/FED members], quite a few of 'em actually, which the [FWWCP/FED] groups have done. They couldn't've done it otherwise. So, they all move on and do [trails off]. I'm quite proud of a lot of our members" ("Mount").[16] The importance of this community—of being in touch—and the pride she had in the FWWCP/FED remained a recurring theme throughout our chat.

Being invited into Sally's home and moving within the local spaces she wrote about immersed me into this community in new ways. This new status (as not just a researcher) granted me access to a history and to materials that were inaccessible and often undocumented elsewhere. Sally's restricted mobility made meeting at her home easier for her, but it also allowed her to curate her story with personal artifacts in the way she wanted. For instance, in one collection she pulled out, I saw a poem, "The Brick Lane I See," which mentioned spaces I passed to get to her home:

> Brick Lane is a mixture
> Of aromatic spices
> Curries, onions and bad drains
> Pakistani restaurants
> Jewish trimming shops
> And betting shops
> Down-at-heel workers [. . .]

Pavements and gutters
Are littered with overspill
From dustbins and shops
This is where the immigrant
Looks for fulfillment! [. . .]
This is Brick Lane. (*Window on Brick Lane*)

Throughout this poem, and in many other pieces, Sally remarks on the unpleasant material conditions around her in the borough of Tower Hamlets. Over the years, Sally wrote prolifically, during in-between moments, while caring for her children and while at work. And by visiting Sally at her house, I got to read the text she produced, hear the stories about it, and see where this work emerged.

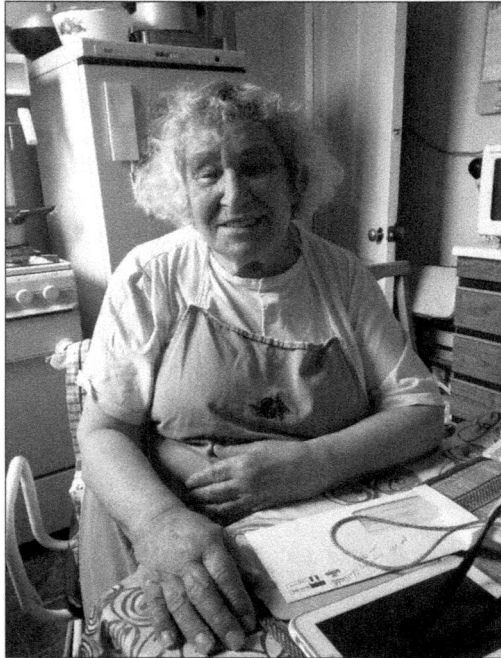

Figure 6: Sally at her home. Photo by Jessica Pauszek.

In the spaces of her home, Sally could conjure memories from her family and the embroidery factory—memories about her past and hopes for the future. Understanding the location and physicality of where this work and writing happened adds another layer of crucial embodied knowledge. Indeed, as Mike Rose reminds us, if we want to take seriously the value of working-class experiences, we must be "vigilant for the intelligence not only in the boardroom but on the shop floor . . . in the classroom, the garage, the busy restaurant, vibrant with desire and strategic movement" (216). And Sally showcases how her knowledge of working-class living and working spaces contributes to what she shares as a writer and storyteller. In addition to Brick Lane, we talked about some FWWCP publications about the Battle of Cable Street, an event new to me but that I soon learned was a moment when the East End community came together to protest a fascist march in 1936. Sally and I talked about writing's ability to document the past across geographic spaces, cultures, and languages. Sally shared stories of how her life was impacted by her father immigrating from Russia to England under political, religious, and ethnic duress during the anti-Semitic pogroms. Here, alongside her familial story of migration, she also offers context for how work and language practices played out in her life:

> I was born here, but my father was born in Russia. But he came over when he was four years old. His father actually came over at the end of the eighteen hundreds but he couldn't get his family over until 1902 because you had to have a job and house and a wage for his family to come over into the country in those days. That's when the pogroms were going on [in Russia]. My grandparents never spoke a word of English. My grandfather was a Hebrew teacher and he was a rabbi at the shul.[17] ("Mount Terrace")

Sally was specifically aware of her Jewish background and remembered not wanting people to know about this: "We were brought up not to tell anyone anything because it was bad times . . . and I used to do a lot of writing because a lot of things that were happening as a child didn't make sense to me" ("Mount Terrace"). We then discussed how some FWWCP publications were written by immigrants who had just come to England and drew from their home languages and experiences to form a community. Writing became an outlet to process these experiences.

Sally then described to me how, as a child, she was evacuated from London twice for multiple months during bombings in World War II, once to Norfolk and then to Torquay. When she returned after the evacuations, Sally thought she might take classes to become a teacher, but her mother decided against it, telling her to become a machinist. Sally left school at fourteen and was, indeed, a machinist for most of her life. While Sally enjoyed writing throughout her early life, she was discouraged from furthering her education and from pursuing activities such as writing and poetry; working and raising a family were supposed to be the main priorities. But that didn't stop Sally from writing as an adult at her machine in a factory in East London. While Sally's stories are personal and unique to her, they also provide examples as to the social reproduction of working-class life—what Paul Willis in *Learning to Labor* has described as "how working class kids get working class jobs" (1), suggesting that "[t]he language in the home reproduces . . . that of work culture" (73). Indeed, Sally's story parallels how many working-class people (not to mention women and those with immigrant families or immigrants themselves) have been pushed away from pursuing writing or education in order to continue doing working-class labor.

For Sally and many other working-class writers, the materials they wrote with, what form their writing took, how their writing was produced and published, and even where they wrote were all connected to the precarious material conditions of working-class life. Take Sally's interest in the genre of poetry, or what Audre Lorde in *Sister Outsider* describes as "the most economical. It is the one which is the most secret, which requires the least physical labor, the least material, and the one which can be done between shifts, in the hospital pantry, on the subway, and on scraps of surplus paper" (116). Working-class studies scholar Emma Penney[18] helped me see these connections in relation to the FWWCP as she described her introduction to working-class women's poetry groups in Kilbarrack, Ireland. About using poetry as a means of expression in these communities. Penney argues, "This speaks to the fact that even form is a class issue. Working-class women's decision to pursue poetry may have been informed by its capacity to mirror their speaking patterns" (n.p.) Although the groups Penney describes were not explicitly part of the FWWCP, Penney and I have been excited to discover how similar working-class writing groups were operating in both England and Ireland during the same period. Through poetry, Sally was able to explore and negotiate her identities—East Ender, working-class, machinist, female, mother, with an immigrant father and a Jewish background—during moments away from work and kids. In many ways, these identity markers—accent, location, class, occupation, gender, ethnicity— negatively positioned Sally in regard to her literacy skills. However, the marginality she felt became integral to her writing. She wrote in spare moments on scrap paper, whenever and wherever she could, first producing ephemera we will never see.

While these moments of writing were individually meaningful to Sally, they took on new meaning when she learned that other working-class people were participating in groups to share their writing. One such group was called the Basement Writers. Joining this group became a turning point in Sally's life, as she went from seeing herself as a machinist to being a worker *writer*. The Basement Writers ultimately provided Sally with confidence and community support that empowered her to keep writing. I could hear the pride in Sally's voice as she described these memories:

Ah, it changed my life, actually . . . I started as a member of the Basement Writers. I had raised 7 children and my youngest was 13 when I saw a flyer in Bethnal Green. I decided to send them [the Basement Writers] a poem, and I couldn't believe it. They published it. And they asked me to join 'em. And that really changed my life. Yeah, because once I became part of the group, it was fantastic. I didn't think I could write, until I joined the Basement Writers. . . . We still keep in touch forty years later. ("FED Festival Interview")

Indeed, the Basement Writers became one of the founding groups of the FWWCP, and so Sally's story offered a perspective on the origins of the Federation and its decades of history.

When I asked how the Basement Writers began, Sally told me another story about how children prompted a writing group. "The Basement Writers began after the children's strike," Sally noted ("FED Festival Interview"). I didn't know what she meant— what children's strike? Sally's account prompted me to look for information in the form of news clippings, interviews, community publications, and more to learn about this history alongside the stories she shared. The "children's strike" that Sally referred to is the Stepney School Strike of 1971. The inspiration for the FWWCP network itself emerged from this protest led by children from the East End who stood up in solidarity for their education. My knowledge of this moment, first learned through Sally, has since become even more textured through archival documents and additional storytelling from FWWCP/FED members. Some of the items Sally mentioned eventually made their way into the FWWCP Collection as archival documents, in effect showing how a moment of storytelling translated to archival choice. These layered stories highlight how FWWCP/FED community members and their histories tangibly shaped the archive that now exists, the histories and publications it contains, and the methods we used to curate it. FWWCP/FED members became knowledge producers and curators of the archival project as they made these histories known to me and others involved.

FROM (STEPNEY) WORDS TO ACTION

In the early 1970s, a teacher named Chris Searle taught at Sir John Cass's Foundation and Redcoat School in East London, England, in a neighborhood environment rife with tensions of race, class, and nationality. But distinctions of class were particularly at the forefront. Sir John Cass School was established just a few years earlier, in 1966 (the same year that scholars gathered for the Dartmouth Seminar that would become a key moment in writing studies lore) with the financial support of Sir John Cass's Foundation, as well as ties to the Church of England. The mission and ethos associated with Sir John Cass's Foundation has a deep history dating back to the 1700s, when Cass, a notable politician and philanthropist, opened his first school with the mission of "educating the poorer children in London" ("Origins and History"). The phrasing here elicits class-based hierarchies that circulated extensively throughout the era of John Cass and into Chris Searle's tenure at the school. Indeed, the use of such rhetoric would stigmatize working-class populations throughout England in the 1970s, particularly in Tower Hamlets, the borough where the school was located and home to the same Brick Lane in Sally's poetry.

Tower Hamlets was marked by overcrowding and poverty during this time as well as being a notable settling place for several populations of immigrants, prompted by events such as the Bangladesh Liberation War of 1971.[19] As in the aftermath of many cases of migration and war, tensions surrounding racial identity and nationality increased, adding to concerns about class and work in an already overcrowded and impoverished community (Glynn). As Searle described in his book *None but Our Words*, there was a "vibrant internationalism" between some students at Sir John Cass School coming from British, working-class backgrounds; others had "origins in Bengal, Ghana, Gibraltar, Cyprus and Jamaica among many other countries" (19).

As a teacher, Searle wanted students to draw from these experiences of class, race, nationality, and more to write about how they felt. He decided to have students write about their lives with the goal of publishing them as a collection called *Stepney Words*. For the first time, many of these students had a chance to write about their lives in a way that was often unavailable to them, pushing past prescriptive grammar exercises and, instead, using writing to describe the world that they saw around them or how they felt in it—even if it meant, as one anonymous student wrote, in *Stepney Words*, expressing the fear of being "nothing special just . . . ordinary" (Searle 1). The feelings this student described parallel the descriptions from other students as well, who felt underwhelmed at the opportunities open to them as working-class kids. The process of creating *Stepney Words* provided a chance for students to be visible, through their words, in a world that often rendered them invisible. This collective experience with writing and publishing, which foregrounded student voices and ideas through poetry, was new to many of the youth involved. The publication presented a way to share their perspectives with an audience both within and beyond the classroom and to circulate their work. Who could dismiss such an engaging form of pedagogy?

During the book's creation, Searle and his students seemed to have the backing of the school; however, this didn't last long. Searle recounts, instead, that support fractured:

> I showed the poems to Trevor Huddleston, the Bishop of Stepney, and he loved them. And it became evident that there was a duality in the church, because the chairman of the school governors who was a priest said to me, 'Don't you realise these are fallen children?' in other words, they were of the devil. But Trevor Huddleston read the poems and then, with a profound look, said, 'These children are the children of God.' So I should have realised there was going to be a bit of a battle. (qtd. in Wells)

With the help of Huddleston and others in the local community, Searle raised £200 (around $488 then) to publish *Stepney Words*. The funds came from "a local plumber, a librarian, a social worker and two other very influential individuals in particular [one of whom was a retired docker, communist, and trades unionist], who were very moved by the students' work" (Searle, *None but Our Words* 20). This local financial support paired with assistance from the student-poets' parents. Warm community support quickly was at odds with the faltering institutional support. FWWCP member Roger Mills interviewed Chris Searle for *Everything Happens in Cable Street* and noted that the school governors wanted something different than the "gritty gathering of work" the students published, which featured "abusive parents, football hooliganism, slum housing, street corner drunks" (94). Poetry itself wasn't the problem in this publication; the problem was that working-class students were writing about the realities of working-class life, and some people didn't want that represented because they believed the poems were "drab" and were written by "fallen children . . . in a state of sin" (qtd. in Mills, *Everything Happens in Cable Street* 94–95). Unfortunately, despite the financial and social backing from students and community members, Searle was fired after the book's release.

The story could end here—with Searle being sacked and the students moving on to their next day at school. What happened instead was a moment where words moved into action—where the concrete manifestation of hope emerged as a protest about working-class writing. Following Searle's dismissal, over eight-hundred students, without his knowledge, skipped school and protested in London's Trafalgar Square so they might "Bring Searle Back" (The gentle author). Alongside the documents Sally had about the strike, she directed me to a blog by a local East End writer known as "the gentle author," who Sally proudly shared had interviewed her as well. The story of the strike made headlines nationally through newspaper stories and television broadcasts. But it also kept circulating through the eventual production of what some students and FWWCP members note as totaling over fifteen . thousand copies of *Stepney Words*. Reality Press, a small Jewish printshop from the East End, initially printed the thirty-two-page book. Searle and students distributed *Stepney Words* around the community, particularly to community centers, libraries, and doctor's offices (Searle, *None but Our Words* 21).

These words of poetry moved the students to take action and inspired multiple community members as well. The circulation of *Stepney Words* and the strike prompted residents of Tower Hamlets to take up writing in ways that would build on these actions, with an ongoing impact.[20] Later in 1976, Centerprise Publishing, a founding member group of the FWWCP, published a reprint called *Stepney Words I & II* with an additional forty pages of text and images, listed with a 35p selling price (about 60 cents). *Stepney Words'* significance is still felt. In 2021, fifty years after the strike, Searle, some students, scholars, and community members gathered in London to discuss the strike, writing, and their impacts. This foundation—of valuing working-class writing and advocating for spaces to be heard—provided community members with a strong sense of solidarity that spurred other moments of individual and collective action. Indeed, this strike was one of the constellating moments for the FWWCP's emergence.[21]

The strike eventually led to the creation of the Basement Writers. As we sat at Sally's kitchen table, she pulled out another batch of documents including *Stepney Words*, showing me newspaper clippings and recounting what she remembered about that time:

> The Basement Writers started with the truants, and then he [Chris Searle] got them writing poetry. He published it [*Stepney Words*]. And they sacked him. The first I heard of it was when it was in the *East London News,* and it showed Chris and showed the children had come out on strike. Thousands of them marched to Trafalgar Square, demanding that he be reinstated. And he started the Basement Writers for the truants. Alan Gilbey was one of the truants and he [later] won a BAFTA award. ("Mount Terrace")[22]

Sally described how the strike motivated her and reflected on why she believed Searle was fired for prompting students to publish poems about their lives that included poverty, loss, and struggle: "They didn't want to give the children a voice, actually! That was the truth of it!" ("Mount Terrace"). Watching the news unfold around her, Sally's own act of writing poems at her embroidery machine suddenly took on new meaning. For Sally and other locals, this suppression of working-class voices was all too familiar. But the children's words and actions influenced Sally and others from the community to find more public venues for their writing. She explained that the protest garnered attention from media outlets such as *The Daily Telegraph* and *The Sun,* which circulated the story throughout the city, particularly to East Londoners who identified with the students and expressed a great sense of pride and support for these children standing up for themselves ("Mount Terrace").

This belief—in the possibility that all people can produce meaningful writing—became the impetus for Searle and others to continue pursuing collaborative writing opportunities that went against dominant ideas of literacy for working-class youth in 1970s Britain. Searle explained the power embodied by the students in his poem "A Strike of Words":

> Anyone can write a poem, I still hold that,
> But you children, sharply organized,
> You made your words strike,
> The words of your class march
> Past middle-class poet-cynics
> Shaking their heads, declaring
> 'Poetry can do nothing,
> It makes nothing happen.'
>
> Yes, *their* poetry can do nothing
> Morosely making nothing of the world,
> But yours, wed to action
> Can take it over. (*Classrooms*)

The capacity to effect change through writing and organizing that Searle describes cannot be overlooked. Here, Searle calls attention to the class-based tension between the commanding words of the working-class students—words that "march past middle-class poet-cynics"—and the diminishing rhetoric of some of the school's leaders who don't believe poetry from students can matter. Referencing W. H. Auden's well-known take on poetry's real-world efficacy and ability, Searle pushes us to consider the possibilities of poetry beyond aesthetics and toward its potential political and social impact. In fact, Searle emphasizes that power emerges from the union between writing and action.

Stepney Words and the school strike began with a valuing of working-class writing and small financial contributions from community members, but its impact lives on today with working-class people who identified with this story. From this history, we see how writing can connect to locally based social and political issues with widespread effects. The production of *Stepney Words* impacted students, Chris Searle, and the East End community;

it also prompted the emergence of a much larger movement of alternative publishing. In fact, *Stepney Words* emboldened working-class people to write about their own experiences—something that unpredictably grew into a worker writer movement. Such an example illustrates how literacy—as a rhetorical act of collectivity, defiance, celebration, and respect—was as empowering for students as it was threatening to the structure and power of institutional support that the school administrators maintained. In this way, through the circulation of the physical book of poems and the news spreading through the protest, these students became part of a conversation in which working-class people of all ages challenged the status quo.

FROM THE BASEMENT WRITERS TO THE FWWCP

The Stepney School Strike served as a catalyst for a larger movement centered on the production of working-class writing through individual groups, starting, in its immediate context, with the Basement Writers. But shortly upon learning that other working-class writing groups around London, Liverpool, and Manchester were gathering, the Basement Writers decided to join them to see what they were doing. About this first meeting, in 1976, Sally notes:

> There were eight groups when we all got together to form a federation. I was there. We were in the pub. I don't drink normally, but we were all there. Scotty Roads from Liverpool, Centerprise [from London], Commonword from Manchester. What we did . . . we had a reading in Centerprise [the East London bookshop], and it was wonderful. It was the first time we all got together. We had a great time. ("Mount Terrace")

Through this collaboration, the Basement Writers became a founding FWWCP group. Now Sally and others had a space in which they could contribute to an even broader writing community—one that would expand further to include groups of multiple generations across continents and languages.

According to Sally, her entry into these writing communities gave her access to new public rhetorical spaces. Rather than ripping up her poems like before, she found a growing audience to support her voice, even when political and labor structures diminished her class: "I ended up reading at the Festival Hall and the Globe, places I would've never dreamt of before. So . . . the [FWWCP] has definitely changed my life. And I'm still part of them" ("FED Festival Interview"). One factor in this success was that Sally gained new "confidence" in herself within the FWWCP ("FED Festival Interview"). In other words, the community ignited a feeling of empowerment and enabled her to circulate her writing. Being part of the Basement Writers and the FWWCP also changed the material conditions of Sally's life in poignant ways that shifted the type of work she did daily. Through the FWWCP, for instance, Sally and another member, Gladys McGee, started teaching a writing course at a rehabilitation center. Members enjoyed it so much that it prompted other groups, such as Age Exchange, to ask them to teach writing for them at hospitals and homes. Sally explained that she had been offered enough writing opportunities to allow her to quit her factory work later in life:

> I must tell you I went through a phase . . . where I was teaching because I was writing and eventually had to give up being a machinist and had to become . . . you know . . . teaching creative writing, reminiscence and that type of thing . . . so I didn't need to sit behind a machine. That was in later life. And that would never have happened without the Federation behind me 'cause I wouldn't have the confidence. But, yes, they've given me a lot of confidence. ("FED Festival Interview")

Writing was the way that Sally and others formed solidarity beyond the workplace because they were able to identify with each other through complexities of work and class. Without such a community, it is all too likely that Sally and others would never have had a choice to leave their machines (if they wanted) or publish their writing.

Sally showed immense pride in her laboring and the skills she had, noting that she "enjoyed machining. I did embroidery, and it was lovely work, and I did dressmaking as well" ("Mount Terrace"). As she described this work, though, she also explained how she was deeply impacted by its physical demands. Looking at her swollen and arthritic hands, Sally explained:

> It hasn't helped me much, though, because of the way you have to hold your hands and it all affects you eventually, then use your knee for the wits. You use every part of your body. . . . I'm proud because I've been able to work and support my myself and my family, and I've never asked for handouts. Whatever we got, we worked for it, and it does give you a pride in what you do. I believe in work. ("Mount Terrace")

Sally's description of the ways embroidery machining impacted her body and caused her hands to become arthritic, alongside her pride in the work she did, embodies a paradox that many working-class people experience. Sally's testimony closely recalls Mike Rose's nuanced account of how work inhibits the body and yet becomes a part of your life as well as your livelihood: "[E]ven as work threatens body and dignity— people tend to seek agency and meaning within the constraints placed on them" (xlviii). Sherry Lee Linkon describes a similar dichotomy in industrial work, which she calls "at once problematic and productive, a source of hardship and a good living, humiliation and pride, alienation and solidarity" (22). While Sally was able to leave her factory job later in her life, many FWWCP members stayed until they were forced out because of deindustrialization. In each of these examples, tensions between a pride in hard work and the toll it takes on the body are consistent.

The trajectory that Sally shared from *Stepney Words* to the Basement Writers to the creation of the FWWCP is certainly recognized by numerous FWWCP members; however, I want to acknowledge the complexity of this perspective (told through Sally's account) when the FWWCP includes many people and memories across decades. Other members might highlight different moments alongside the Stepney Strike to tell additional versions of the FWWCP's formation. For instance, in group interviews that we conducted, Jennifer Harding, Steve Parks, Nick Pollard, and I learned of adult literacy workers such as Sue Shrapnel in London and David Evans in Liverpool who prompted writers in each location to realize they were "doing the same thing," which led to meetings, public readings, and writing groups (qtd. in Harding et al. 15). We describe these as "assemblages . . . of publications, events, travels, and meetings" (17) that made up the FWWCP as opposed to one categorical event, person, or moment that can stand as the origin of the network. Similarly, my goal here is not to say that Sally's story is *the* story of the FWWCP but rather *a* story that is recognizable across many members and has corresponded meaningfully with others' recollections—Sally's is also a story that has shaped my own learning of these histories, given my access to her and the reality that many original members are no longer alive. Not all writers in the FWWCP were able to switch jobs because of their success, and perhaps not even all writers felt entirely positive about the FWWCP. But this vision of the FWWCP network inspiring confidence and belief in worker writers is overwhelmingly described by members across decades.

The complexity of sharing the history of a federation made up of many members is further complicated by the way that members often describe the FWWCP in collective ways. Take for instance, how Sally seamlessly moved between herself and the community she joined. She would say "they asked me to join 'em,'" followed by an indication that she was then part of the group: "We still keep in touch." This movement from the personal "me" and "I" to the collective "we," "us," or "our" is something that Sally constantly did, as she invoked the solidarity she felt. Many times, Sally's personal stories merged into one with the community: "I write about everything. . . . We write in truth" ("Mount Terrace"). This spirit of solidarity highlights how FWWCP members actively embody what it means to be a *community*. Analyzing the possibilities for solidarity in *Social Poetics*, Mark Nowak draws attention to the language working-class writers use:

> *Us* broadens the world of *me, we* opens spaces of solidarity for *I*, and *they* broadens the binary. The plural is a collective with innate potential to embrace, augment, and amplify our

imaginings in ways impossible for the singular. If capitalism, neoliberalism, and empire place their sole emphasis on *my* and *mine,* the social (within any socialism and any social poetics) must insist on shifting emphases in the direction of the pronouns of the first-person plural, toward *we* and *us* and *they,* toward *our, ours, ourselves.* The result of this social shift will be that my burden becomes our burden, my precarity becomes our precarity . . . my joy becomes our joy. (177)

Nowak's analysis captures exactly how individual writers like Sally articulate their relation to the FWWCP. While Sally is one individual *I,* she is also part of the collective FWWCP that purposely positions itself as an *us* and *we.* The FWWCP and now FED members consistently enact this use of the first-person plural to emphasize what the community as a whole represents, which I further explore in later chapters.

Ultimately, through the FWWCP/FED community, Sally gained confidence about her literacy because she saw herself as a writer with valid stories to tell. This began with her membership in the Basement Writers and continues even today. Sally's personal account of the FWWCP/FED is a life-altering sense of community that enabled her writing to be published, gave her confidence, and changed how she participated in the world around her. Leaving school early did not deter Sally from succeeding in the FWWCP and building her network to become a published author, a teacher of writing for other groups, and an advocate for working-class writers. But this boost in confidence was also rooted in the material practice of publishing. For instance, Sally published multiple booklets of poetry including *Window on Brick Lane* and *Paper Talk*; took part in anthologies such as *Move Over Adam;* went to workshops and published with groups such as Age Exchange and Newham Writers; and wrote for the *Federation Magazine* on multiple occasions. Sally was a part of the FWWCP and FED executive committees for many years and shaped the network through its constitution, publications, policies, as well as in less formal ways. The FWWCP shaped Sally and, in turn, Sally shaped the FWWCP. I close this chapter by explaining how Sally (and the FWWCP)'s stories have since impacted the FWWCP Archival Project in tangible ways.

EMBODIED METHODS AND A KITCHEN-TABLE ETHOS

As I think back on sitting at Sally's kitchen table, the way she had curated documents for me, and the way she started our time together with a story, I am reminded of Anne Ruggles Gere's idea in "Kitchen Tables and Rented Rooms: The Extracurriculum of Composition" to include narratives of writing that extend to extracurriculum examples or non-academic writers and non-university spaces, such as a writing club or a group at a local center. Sally brought to life a key component of the extracurriculum or what Ruggles Gere describes as the "cultural work undertaken by various groups of writers" (80). And, just as Ruggles Gere advocates for pushing beyond histories circumscribed to schools, universities, and textbooks (90), Sally's stories pushed me to "consider the various sites" of extracurriculum writing, as well as "the local circumstances that supported its development, the material artifacts employed by its practitioners" (90). I learned from Sally's expertise, in her own home, through the materials she curated for me; through these pieces, I saw firsthand how the FWWCP/FED functioned as its own extracurriculum. With Sally, this idea became embodied through the ethos she shared about the FWWCP/FED on a national and international scale. Sally donated many of her materials, and she also took part in the creation and curation of the official FWWCP Collection, which was significantly impacted because Sally and FWWCP/FED members allowed us to share in their private spaces and stories.

The combination of these intimate and community-based moments has led me to describe this process of learning, interacting, and sharing as not just a form of community listening but also as embodying a kitchen-table ethos, a term that indicates a learning process that accounts for personal moments, often shared in community spaces and *in community with* each other. The content of Sally's stories is significant, but the significance emerged in critical ways through listening and learning that happened in her home, shaped by her memories and artifacts. Community listening is deeply connected to how I see a kitchen-table ethos because it focuses on the possibility of community narratives—the way Sally and other members sought to continue building, circulating, and reanimating them. The ethos, or spirit of the FWWCP/FED revolves around shared moments appealing to a sense of community and inclusivity: as members write together at long tables and share tea and biscuits during their meeting, often within the ordinary spaces of their home and communities. The ethos depends on shared respect and belief that all people should be heard; in these kitchen-table spaces, the FWWCP/FED writers were archiving in recursive ways as they built on collaborative moments of interaction and storytelling. A kitchen-table ethos represents the values, practices, and connectedness that drive the relationships that I've formed with FWWCP/FED members and our work together in the FWWCP Archival Project.

Within the FWWCP/FED, this kitchen-table ethos manifests more specifically in a shared feeling of empowerment, agency, and confidence through writing as part of a group that believes in the power of storytelling, regardless of traditional education, gender, race, nationality, or even ability to read and write. Importantly, though, these moments of community are not dependent upon absolute agreement. In fact, many people noted that during meetings and performances, members could vehemently disagree with each other. Yet whenever they shared writing, everyone applauded, understanding the importance of telling your story. A kitchen-table ethos, in this case, emerges through the FWWCP/ FED's promotion of inclusivity, confidence, collective struggle, and love over the past four decades. This ethos also led many members to open their homes to me during my visits to England. Before my first FEDFest, I was welcomed to Roy and Lucia Birch's home with another FWWCP/FED member, Ashley Jordan. Lucia cooked dinner and baked a Victoria sponge for us to enjoy before we went to the Stevenage Survivors Writing Group, where I met new FED friends who encouraged me to write about my own personal life— not just my academic work—through poetry. We came back after our writing group to chat into the late hours of the night as Roy, Lucia, and Ashley told me their histories of joining the FWWCP. These shared meals and opened homes were not exceptions; rather, they typified the way the FWWCP/FED was built into the texture of everyday life. This shaped my relationship to this work, this community, and my research, making it not an objective thing to study but rather a deeply personal, embodied series of experiences, observations, and stories.

Accounting for such moments, I believe, encourages discussions about the embodied choices we make—choices that have consequences for what we understand as research, materials, and practices, as well as how those practices affect, enable, and sometimes stall our community partnerships. At the heart of the FWWCP/FED are community action, solidarity, and a networked sense of support, bolstered by storytelling; storytelling is a vehicle through which FWWCP/FED members share these moments and encourage each other to live on. To tell the FWWCP/FED's history requires a complicated weaving together of these snippets that showcase how they collaborated and the impacts of creating space for working-class writing.

WHAT WE LEARN AND HOW WE MOVE FORWARD

As I'll continue to show throughout this book, listening to stories and valuing literacy in the FWWCP Archival Project required a new take on the methods that we engaged in to gather, circulate, and preserve information. Community listening is central to the FWWCP Archival Project's methods and methodology—as well as my own. Barbara E. L'Eplattenier articulates the important ways that methods connect to the materiality of research, and I extend this discussion to include the process of curating archives with community members. L'Eplattenier writes,

> Methods are about achieving access to information, about finding aids, about reference materials, about archive locations and restrictions, about the condition of the materials, about the existence of evidence or the lack of evidence, and about the triangulation of information. (69)

L'Eplattenier points out how methods connect to the access we might have and the spaces where we find information—as well as making visible the "time and care used to put that information together"

(75). Methods, when viewed this way, become intertwined with the labor and materiality of archival work.

My research and primary materials were dependent upon me being invited into the homes of FWWCP/FED members—because there wasn't an archive to locate the materials at the beginning. This process of locating and collecting materials and sharing histories involved a commitment to the process of listening and learning from the FWWCP/FED members; drawing attention to this process also makes visible the work that had to happen before I could go to an archive and enact archival methods. Instead, Sally's stories and the process of learning them become part of the *methods* and *methodology*, part of the *recovery*, part of the *history*. These stories allow research to happen, and they fundamentally shift the nature of this project. This approach to archival methods is also deeply connected to the democratic, community-based ethos of the FWWCP and the structures they created as their mission to "make writing and publishing accessible to all" (Federation, "Constitution"). The FWWCP/FED self-sponsored literacy in everyday spaces and created new publics for working-class writers and audiences, even when they were doubted. In doing so, the FWWCP/FED was able to respond to intense social and political environments and invoke an ethos of working-class solidarity. The creation of the FWWCP/FED symbolizes more than any one person, one book, or even one archive.

The embodied nature of the FWWCP Archival Project illustrates how stories like Sally's might travel—from a poem on scrap paper written in a factory decades ago to her kitchen table to a transnational community archive. Sally published her poems to be sold for fifty pence (less than one dollar) at community spaces—publications that became part of the FWWCP Collection (see Chapter 4). Over the decades, Sally performed readings, gave interviews, and even taught reminiscence writing—work that allowed her to quit her factory job. If we read Sally's poems about the "exploited" working-class and "down-at-heel workers," we see that her story is an expression of the physical, mental, and financial hardships felt from a perilous class existence (*Paper Talk*). The tearing up of

Sally's poems becomes a metaphor for the ephemerality of working-class voices still unknown. Together, these texts epitomize the lived experience of the FWWCP/FED and shape the values brought to the task of preservation.

Within Sally's stories, the interplay of governmental and educational power, as well as social/economic influence, deeply impacted perceptions of literacy. In her stories, institutions, individuals, and groups often position the working class as intellectually lacking. Sally recounted this feeling, stating, "Most of our FWWCP writers come from poorer districts and they can tell a very different story. . . . When we first started writing, they told us that it wasn't literacy. Because it was coming from *the wrong class*. And we proved them wrong" ("Mount Terrace," emphasis added). The FWWCP/FED proved many doubters wrong by developing social awareness of class struggles at the local level, producing change with inclusive writing/publishing practices, and advocating that working-class people produce writing that matters. But through the FWWCP Archival Project, we also had the opportunity to grapple with the material challenges of processing these texts as well as the ideological power of what it means for communities to have a say in their own archiving. Privileging the FWWCP/FED as knowledge-makers and curators of their own archive becomes a way to make precarity visible and respond to it collaboratively through our methods of interaction and archiving.

Chapter 3

Biscit Politics

IN 1984, A GROUP OF ABOUT eight working-class, adult learners in West Yorkshire, England, most of whom had severe difficulties with reading and writing, were banned from the premises of their adult education center, Horton House, for a spelling error on a poster: "biscits." After experiencing years of social and educational marginalization, these learners were dismissed from the very structure meant to enable their learning because of this misspelled word. The funding and support for their weekly magazine group was cut off, and they could not be admitted to Horton House without a tutor present. Although these events could have been devastating, the "biscits incident," as it became known, represents a pivotal moment of collective organizing in support of these learners' intellectual and political vision of themselves as citizens and literacy users—a moment of "powerful literacies," enabling them to "ac[t] back against the forces that limit their lives" (Tett et al. 5).

The biscits incident set many events into motion. First, the adult learners within the magazine group at Horton House went to the town hall to try and save their group. They were given a one-year reprieve; however, this still meant they would soon be out of a working space and financial support. The adult learners and their tutor were unhappy with this situation and wanted to find a different structure for their work over the next few months and for their long-term educational ambitions. The desire for increased agency and decision-making led the group to brainstorm how they might create a new learning environment. These changes occurred in multiple steps over the next few years: The group held meetings in people's houses as they planned how they could support their

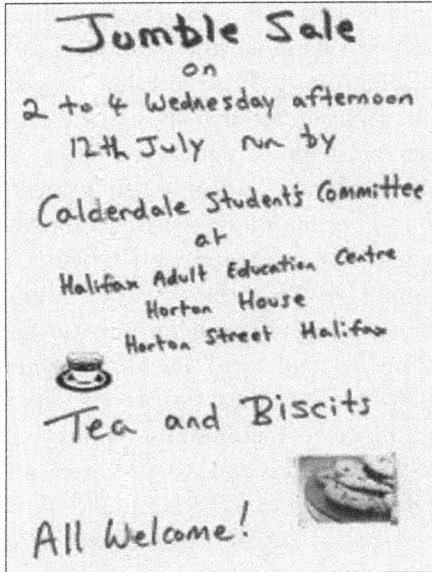

Figure 7: Biscits poster, courtesy of
Pecket Learning Community.

own education; they raised funds through rummage sales; and
they made connections with local organizations in order to acquire
a more permanent space to meet. Through these practical steps,
they also began to establish a community that valued collaborative
learning and challenged power dynamics that privileged only some
learners. In fact, these values prompted the learners to form activist
networks, advocate for an expanded sense of agency for themselves,
and ultimately create Britain's first user-led residential college for
adult learners: Pecket Well College (hereafter, Pecket).[23]

Pecket was both an individual organization, with policies
unique to itself, as well as a member group within the FWWCP
network from 1991 through 2007. It continued to be part of the
new formation of TheFED until 2014 when Pecket ended as an
official organization. Individual members from Pecket (known as
Pecket Wellians) were also part of the FWWCP before Pecket's
entry as a member group. While the previous chapter focused

on how Sally Flood and others experienced the growth of the FWWCP to become a national (then international) working-class network, this chapter turns to West Yorkshire, England, showing an example of solidarity on a regional level that then also connected to these broader transnational endeavors. Pecket emerges within these discussions as a group not only firmly rooted by working-class ideals but also deeply influenced by its members' identity as adults in basic education, or learners with difficulty in numbers and letters. Pecket's membership in the FWWCP was distinct within the network because it was not explicitly a writing group but rather a residential college for adults with learning difficulties. Moreover, in terms of the FWWCP Archival Project, Pecket's trajectory as an organization and members themselves were integral in shaping the FWWCP Collection in print and digital forms, which I'll discuss here and throughout Chapter 4. Pecket is a localized example of a member group that self-built an organization and curriculum and showcased multiple forms of literacy.

Most notable about Pecket's development was that members with various literacy levels and educational experiences were the founders, as well as leaders for the facilitation, teaching, management, and direction of the organization. Put another way, people who struggled with reading and writing, some of whom were even labeled illiterate,[24] created this residential college and kept it going for nearly thirty years. And they did so in a political environment that was actively destroying many working-class institutions in the name of neoliberalism. In this way, the very creation of Pecket can be seen as a form of working-class collective politics.

Pecket demands our attention, then, as it represents the type of history that too often rests at the outskirts of discussions about community literacy and writing studies' disciplinary histories. Indeed, Pecket models an educational community, formed by working-class adult learners that functioned through collective organizing, peer learning, and a belief in equal participation. It demonstrates how such beliefs enabled them to use writing in ways that were useful for their own rhetorical purposes and social needs, including the creation of written products, educational workshops, and courses. Pecket demonstrates how people in marginalized positions have collectively developed literacy and rhetorical skills to combat an educational system that excluded them for years and to resist a political environment that was working to dismantle collective organizing by the working class. Using archival documents and interviews, I illustrate how Pecket's self-directed model of literacy challenges traditional notions of expertise, redefines who participates in intellectual and knowledge-creation work, and reenvisions pedagogical tools and curriculum based on community desires, abilities, and agency.

LOCATING LITERACY EDUCATION IN WORKING-CLASS SPACES

Within writing studies, many scholars are working toward revisionist histories, aimed at uncovering people, identities, and communities that have been disregarded within our disciplinary focus. For instance, David Gold discusses how the field has productively expanded to include "alternative rhetorical traditions and sites of instruction and production" through historiography and archival work that challenges dominant ideologies and historical constructions of the discipline (16). Scholars have used historiographic methodologies in ways that transcend disciplinary, gendered, racial, and sexual borders, by reclaiming writing done from marginalized gendered identities (Glenn and Enoch; Jarratt; Rawson, "Queering") and positioning historiography at the intersection of gender and race (Enoch, *Rhetorical Education*; Royster). In these revisionist efforts, however, little attention has been paid to sustained grassroots literacy sites and communities that were initiated without university assistance. And even less attention has been turned to include a majority of adults who struggled with reading and writing.

Some central examples of such grassroots community organizing for educational purposes are the Highlander Folk School in Appalachia and the subsequent emergence of the Sea Island Citizenship Schools. Myles Horton cofounded Highlander to connect education with social change in Appalachia, to "help the disadvantaged of all races help themselves" and "to challenge the status quo in the name of democracy and brotherhood" (Jacobs 4). This idea of education later prompted the Sea Island Citizenship Schools, which provided assistance to Black community members to develop the literacy skills needed to vote and further support community-organized education.[25] These examples provide clear articulations for how self-motivated and self-directed groups might be founded on the concept of literacy instruction that is disconnected from formal institutions (see Branch; Kates; Lathan; Schneider) and aligned instead with more informal spaces of writing development. These examples highlight organic approaches toward literacy. These communities had to respond to the exigencies around them and push back against oppressive forces that excluded them; they developed skills and structures that fit their needs within a given moment. In effect, they used literacy rhetorically to achieve a particular social purpose, such as to vote or to create different educational spaces.

Yet, beyond these examples, our field knows little of such work, despite its potential. Susan Kates argues that scholars must still do more to explore the origins of literacy practices beyond the university, particularly "the ways in which individuals who were pushed to the margins of our educational system, in various historical moments, learned to read and write" (500). Kates suggests the importance of community literacy practices that exist "outside the boundaries of traditional educational institutions" and include how "individuals who did not have access to mainstream education learned to read and write within the context of larger political and social goals" (500). A full understanding of literacy practices and the politics of literacy must include alternative models of self-organized and self-sustained collective literacy and education efforts. Our failure to study such models comes, too often, at the expense of recognizing the people and histories that are still marginalized in our classrooms and our scholarship—particularly the working class.

Writing studies and working-class studies scholar William DeGenaro has argued that class is often overlooked, even under the best of intentions, and has called for a more nuanced engagement with working-class rhetorics—specifically, to "confron[t] the elitism that has characterized educational, political, and civic institutions throughout the Western tradition" (*Who Says?* 6). John Russo and Sherry Lee Linkon also note the importance of class "as deeply interwoven with other formative elements of society—race, gender, work, structures of power," but they acknowledge that class is "the element that is often least explored and most difficult to understand" (*New Working-Class Studies* 12). Pecket and its members align with stories of working-class exclusion and resistance—of literacies and people that have been at the margins and have sustained themselves. Class, as we see with the FWWCP, is deeply embedded within power structures and other identity factors. But class is also not always visible: Sometimes, it is a felt experience, often easily hidden or glossed over. Pecket provides us with another context in which to explore the intersections of literacy and class at the grassroots level.

AN ETHOS OF CLASS COLLECTIVITY: FROM SPONSORED TO SPONSORS

Pecket's "origin" story is both interesting and complex, since many would locate the group's beginning in different instances between 1982 and 1992. But other important moments in its history date back to the 1970s, including the creation of the FWWCP. These dates trace the beginning of Pecket from the small-group meetings (emerging from the Horton House magazine group) through its eventual transformation into the user-led and directed Pecket Well College. At the heart of these formative occasions was the democratic ideal and the hope for what Pecket's oral history describes as "more inclusive education," especially for people who had limited access to education or were "tackling difficulties with the written word and/or numbers" (Ross 3). Throughout Pecket's tenure, these learners fought for the rights to expand their education and, in turn, structured a learning community with *their* interests at the forefront.

It would be easy to frame Pecket with a romanticized view of its heroic efforts against educational marginalization; however, the struggles they faced are part of an ongoing public battle between educational access and social realities for many working-class learners. As Pecket Wellians noted on their digital archive, "Most of us are working class adults who missed out on education. . . . This reality has affected every area of our lives—social, education, financial and our health (physical and emotional)" (Pecket Learning Community). Indeed, material constraints and inadequate resources continued to impact Pecket just as they affected the larger FWWCP network. Pecket and its members were struggling with shifting governmental policies and deindustrialization in a particular geographic area that was reliant on the very industries being dismantled, such as coal mining and manufacturing. Although I'll describe many locations where Pecket existed, all were within the Yorkshire region. Between the late 1970s and 1990s, Yorkshire experienced industrial changes that would affect the social environment for years to come in the predominantly working-class region. For instance, in 1984–85, Yorkshire was plagued by coal mining pit closures that caused strikes across the nation and led to solidaristic working-class political action. Amid Margaret Thatcher's neoliberal rhetorics and policies, focused on personal responsibility and self-interest, FWWCP members and Pecket Wellians came together as a community to represent working-class experiences in writing and publishing. But they also endured the material impacts of these industrial actions.

Tom Woodin addresses how this political landscape inspired adult education and publishing efforts in the United Kingdom, noting the "On the Move" campaign that arose from a belief that learners could participate in their own literacy development, and even in the production of educational texts, to increase their sense of educational agency ("Building Culture" 358). During the 1980s, this mission was advanced by organizations such as Write First Time and Gatehouse, which were part of the adult basic education students' movement and shared connections with Pecket Wellians ("A Beginner"). Each of these organizations attempted to provide opportunities for all learners, especially those regarded as requiring "remedial education," to participate and experience workshops and other social activities focused on literacy such as in public writing or reading events, publications, and writing weekends (Ross 11). Pecket, then, grew out of a period of social conflict and anxiety. The external political and social exigencies compelled these learners, in the face of a radical destruction of working-class institutions, to create a space where working-class individuals would be able to take part in their own education through a profound restructuring of education as a user-led initiative and a space for civic agency.

For many Pecket Wellians, the biscits story illustrates an ideological stand against the authorities, a moment of educational agency. It also encapsulates many of their (and the general movement's) values, particularly a belief in taking action through collective organizing, and the idea that everyone deserves a say in their education. Horton House had been a space where adults with reading and writing difficulties came together in a cooperative learning environment to publish a magazine, *Not Written Off*. The goals of this group were not only focused on improving literacy but also on providing a public component for adult education. Between 1982 and 1984, six issues of the magazine were published, each issue crafted, edited, and formatted by the learners themselves with the help of an adult educator, Gillian Frost. This collaboration allowed the group to negotiate literacy development as a communal activity and gain confidence in their ability to participate in an educational project without being written off, as their magazine title suggests.

Although Horton House participants felt very positive about these experiences, a changing managerial structure in 1984 led to the pivotal biscits moment. Frost explains this incident in Pecket's oral history, *Telling It*, noting that the adult learners hoped to raise money to purchase a tape recorder to make taking minutes for meetings easier. The events transpired into something much different when the adult learners started advertising their jumble (rummage) sale to raise money:

> I got a phone call one day from the education shop worker. . . .
> He said, what's this, what happened, how come you've allowed out this poster with a spelling mistake in it? It was biscuits, it's very easy to make a spelling mistake with biscuits,

and leave out the silent 'U.' *I said it's nothing to do with me actually, if they want me to correct it they know they can come and ask me and I'll do it, but they haven't done and I haven't got authority over them.* I suggested that this was a good way of learning that, as with the fruit and veg stall holders' labels in the market, it doesn't have to be spelt perfectly to achieve its objective. This was too mind blowing for adult education. Here was a group in adult education . . . your job is to get it right. *But a tutor didn't have authority over them* . . . (qtd. in Ross 20–21, emphasis added)[26]

As we see from Frost's retelling, the worker at Horton House believed that circulating posters with a misspelled word diminished the center's value and would not sponsor it. Frost and the group, however, felt it was their right to use their own language, to view it not as a mistake but as a rhetorical choice that still functioned adequately for the poster's purpose. After all, would anyone really not know what biscits were in this context?

It might seem like a foolish choice for Frost and the adult learners to reject changing the spelling simply for the sake of retaining Horton House's sponsorship. However, as an advocate of democratic and reciprocal learning, in which each student gets a say in the group's decisions, Frost saw herself as a supporter of the group's collective efforts, not as an enforcer of rules. This view also aligned with the ethos and agency the adult learners wanted for themselves. To be sure, this confrontation went deeper than a simple spelling error. Rather, it pointed to the intersection of language standardization, authority, and the marginalization of working-class individuals.

This was a moment of resistance and solidarity—a moment when people who had been marginalized for many years in their educational experiences decided to take control and renegotiate authority to their benefit, a moment when the *un*authorized authorized themselves. Acting within the political milieu of the time, this self-authorization enabled the learners to negotiate sponsorship and promote their own agendas. In doing so, these learners also enacted power over the standard of spelling (and the ideologies that went along with it) to show their ability to function successfully through their own ways of writing and communicating. For these people—some of whom grew up illiterate or who had difficulties with learning and were subsequently marginalized from educational opportunities—standardization was their adversary, not their motivation. Consequently, the biscits incident marked a shift in their collective desire to change the conditions surrounding their authority as learners. As Pecket Wellian Billy Breeze describes this confrontation, "I said to the Education Centre, yeah, because it's the way we spell it. You can't alter it" (qtd. in Ross 21). Here, Breeze draws attention to a dialect difference between "the way we spell it" of the adult learners and the education center's standard, which led to a sense of collective agency for the group, as well as an active attempt to change the hierarchical structure of their environment to one that privileged the learners.

This spelling dispute was the fuel that pushed Horton House participants to advocate for a learning environment where they could determine the rules. Eventually, this meant prioritizing working-class people and ideas within leadership, finding a new space, and developing a new educational structure based on participants' desires. Moving away from a traditional adult education center represented an evolving sense of sponsorship that departed from simply relying on the often-middle-class management and perspectives. It also moved away from neoliberal ideas that focus on individual attainments and responsibilities. Instead, learners framed their work within the possibilities of forming a collective in order to create and sustain a model of self-directed and user-led education—a collective self-sponsorship. This was the beginning of building Pecket—a group that defied a system based on social status and previous education and instead began working outside of an established educational paradigm toward one that respects learners' choices and rhetorical agency.[27]

At this point, however, Pecket as an officially named establishment did not exist. Yet the individuals from Horton House's magazine group continued to meet and discuss how to improve their educational experiences. Reflecting on this time, Pecket Wellian Michelle Baynes describes the group's dream of redefining education to enable a student-led enterprise and create their own college:

> [W]e talked about our idea and asked if people thought it was feasible to run a college that was "student led"—run by and for people who couldn't read and write—they said yes! Lots of other people thought it couldn't be done and some today probably wouldn't believe we did it but we had already had a taste of that freedom and—we wanted that for other people like us. (qtd. in Ross 24)

What emerged during these meetings was a desire to generate a user-led environment through a collective community and equal participation rather than one that focused on traditional models of education and institutional partnerships. This model complicates notions of literacy sponsorship, described by Deborah Brandt, because the community both actively denied Horton House's financial and educational sponsorship and then aggressively pursued a means to develop their own version of sponsorship as a community enterprise. Brandt notes that literacy sponsors "set the terms for access to literacy and wield powerful incentives for compliance and loyalty" (166–67). Sponsors, Brandt writes,

> are a tangible reminder that literacy learning throughout history has always required permission, sanction, assistance, coercion, or, at minimum, contact with existing trade routes. Sponsors are delivery systems for the economies of literacy, the means by which these forces present themselves to—and through—individual learners. (167)

Brandt's examples here emphasize how the outside sponsor is often cast as authority. Pecket subverted this power structure and, instead, chose to form their own internal collective and oppositional sponsorship network based on "economies" (read non-neoliberal economies) that were relevant to and supportive of them.[28]

To succeed, then, Pecket had to create a sponsorship network where they were the authority. Importantly, the adult learners of *Not Written Off* recognized there was a growing network that might support (and join) their efforts at gaining full agency of their education. Many of Pecket's founding members, including Ann Greenwood, Michael Callaghan, Portia Fincham, Joe Flanagan, Peter Goode, Betty Legg, Joan Keighley, and Gillian Frost, were each involved in other educational projects that were aimed to push the boundaries of Britain's educational system.[29] The activist political climate of the time fed into their belief in an education pointed toward civic engagement where all learners were central. During this time, too, they realized Pecket needed a physical presence in the community—a college building to call their own. This desire inspired them to apply for grants from the Yorkshire Arts Association, the European Social Fund, the Rural Development Commission, the Lottery Fund, and a New Directions Programme through the University of Bradford Access Unit, which supplied enough funds to remodel a building in Hebden Bridge, West Yorkshire, that would become the physical structure of Pecket. This work was done through what I will later refer to as "the humbling of traditional intellectuals"—that is, while using financial, physical, and intellectual resources from multiple supporters, Pecket Wellians retained power over their vision. Importantly, the funding that Pecket received differed from that of the broader FWWCP network, because they were able to rely on more localized funding networks rather than solely national institutions such as the Arts Council.[30] The focus on adult education also shaped the funding available and called up different associations than applications centered on arts or literature. In this way, Pecket was able to reshape what adult education meant for them.

Pecket's Archive Project Director Pol Nugent, who housed me on my first visit to England, explained in a conversation how the group's significant accomplishments grew out of this self-directed environment. They worked tirelessly to raise funds for modifying the building, accommodating wheelchair needs, and sustaining their unique learning practices. Such direction, Pol said, led to the physical creation of inclusive learning spaces, which provided the "courage and support to help learners begin writing and reading again" in their adult years (Nugent). And, in effect, many Pecket Wellians left with "a sense of confidence" gained from these interactions—confidence that cannot be discounted, as it also transferred in material ways to people traveling for the first time beyond West Yorkshire, managing budgets, having director roles, and sharing their skills (Nugent).

These accomplishments officially manifested in 1992, when Pecket opened as a user-led learning community housed within a physical building. Over four hundred people celebrated Pecket Well College's opening as Britain's first residential college for basic education (Pecket Well College, *Opening Day*). At Pecket, learners could now attend various courses and stay overnight in the building for the length of the courses, which usually lasted a few days at a time. In a poem written on the opening of the college, Pecket Wellian Corrine John evinces both the struggles and joys of what this day represented for many community members. She describes the intense labors that went into establishing Pecket as well as her shift from seeing literacy as "frightening" to something she could actively take a part in and develop with Pecket's educational model:

> For seven long years a fight we've had
> with lots of troubles but now we are glad
> The openin day of Pecket Well
> Is here to stay so ring that bell
> We thank the people who have fought
> For those in need of being taught.
>
> Don't be shy and hide in a cold corner
> Come and make friends its [sic] also warmer
> Learning can be hard but please don't run
> At Pecket Well you are taught by fun
> Once you start learning you'll want more
> So please do come and knock on the door.
>
> Words that look long and frightening too
> Soon learning comes easy for me and you
> With numbers and letters, reading and writing
> Not knowing where it might be leading
> Extending our skills Thirsting for knowledge
> You never know we could make it to college.
> (Pecket Well College, *Opening Day*)

Pecket Well College, Nr Hebden Bridge

Pecket Well College was set up
and is run by people working on
things in their lives which hold
them back, such as reading and
writing. It is for people who have
missed out on education.

If you would like to work with
others like yourself to overcome
your fears and share your
strengths, then
Pecket Well College is for you!

Figure 8: Pecket Well flyer, courtesy of Pecket
Learning Community.

For many other members as well, this opening was the defining
moment in Pecket's legacy because it established a physical presence
in the community, legitimating both a physical (the building) and
discursive structure (user-led curriculum) premised on the interests
and needs of the learners themselves. Pecket sustained this work
from 1992 until about 2011,[31] with thousands of people involved

in Pecket's courses as "founder members, participants, Directors, volunteers, paid workers or partner organisations" (Ross 3).

LEARNING "THE PECKET WAY": DEMOCRATIC PRACTICES AND ORGANIC INTELLECTUALS

After establishing the physical college space, Pecket was able to expand their collective approach to learning. "The Pecket Way" became a fluid set of pedagogical tools for learners to enact a democratic vision of participatory learning—a model that has implications both within and beyond traditional educational spaces because it introduces a unique sense of community-based power and agency.

Before discussing "The Pecket Way," however, it should not be forgotten that many of Pecket's members expressed severe difficulties reading and writing. I argue, through their embodied work of developing their own curriculum and college, Pecket can be understood as exemplifying a version of what Antonio Gramsci calls *organic intellectuals*. He writes,

> All men [sic] are intellectuals, one could therefore say: but not all men have in society the function of intellectuals. When one distinguishes between intellectuals and non-intellectuals, one is referring in reality only to the immediate social function of the professional category of the intellectuals . . . (9)

Indeed, Gramsci notes how intellectuals are often categorized through their schooling and the vertical nature of moving up in gradation or levels; this represents the stratifying nature of traditional education and a version of sponsorship that relies on an authoritative institution and person (or group). However, as Gramsci notes, organic intellectuals materialize not in the "social function" of what jobs people do but rather through their participation with the masses, through important collective organizational efforts to meet their real-life needs (9). In effect, the foundation of organic intellectual work comes from groups, like Pecket, that actively engage with the needs of a community and produce structural change, like a residential college, though perhaps not the complete economic change Gramsci might have ultimately sought.

Gramsci's discussion of traditional and organic intellectuals provides a valuable framework for understanding Pecket's impact, although it does not account for the importance that people of various positionalities (and not just men) played in Pecket's success. The framework of the organic intellectual represents the belief that all people have meaningful experiences, which can inform and contribute to the organization's collective effort. As Pecket Wellian Joe Flanagan notes:

> The first thing people want to know is "who's in charge," but we have to make it clear, we all are. I'm responsible for what I'm doing. The help is there if I need it. We are not here as students or tutors. We are all here to work together and to learn from each other. Those labels have gone out the door. (qtd. in Pecket Well College, "Forging a Common Langauge" 229)

In essence, what made Pecket distinctive was that a group of community members self-organized, identified their goals and needs, and created a learning environment that focused on the assets that all members bring. They were organic intellectuals who saw the affordances of social organizing in order to build a collective educational structure to benefit adults who had been unjustly excluded based on their working-class identity and educational difficulties. For the remainder of this section, I will draw on Gramsci's concept to articulate three strategies that were central to Pecket's success: (1) recognizing organic intellectuals; (2) humbling traditional intellectuals; and (3) building a new common-sense curriculum.

Recognizing Organic Intellectuals

Most Pecket Wellians were working from severely disadvantaged economic conditions as well as challenged educational and personal backgrounds. But Pecket operated under "a belief that everyone had skills" (Ross 47), which meant the courses were most often led and directed by individuals who were themselves working on their writing and reading. Therefore, they were able to take the idea of organic intellectuals and organize and build on that through their peer learning strategies, to dispel the idea that only certain people have the expertise to teach. In effect, the awareness and belief in their own abilities allowed Pecket to operate on an asset-based model of learning. This ideal was represented in the structure, naming, and daily activities of the organization.

One way Pecket distributed learning instruction was through the use of tools aimed at inclusion. Because all learners had different needs, Pecket Wellians were devoted to discovering ways of enabling productive learning environments. One such tool was a "writing hand" (or a scribe) who volunteered to write down the words of someone who may not have been able to write or wanted someone else to assist in this process (Ross 49). A writing hand was not meant to standardize or diminish the person speaking but rather to provide a method for support that allowed everyone a chance to get their speaking into writing. The role of a writing hand required a professional and caring relationship with the learner, one formed out of mutual respect. As described by Pol Nugent, the writing hand was important in helping learners find their own confidence in their education: "There was a very acute awareness of how people's confidence had been knocked down by educational institutions and other life experiences. The Pecket Way of working was about not making those situations worse" (qtd. in Ross 50). Here, the writing hand was a rhetorical approach—a response to the needs of the learners in order to allow everyone to participate in learning, especially by recognizing that learning and rhetorical work can happen through variations of orality, writing, and collaboration.

Pecket also used other teaching techniques to encourage each learner to interact with others and learn through doing. "Journey sticks," for instance, were used as a physical reminder for learners when they went on group walks (qtd. in Ross 50). Members could pick up sticks (or other objects), bring them back to the building, and use them for memory aids when sharing their stories. For instance, members would attach objects to their stick that represented key moments along the way. The goal was to use the objects as a physical reminder of their embodied learning experience and to encourage personal reflection and emotions in their own learning development—something few Pecket Wellians ever experienced before. That is, Pecket Wellians often tried to make learning more tangible through kinesthetic activities, such as creating posters, magazines, quilts, and banners, which allowed them to express ideas with multiple materials and moved beyond a solely text-based method of learning. Of course, within writing studies, scholars have done exciting work connected to the affordances of multimodality (Shipka), zine making (Luther), and crafting (Gruwell) in more recent years; however, these early examples show Pecket Wellians interpreting their own needs and organically developing tactile learning strategies to assist each other and learn through actively gathering, collecting, and curating materials.

Pecket also believed in the benefits of life stories, in which learners would narrate their educational and personal histories. These written productions functioned as a form of testimony of working-class experiences and education, representing, for many, the first time they were ever asked to talk about "what mattered to them" (Nugent). Indeed, life stories were the first opportunity in their educational history that gave Pecket Wellians a chance to describe their difficulties in a safe environment and to contribute to something on their own, showing that their life experiences mattered. Eventually, life stories became a way for Pecket to publish and circulate their writing as a collaborative endeavor. This represented the first significant written work many of these learners had ever accomplished in their life. The pedagogical aim was to enable people to discuss and reflect on their experiences and learn from each other. Such methods emphasized that everybody is an active participant—an organic intellectual—as they worked together as cocreators of knowledge.

Notably, these learning practices often transformed lives in both material and ideological ways, prompting altogether new opportunities for Pecket Wellians. For instance, Pecket Wellian Florence Agbah describes how growing confidence led to additional life changes. After immigrating from Ghana, Florence joined Pecket, where she took classes and worked with writing hands, who helped her transcribe what she wanted in her own words. Community publishing was key to building Florence's journey as a writer, and she was able to take part in it first through a local group called Chapeltown Community, where she published her life stories *The Survivor* and *Ways of Learning*. In these stories, she details family struggles as well as her working life as a janitor who could not read, write, or speak much British English. She also writes about the impact of personal trauma, social stigma, financial constraints, and geographic changes on her educational development. Moreover, in an interview on Pecket's digital archive, Florence explains how difficult daily life was for her with her limited reading and writing skills. Going to a bank was hard because she couldn't read or write. Then, when banks switched to ATMs, she couldn't understand the machines, and when one swallowed her card, it left her embarrassed at the need to ask for help (Agbah, "The Hole"). Florence shares these accounts because she sees what supportive communities have enabled her to do and how they have encouraged her to take matters into her own hands with her education. While Florence claims that her reading and writing did not always progress as quickly as she had hoped, her experiences represent the rhetorical literacy skills she acquired throughout her years. For example, the process of collaboratively talking about, creating, and publishing her stories enabled her to share her testimony with a broader group of people and also spurred material results (publications and, later, a paid job).

Eventually, Florence became a director at Pecket and a member of the FWWCP executive committee. She was Pecket's first paid outreach worker because she understood the needs of adult learners. She described the importance of this position stating:

> My job was working with people like myself. Finding them and bringing them to Pecket to work on their reading and writing. It wasn't easy. . . . It is frightening to be going somewhere to work on your reading and writing because you always think you are the only one. . . . I was treated equally— sometimes I forgot I couldn't read and write! I know what

other participants feel like—I can relate to them. But if you are someone who has had a good education you can't do that. (qtd. in Ross 44)

In this way, Florence's story represents how Pecket embodies organic intellectual work: by privileging her knowledge and ability to do outreach over that of a traditionally educated person. By paying Florence to do this work, Pecket also illustrates a commitment to knowledges formed from life experiences and the recognition of intelligence beyond the "social function" of individuals (Gramsci 9).

Humbling Traditional Intellectuals

Since its emergence, Pecket has demonstrated a commitment to valuing all learners and building from their abilities to make the organization run effectively. While working to improve their own reading and writing, members maintained agency over decisions throughout the process of organizing Pecket's learning community. Pecket Wellians designed the board of directors so that community members outnumbered traditional intellectuals. As stated in their constitution, "a majority of directors must have reading and writing difficulties themselves and other directors should be people who suppor[t] our aims and ways of working" (qtd. in Ross 32).

Significant here is how forcefully Pecket Wellians advocated for the dismantling of the hierarchy of traditional expertise. This does not mean that professional workers or scholars were not welcome. In fact, members from universities were involved in Pecket in a number of ways. Rather, it represents a valuing of Pecket's agency. As one member expressed, even when there were traditional intellectuals around, "You didn't call them tutors, you called them on a first-name basis and if they didn't like it they had to just lump it you know. Anyone said I'm a tutor, ah—no, not going to call you tutor. We didn't want to be called students because we wasn't students, we was learners. So they were workers and learners—that was the language" (qtd. in Ross 47). Here, the change in discourse from "tutor" to "worker" and from "students" to "learners" signifies a deeper ideological valuing of all participants. The extent that

Pecket Wellians felt valued and invested in their development as an organization became clear to me in an interview with Florence Agbah, Corrine John, and Billy Breeze, who all explained that, for them, "Pecket means life" ("Hudds Interview"). Following up on this, Florence explained,

> Pecket is self-respect. Something to live up to. Something to make us feel a part of the world . . . because before then we were all feeling useless. But Pecket taught us you don't have to feel useless, because we all have a part to play. And, when we go there, we play our part. We didn't have managers. There was no one in charge. We were all in charge, so whatever happens is important to all of us. So we take care of each other. ("Hudds Interview")

This vehement belief in valuing each other's experiences to the extent of placing everyone in a role of power defined Pecket throughout its tenure and created an ethos of solidarity.

Instead of treating one person as the standard of knowledge, Pecket actively worked toward emphasizing every person's ability to share different knowledge and skills—a method that was put to test many times throughout its tenure. For instance, while looking into a charitable status, Pecket hired John Coles, later deemed "Uncle John," because the group needed someone to "put gobbledygook legal language into everyday language so that those of [us] who were going to be a director of Pecket would understand what were required of [them], what [they] had to do by law" (qtd. in Ross 30). Here, Pecket Wellians asked the legal professional (or "expert") to assist them in taking an active part in understanding all aspects of the organization. In this way, there was a distinct attempt to negotiate authority so their desires would not be co-opted; put another way, although Pecket had multiple financial, educational, and professional sponsors, the goal was always for Pecket to maintain agency. Here again, Gramsci might usefully articulate the importance of such a strategy:

> One of the most important characteristics of any group that is developing towards dominance is its struggle to assimilate and conquer "ideologically" the traditional intellectuals, but

this assimilation and conquest is made quicker and more efficacious the more the group in question succeeds in simultaneously elaborating its own organic intellectuals. (10)

In this way, Pecket represents a practical effort to enact this Gramscian project, developing their own organic intellectuals and using that base as a means to convert traditional intellectuals to their cause.

For Pecket, the humbling of traditional intellectuals was rooted in solidarity, particularly through advocacy and access for all members. For instance, as Pecket developed courses and expanded their network, they constantly reflected on how to highlight their own strengths. In their policy document "What We Mean By 'Access,'" Pecket Wellians write, "What we are about is self-advocacy and self-organization. We work alongside carefully chosen professionals when we need their knowledge and advice . . . [W]e value our own knowledge and experience, and that of others like ourselves" (Pecket Learning Community 1). Self-advocacy, here, means that Pecket privileges the experiences and knowledges they have; however, they build on this with the assistance of others. One way that Pecket relied on their own knowledge is by developing courses based on members' own experiences and needs. For instance, one member of the Management Committee relied on wheelchair access and expressed the importance for those with physical disabilities to have a space where they could "be safe and able to find where everything is for ourselves" (Pecket Learning Community, "What We Mean" 1). Alongside physical accommodations, Pecket foregrounded the belief that access included an ideology and practice of respect in everyday choices: "Access is about . . . our attitudes, how we talk to and treat each other, decisions we make, and planning ahead" (1). For those who might doubt the effectiveness of such a strategy, Pecket responds with their ability to network locally, nationally, and internationally, stating:

> Don't think this means that we are unable to work in a "professional" way. We are organized and are spreading our ideas and ways of working locally, nationally, and internationally. By networking (making links with others to

share ideas, experience, contacts, and resources) we can get a clear picture of advances being made in adult basic and community education. (2)

Through this statement, Pecket confirms their ability to build on their own ideas, collaborate, and develop their organization in meaningful ways.

Finally, Mary Hamilton, Pol Nugent, and Nick Pollard highlight the choice of the term "college" in order to challenge traditional perspectives on learning. They note Pecket Wellians' claim that Pecket is "not an ordinary college" and that learning "could take a lifetime" because everyone learns at different paces, a key reason why Pecket was about "every participant . . . having a say in their own learning" (Hamilton et al. 17). In effect, Pecket Wellians organized and negotiated their own methods of support, evincing the ability of working-class individuals to mobilize and create spaces of agency for their own learning. Therefore, we can see how Pecket adamantly pursued an expansive notion of *intellectuals*, even naming their learning community Pecket Well College, flipping the expectations associated with traditional educational structures.

Highlighting organic intellectuals and humbling the power of traditional intellectuals, Pecket demonstrates a new model for collective self-sponsorship in which the community members have an expanded sense of agency. Each of these examples shows how Pecket Wellians successfully navigated responsibility in the growth and development of Pecket. Even more, these moments represent numerous rhetorical tactics Pecket Wellians used in order to maintain their own sense of sponsorship. To be sure, Pecket did receive assistance from traditional intellectual and institutional sources of funding, but they did so while staying true to Pecket's values, ethos, and structure. In fact, Pecket represents a model of partnership work that relied on the agency, organizing efforts, and rhetorically savvy skills of the learners themselves.

Building a New Common-Sense Curriculum
Ultimately, Gramsci saw the need to reframe "common sense" values in working-class terms against hegemonic structures (199),

and Pecket did this. Just as, for Gramsci, individuals do not need to have the social role of an intellectual to *be* intellectuals, Gramsci's "common sense" proposes a critique of hegemonic ruling structures, dismantling the status quo to establish a new "common sense." Pecket Wellians' rejection of the standard educational structures and creation of their own curriculum represents just such a new common sense. It is this organizing strategy that separates Pecket from most traditional learning models during this time in the United Kingdom as well as in the United States.

For Pecket, this new common sense came in the model of residential education courses and a curriculum that emerged from the community. Pecket became part of a network of residential experiences held at various locations, where learners would stay overnight or for multiple-day workshops as part of an immersive learning experience. Pecket's history includes residential events such as "Sharing Dreams," "One World to Share," "As We See Ourselves," and others. These workshops were geared toward participant engagement with themes of identity and community, in which participants understood themselves in relation to the world around them. "Sharing Dreams," for instance, was a weekend residential course in 1987 at Northern College in Barnsley. During this time, the participants co-facilitated workshops on topics ranging from "photography, poetry, life stories, what matters to you, art, sing out, Handicapped Awareness, Black writers, Young Writers, Women's writer groups" (Pecket Well College, *Sharing Dreams*). These workshops culminated in a publication entitled *Sharing Dreams,* which was sold for £3 (around $5) to help with fundraising efforts. Thus, the workshop's effects extended beyond the weekend, as the community publication gave Pecket Wellians material to circulate and to continue dialogue about the importance of adult education. In this way, residential education offered sites of learning that moved beyond traditional educational spaces and into community spaces and activities; this model emerged from a democratic sensibility that held that all participants could contribute to the learning at hand, actively shaping the cultural conditions around them.

These attempts to support a new common sense, a new curriculum, expanded as Pecket grew. Over time, local newspapers, the

BBC, and even international organizations recognized Pecket's success as a new learning structure and activist organization for basic education. One of the main examples of Pecket's active intervention in the conservative educational system came in 1990, when Pecket Wellians Corrine John and Peter Goode were invited to Holland for a literacy conference. Hosted by the Bossche School voor Volwassenen, this conference brought together an international network of adult learners to discuss their experiences and to highlight the ways adult learners across the world were breaking down barriers in their communities. This conference solidified Pecket's advocacy for adult basic education and represented an official moment when Pecket was not in a marginalized position but considered a valid and legitimate group to be honored and invited to share its learning techniques. In essence, this was a moment where traditional intellectuals realized that organic intellectuals like Pecket Wellians were doing valuable work. To be sure, Pecket Wellians already saw themselves as legitimate. This conference, however, represented a changing paradigm in international views of adult basic literacy among traditionally defined intellectuals.

As a result of their conference visit, Paulo Freire endorsed Pecket's work in a documentary called *Liberating Literacy*. And it is easy to see why, since Pecket's model highlighted the connection between democracy and liberation, what Freire calls elsewhere "that specifically human act of intervening in the world" (99). Freire's view of education centers on changing a society—not only through our thinking but also through the material realities and challenges faced each day—to understand that economics and rights and access to education and healthcare or employment are all a part of the socially constructed world we live in. Moreover, Freire insists that education can have "a 'directive' vocation," which "addresses itself to dreams, ideals, utopias, objectives, to what [he has called] the 'political' nature of education" (100). Education, therefore, embodies not only material constraints and challenges but also the immense possibilities afforded through human interaction. Pecket adhered to a similar vision of activism focused on improving educational opportunities for adult learners—significant for learning development, occupational skill improvement, and community literacy growth—and used those same skills to engage in daily civic participation. Intervening in the world, for Pecket, was also equally about creating a self-sponsored community of learners that could (and did) experience personal and political change as part of this supportive educational environment.

Pecketwellian Corrine John explains the personal significance of Pecket on her life as well as the material changes it prompted. She states,

> Oh [my life] changed a lot. I ended up getting a job after 12 years out of work. I ended up passing me driving test. And I got certificates for IT work. Pecket opened the door for me and it just kept opening, just kept moving to doors that opened. When you went to Pecket, we were all one. We were all the same. There was always something that someone else could help me. And we got the answer in the end. We didn't have anybody over you. You decided what you wanted to learn. (John)

Here, Corrine notes just a few of the defining factors of Pecket's organizational structure and how this community model was central in providing her with confidence, a support structure for her learning, and ultimately a renewed sense of her abilities. First, it was built around a democratic view that represented the interests of all learners, regardless of their educational experiences or personal identity. Next, Pecket's solidarity and sense of collective ownership created a base for seeing literacy as a collaborative and reciprocal learning endeavor, as well as rhetorically contingent upon what the community wanted to accomplish. And finally, each person who came to Pecket was met with the acknowledgment of the right of people to learn. Pecket, as a community of learners, helped Corrine push past the stigma of literacy difficulties and enabled her to get a job and a license, become a peer-learner and leader within Pecket's workshops, and attend an international literacy conference as an invited guest. Another founding member described Pecket in the highest possible terms: "It's meant the privilege of witnessing and of experiencing myself the transformation, and for me Pecket was a little utopia, it was how society should be. It was how people should relate to each other. It was power used together and for something, rather than power used over above and against" (qtd. in Ross 94).

IMPLICATIONS FOR WORKING-CLASS LITERACIES AND ALTERNATIVE COMMUNITY HISTORIES

Pecket's story, focused on working-class British adult learners, provides a version of a history of individuals pushed to the margins of education. And I would argue that by exploring how Pecket generated a new vision of agency and organic intellectuals, the work of these writers reorients what histories we include in our field and provides an expanded sense of how we understand community literacy efforts within working-class communities. Indeed, through Pecket, we see valuable examples of how working-class communities develop literacy skills in highly rhetorical ways—by creating a unique and democratic model of education, by recognizing themselves as organic intellectuals, humbling the authority traditional intellectuals had over their organization, and by building a curriculum for themselves. Each of these examples had affective impacts and created material differences in the lives of Pecket Wellians.

Pecket also expands our sense of community literacy practices. That is, it provides an important self-generated example of literacy practices in which non-experts create an alternative educational space with new criteria for literacy and education that are often not recognized in our scholarship. Three main insights follow from Pecket's history:

1. We can see *organizational literacy*: Members consistently organized as a group in order to learn how to build and manage their own educational program, establishing ways to fundraise, providing outreach, and ultimately developing from a small magazine group into a residential college under their own leadership.

2. We can see *vernacular literacies* represented from the earliest moments of the biscits incident, where members advo-

cated for writing and language that was representative of their dialects and experiences, even if that went against standardized language rules. David Barton and Mary Hamilton define vernacular literacy practices as those "not regulated by the formal rules and procedures of dominant social institutions and which have their origins in everyday life" (247). Vernacular literacies are represented on a larger scale as well through Pecket's collaborative publishing of life stories, which focus on each writer's personal testimony. This work was also expanded through collaborative publications created after residential sessions. Each of these publications focused on celebrating the language of the learners in their own right and often provided an outlet to discuss important social and political issues.

3. Finally, we can see Pecket's *pedagogical literacies* developed through years of creating their own curriculum and teaching "The Pecket Way" through the use of learning tools such as journey sticks, writing hands, and other collaborative techniques that enable learners to engage in knowledge-production in multiple ways.

To be sure, these examples of organizational, vernacular, and pedagogical literacies create an expansive understanding of literacy that might even be criticized as relying on overly broad statements about the term. My goal, however, is not to generalize literacy to mean everything but rather to broaden where we look when we think about literacy and who we include in literacy discussions. If we understand Pecket in this way, we see a community located at the margins, which challenges traditional models of agency that often rely on university sponsorship and authority, as well as redefines who can be intellectuals by embodying organic intellectuals themselves. This provides an expanded sense of agency that we don't often see in moments of community partnership, where the community is in charge and negotiates their wants, needs, values, and skills.

When we recognize its agency, Pecket also demonstrates a working model of how communities can create new strategic spaces that interrupt our usual stories about community partnerships.

While many scholars have already troubled the idea of partnership work, arguing for approaches that focus on community needs rather than university interests, none of these models emerged organically from the community.[32] Often, we "trouble" university-directed efforts—humbling our goals but not our intellectual dominance. Pecket's model reminds us of the importance of community-generated values and curriculum, meaning scholarly interests take a backseat to community interests and desires; it demands that the community hold the power. Pecket's model emerges from the learners themselves. With Pecket, we see how communities can and do organically create their own model of collective self-sponsored learning, as well as some challenges they face along the way. A strong belief in the agency of a collective organization gave Pecket power to dictate what they wanted, thereby flipping the model of interaction to fit their needs.

At the heart of the biscits incident was an understanding that working-class, adult learners have rhetorical agency that does not have to adhere to standardized or traditional notions or expectations of education. In community literacy work, we can continue to expand our understanding of literacy by highlighting people, literacies, and the knowledges that circulate within communities but that are continually pushed aside—particularly that of the working class. Rather than thinking of this as a hierarchy of knowledge, a community organization model such as Pecket shows us how they reframed legal, tutoring, and funding expertise (among other things) in order to be of use *to* the community. This resists positioning communities as lacking: Pecket shows what is possible with an entire population of learners who were systematically described in negative ways based on their educational experiences and socio-economic status. It seeks to reframe or negotiate a model that pulls from all the available means of collaborative enterprises.

Many times, we might see ourselves as bringing in a curriculum, but Pecket built their own. We might see ourselves as being leaders, but Pecket directed themselves. And we might see ourselves as dispelling hierarchies of education, but Pecket already created a college to do that. In effect, to promote more sustainable environments, it might first take a shift in what histories we explore and how we understand our role within the community in relation to the agency that they have already created.

A CODA: PECKET AND THE
FWWCP ARCHIVAL PROJECT

The FWWCP Archival Project is intertwined with Pecket's archival history and its own modeling of community archival work. A downfall of both Pecket and the FWWCP was they never fully integrated a newer generation of members to continue their legacies. Instead, as most original Pecket Wellians aged and the cost to sustain Pecket increased in the 2010s, they began considering their future and decided to develop an oral history and digital archive. They gained enough money to fund both through the sale of their building. Pecket hired someone who could do the technical web work, but Pecket Wellians were involved at every stage, deciding how they wanted to be represented digitally. In fact, during my first visit to Pecket, I sat in on meetings where they discussed the accessibility of the website, thinking about how the text might be enlarged for people with trouble seeing, or how sound might accompany images to highlight nuances of language usage and dialect. The digital archive eventually housed interviews, videos, publications, images, and curriculum tools from Pecket's history. In effect, the vernacular, organizational, and pedagogical literacies Pecket used were able to be circulated through their digital curation. The goal of this digital archive was the preservation of their legacy and the continued circulation, use, and improvement of their learning tools. This process of community input spurred the print and digital archival work in the FWWCP Archival Project.

Being able to write this chapter is a testament to Pecket's work developing, organizing, and funding its own digital archive between 2011 and 2014. But loss must also be recognized: The only way Pecket was able to create the digital archive was by selling their physical building. In other words, their digital preservation was dependent on getting rid of the physical space they had secured in the community. Furthermore, if you were to search online for Pecket's digital archive today, you would only find remnants, because the money to fund the site ran out after five years. The lack of long-term sustainability for Pecket's digital archive serves as another reminder that conversations about class, materiality, and precarity need to be part of our academic archival discussions. For all the work Pecket Wellians did, much of their digital legacy is now inaccessible to most people unless additional funding emerges in connection with developing the FWWCP Digital Collection. Most Pecket Wellians are elderly and do not have the means, resources, or physical health to assist this work. Thankfully, between 2013 and 2015, when I visited TheFED and Pecket, Pol Nugent and Nick Pollard provided physical copies of many of Pecket's textual artifacts, and I was able to physically transport several dozen of these publications and documents in my luggage, via two trains and tube lines, so they could be preserved as part of the FWWCP Collection in London, housed with other groups from Yorkshire.

The valuable oral history and digital archival preservation work Pecket did greatly influenced my own work with the FWWCP Archival Project, as I learned from Pol Nugent about how they prioritized community values and input at every stage of the process. But I'm constantly reminded, too, of the harsh realities and difficulties of creating something sustainable. With Pecket's digital archive project out of money and out of date with technology, its online presence is now reliant on the FWWCP Archival Project. To have more than fragments of Pecket's history exist online, we will have to invest significant time, labor, and resources into this endeavor—and we will have to hope that enough digital files can be converted to newer technology without error.

Chapter 4

Archival Labor

> Thinking like an archivist also means . . . that we as a field need to learn more about the process of archival work and create disciplinary space for bibliographic scholarship and other aspects of archival research that can, in turn, expand the field's historical knowledge.
>
> —Chris Warnick

> Why do we not have articles about finding aids?
> —Barbara E. L'Eplattenier

FOR MANY SCHOLARS, THE PROCESS of archival work today might look something like this: First, you plan a trip to an archive (or special collections), often by looking at finding aids on a website. These finding aids can help you choose which documents to examine. You contact the archivist or librarian via email with a request to book an appointment, and you provide a list of the specific boxes, fonds, documents, or materials you'd like to see, asking questions about the inventory if needed. You travel to the archive/collection, hopefully with time to explore the documents for a couple of days or perhaps longer if you're fortunate enough to have time and funding for transportation, lodging, and meals away from home. Of course, many people might also have similar experiences to mine: on a budget, asking favors from friends, staying in their spare room or on a couch, and finding the cheapest form of transportation possible. Archival work is certainly not accessible to everyone, with so many needed resources and physical demands. But, unless or until a collection is digitized, this tends to be a model.

Often, while at the archival location, you receive further help from a professional staff member who has pulled out materials for you and offers additional recommendations. It is often an iterative process, where one find leads to another and another, if you're lucky. Sometimes, as Gesa E. Kirsch and Liz Rohan thoughtfully remind us, archival findings can be "intuitive, coincidental, and serendipitous" (4). Even an absence of something or someone might offer clues. As you're there, you attempt to document your findings making notes in pencil in a notebook or on a computer or taking pictures with your phone if allowed. Sometimes, photocopying documents for a small fee is possible. There never seems to be enough time. Then, you return home and ideally get reimbursed for travel through your university and begin writing about the findings. Some scholars might even be able to revisit the archive if they have funding to do so.

To be sure, archival research is not as simplistic as this short sketch suggests, given that archives are full of unknowns in the exploration and researchers have varying degrees of resources to do this work. But this is a typical archival process—going to visit an established collection— that most researchers would understand. My own archival journey took a much different process, and I didn't have many models to rely on for what we were trying to do: construct an official archive from scratch.[33] Therefore, this chapter describes some of the step-by-step choices we made to bring an archive together, with the goal of showing how writing studies and working-class studies scholars might learn from precarity and make productive use of a kitchen-table ethos when engaging archival methods.

The FWWCP Archival Project began with a hope, but none of us involved really knew the reality of what it meant to construct an archive. If I'm honest, I never realized I'd end up doing most of the inventory labor—and this work has drastically shaped my appreciation for the time and precision involved. We did, however, have guiding values and goals. Community building remained integral for the FWWCP/FED and its member groups such as Pecket throughout its tenure, and we were hoping to build a community archive with insight from members who were still living.

In this way, we were blending principles of community archives and institutional or scholarly collections. This chapter explains the history and realities of how we did this work. I also reflect on our methods and goals while considering several key questions: What does it mean to construct an archive with community members? What resources, tools, technologies did we use and why? Where, with whom, and with what labor? Under what conditions?

When I began working with the FWWCP/FED, no formal archive existed. It wasn't even the case that documents were housed but unprocessed somewhere, which often happens once archival materials are donated if there are not enough resources to process them quickly. Rather, there was no singular place for me to visit and look at documents, no particular archivist or finding aids to help. Most FWWCP/FED material sat in members' homes, garages, and attics. Over time, some publications or administrative materials and ephemera (such as minutes, reports, or flyers) had been inherited by family members, while others had been donated to community bookstores or centers, changing their provenance. New owners sometimes threw out publications, perhaps not knowing (or caring) what they were or perhaps because of their deteriorating condition. Some texts might be lost forever. This dispersion of materials meant that for an official archive to exist, we would have to do the work of gathering and organizing publications and documents. This chapter, then, is about the process we developed for the FWWCP Archival Project and the ways we attempted to "thin[k] like . . . archivist[s]" collaboratively, drawing on insights of each person involved (Warnick 99). Thinking quickly turned into acting as archivists and librarians alike. Without an official archival title, FWWCP/FED members such as Nick Pollard, Tom Woodin, Sally Flood, Roger Mills, Pol Nugent, Roy and Lucia Birch, Ashley Jordan, Florence Agbah, Billy Cryer, and Corrine John guided me toward what documents could be significant to find and preserve, with the hope that future writers, learners, students, and scholars would use them.

We started this process in 2012, and it remains ongoing. Our experience began with determining a space that might house materials and locating, gathering, and moving materials in purposeful ways in order to create the collection. Then, since 2014, I have led the effort to sort, organize, box, develop metadata, digitize, publicize, create finding aids, and circulate the collection through remixing the contents into podcast segments, digital exhibits, and more. The FWWCP Collection now exists at the TUC Library Collections at LMU, housing over 2,350 individual print publications in over seventy acid-free clamshell archival storage boxes, plus more than twenty boxes' worth of administrative material including meeting minutes, membership files, mission statements, constitutional documents, letters, cassettes, VHS tapes, and more. These materials—some perhaps the only remaining versions—are the textual memory of the FWWCP/FED, but they also represent the lived experiences of thousands of working-class members and the many hopeful iterations of archives whose history the FWWCP/FED attempted to preserve.

The work of constructing archives with FWWCP/FED members involved embodied *action*—doing, building, making, laboring, and working—to create a physical collection in London. This process of archival creation was, just like writing itself, a recursive activity, shaped by contexts around us, different audiences, and rhetorical situations. However, as Janice Fernheimer et al. have argued, "relatively few rhetoricians have embarked on the practice of building an archive—to generate and preserve stories—with reciprocal growth and rhetorical pedagogy as integral and explicit components of the collection's sustainable existence" ("Learning" 232). Importantly, to understand the products of the FWWCP Collection, we cannot ignore the processes of becoming and revising, the ways that multiple actions and separate instances of work—performed by various people—impacted the archive that exists today and the intentional decisions we made for future use. Creating a community archive is not a linear process.

To write about the multi-part process of archival curation, I hope, will motivate conversations about the methods behind creating archives for those wanting to do so as well as encourage transparency about the sustainability (or lack) of community-based projects and possibilities for representation. Our methods have responded to the experiences of devalued work and knowledge described by FWWCP/FED members, and our archival curation pushes against these deficit narratives to highlight the value of working-class writing. We often stalled our decisions to reassess our format and revise the work we had already done, for the archive to be more usable. To continue developing ethical community projects, we must work to make visible our processes and practices that can be responsive to precarious conditions. In turn, I believe our disciplinary methods might be (re)shaped when working with/ archiving the literacy practices of disenfranchised populations.

COMMUNITY ARCHIVAL ORIGINS, ATTEMPTS, AND COMPLICATIONS

Before I explain the process of creating the FWWCP Collection, I want to examine some of the nuances of what community archiving entails. I will also show how the FWWCP attempted to create their own archive, long before I was involved. The long lineage of FWWCP archival work provided foundational stones for what exists today.

Community archives in the United Kingdom and the Republic of Ireland are flourishing, with the Community Archives and Heritages Group website that highlights over 760 ongoing projects, but the process of creation is unique and complex for each archive ("Home"). Michael-John DePalma distinguishes community archives "as texts—print, digital, aural, visual, material—that have been recorded, collected, or preserved by individuals or groups who are connected through shared interests, identities, practices, histories, geographies" (213). In conversations with FWWCP/ FED members, we often questioned what good preserving the materials would be if no one knew about them or used them. We wanted them to be part of a living archive connecting past histories with current and future users. Our choices were both materially motivated and deeply ideological, involving the pragmatic aspects of what to gather, save, and curate as well as thinking through how to avoid reproducing the marginalization felt by working-class people in the archiving process. In turn, we accounted for the contributions and knowledge of working-class community members in the production, processing, terminology, and usage of the FWWCP print and digital collections. Such processes fall under the definition for what Andrew Flinn, Mary Stevens, and Elizabeth Shepherd describe as community archives based on "active participation of a community in documenting and making accessible the history of their particular group and/or locality *on their own terms*" (73).

The collaborative nature of this archival construction aligns with the nuances that Jimmy Zavala et al. articulate in models of "community-based archives that have partnered with academic institutions" (213). Zavala et al. argue that "community archives . . . challenge hierarchical structures" and that "new forms of archival practice are created when community members from under-represented communities may engage with mainstream archival institutions and may provide feedback on how to describe collections" (212–13). While much of this scholarship came out after we had already begun developing the FWWCP Collection, it helps give language to the processes and rhetorical decisions we were making. And it enables me to reflect on this process and consider how the FWWCP Archival Project might inform new archival partnership work involving community members, academic institutions, and other organizations as well.

This language is particularly relevant to how the FWWCP/FED maintained agency throughout our process, and I believe we must share not only the results of this but also the untidy steps along the way. Making the process visible can also make transparent the impacts of funding, technological resources, physical labor, sponsors, and the use or engagement of archival materials. We shaped methods to be responsive to our partnership, inclusive of community knowledge, and accessible to the FWWCP/FED and other communities. In this way, the FWWCP Archival Project illustrates a model of class-based literacy practices and archival methods that draws attention not only to texts written about precarity but also to the conditions that shape how archives emerge and are constructed collaboratively.

Before my own entry into this project, FWWCP/FED members made attempts across decades at creating an archive. Unfortunately, their efforts encountered complications. Yet, without these preliminary starts or archival drafts of sorts, we would not have the result we have today. These attempts kept the hope alive that someday an archive would happen, and they provided early moments of self-documentation by the FWWCP/FED members, so their histories would not be lost. From its earliest days, the FWWCP Archival Project has had an open understanding of provenance or what archival scholar Michelle Caswell describes as

> an ever-changing, infinitely evolving process of recontextualization, encompassing not only the initial creators of the records, but the subjects of the records themselves; the archivists who acquired, described, and digitized them (among other interventions); and the users who constantly reinterpret them (par. 13).

In other words, the process of archiving the FWWCP/FED has involved a network of relationships that contribute to its meaning, and these shifting moments of provenance nuance the collection's decades-long history.

The original 1976 FWWCP gathering at Centerprise Bookshop in East London represents the first moment of provenance or origin for the network. FWWCP writers committed to publishing and circulating their writing as an act of resistance against people and institutions who dismissed the value of worker writers' testimony. As the network grew, the FWWCP recognized the importance of their work as something more than ephemeral: They kept minutes documenting the agendas and discussions at meetings; produced annual reports; developed monthly broadsheets, newsletters, and later magazines; and photographed or filmed large events.

Over the years, the executive committee and members actively sought out support to preserve their publications, and sometimes they succeeded in securing grants for paid labor. On multiple occasions, the executive committee attempted to create an archive in various locations to house the FWWCP's physical publications and administrative documents. For instance, one line of inquiry centered on exploring if organizations such as the London Labor Library might be interested in the materials. Between 1985 and 2007, the FWWCP took inspiration from examples such as the Fritz Hüser Institute for Literary and Cultural Work Studies in Dortmund, Germany, or the North West Sound Archives and other organizations working to archive labor histories, and there were attempts to collect materials in Merseyside as well as Burslem, Stoke-on-Trent, which served as the FWWCP office for a series of paid administrative workers in the late 1980s.

One of the most formal attempts happened in 1988 when Michael Kirkland from the Prescot Writers group became the archival point person. In a note entitled "Archivist" to FWWCP members, he writes:

> I have been asked by the FWWCP executive [committee] to undertake the job of Archivist for the Federation. I am writing to members and other interested persons to outline what I see the job as being and to make a plea for material. . . . One is to collect and preserve everything, and the other is to have materials and information available whenever it is required. I do mean "everything." . . . I mean annual reports, newsletters, national and local, minutes, reports of meetings and of workshops within meetings or at conferences, publicity handouts, reminiscences—you name it. . . . Everything rele-vant to the history of the FWWCP. (1)

Kirkland describes this endeavor as "unknown territory" for the organization and explains the goal is "to amass material and then to produce occasional reports listing what is available with extracts" (1). Kirkland did succeed in collecting some materials, but not much happened beyond collection.

Archival attempts continued when the FWWCP had a paid worker and an office space in Stoke-on-Trent in 2001. However, there wasn't adequate storage space, tools for preservation such as archival boxes that might endure varying temperatures and locations, or the money and labor available to inventory them on top of other necessary work for the organization. These layers of precarity prevented long-term preservation from happening in any sustainable way. By 2004, the conversation had shifted from print to creating an online website or archive to collect the group's periodicals, for example, *Federation Magazine* (produced from 1993 until 2007). Some issues were digitized, but this effort included just a few dozen items out of thousands. Then, in 2007, the organization collapsed—bankrupt and emotionally downtrodden. Without a stable physical space, labor, technological resources, and adequate funding, the documents the FWWCP hoped to save ended up in basements and garages. Many members lost hope for preservation and future access possibilities.

When the new organization, TheFED, a network of writing and publishing groups, emerged from the remnants, the future still seemed bleak. Longtime FWWCP member and chair of TheFED Roy Birch explained about this time that

> The Federation of Worker Writers and Community Publishers died an untimely and painful death in 2007. The New Fed was born in 2008 from the still smoldering ashes of the Old. Lacking the social advantages of its predecessor (funding, friends, credibility, guidance and opportunity) life was never going to be easy for the new organization. . . . Survival was its main priority. (Pauszek, *Preserving Hidden* 8)

While the FWWCP struggled throughout its tenure to get funding from national organizations or to receive recognition from more mainstream literary organizations, Birch notes that the original group did in fact establish a community and secure some necessary resources. In contrast, the new FED flailed for a few years, fearing the complete loss of the FWWCP's network, including the chance to preserve the organization's textual artifacts. However, a deep-seated hope persisted for an archive that could be both, as Birch describes, a "preservation device" and "educational tool" for many who had spent their life as part of this community (Pauszek, *Preserving Hidden* 9). Ultimately, sustained maintenance could only happen if someone (or a group with financial, technological, and labor resources) determined these texts, histories, and people were, indeed, worthy of preservation. Buy-in at this point from non-working-class institutions was difficult to come by. Yet everyone involved felt the exigency that something had to be done before the FWWCP/FED ran out of time, quite bluntly, due to the aging membership, which had already seen the deaths of multiple founders.

How could we build an archive with unstable and precarious resources—when there was no archival space, or archivist, and little money? Could we create an archive while founding members were still alive? These ideological, structural, and material constraints proved complicated, but we were able to turn this hope into a reality over many years. From 2007 to 2014, a new sponsorship structure slowly emerged involving the FWWCP/FED. I learned about the FWWCP in 2012 and shortly thereafter began working alongside Steve Parks, Nick Pollard, and FWWCP/FED members via email and internet correspondence. Together, we discussed ideas for finding a London-based space, ranging from community centers or local archives (May Day rooms) to national organizations (the British Library). Each option came with challenges, not only practical ones such as finding resources but also scholarly and political ones, such as attaining appreciation for the materials on a historical and intellectual level.

When I attended the 2013 FED Festival and met Sally Flood, we expected that it might be my only chance to visit and collect some archival materials and record insights from living members since TheFED was operating with a negative yearly budget. Lucy Parker, a filmmaker and new member, and I were asked to develop a morning workshop at the festival to record FWWCP/FED members discussing the importance and possible structure of an archive. During this two-hour workshop, around a dozen members provided their ideas. There was so much excitement and a renewed sense of possibility with a group willing to do the work to make this happen and an injection of some younger people able to connect with others and perhaps find new resources. By the end of our day, the current members co-opted[34] Lucy and I onto their executive committee, the group leading the decision-making for

Figure 9: Jess Pauszek interviewing Sally Flood. Photo by Ashley Jordan.

the organization. This festival and the moments leading up to it started to build energy around creating a print archive, and the infrastructure of where the archive would be housed became the main priority.

Around this same time (2011–14), FWWCP member-group Pecket was in the process of shutting down. Pecket Wellians were devastated. However, this closure was also a precursor that helped spark the FWWCP Collection's creation. While Pecket could no longer sustain themselves and were forced to sell their residential college building, they used the profits to document as much as possible through oral history and digital archive projects. Pecket Wellians were aware of their distinct educational achievements— in spite of repeated negative framings or dismissals of their capabilities—and felt the best way to celebrate this was to leave a legacy. And they did so with community members leading the decision-making process. Pecket hired Pol Nugent to direct the archival project, and she led them to longtime friend and oral historian Cilla Ross to create the oral history. As a community organizer and Pecket participant, Pol understood the necessity of preserving working-class adult learners' testimony. Nick Pollard was also Pecket's Archive Project chairperson and personally held on to many of the FWWCP publications after the network collapsed.[35] Around this same time, I was studying with Steve Parks in Syracuse and connected with Nick, Sally, and Pol via email. Through these connections, personal relationships, and community/university networks, we began discussing how Pecket's archival structure might become a model for the larger FWWCP/FED community.

This sequence of events led us to consider community and institutional spaces in London to house the archive, eventually focusing on the TUC Library Collections at LMU. Importantly, while this space is associated with the university, the library is open to the public, and FWWCP/FED members knew they could access

Figure 10: Screenshot of Pecket Learning Community's digital archive, unfortunately now defunct.

their own materials. In 2014, thirty-eight years after FWWCP members gathered for the first time, Nick Pollard donated over 5,000 documents, the most extensive collection of FWWCP/FED material, to the TUC Library Collections at LMU. Nick had saved these materials, hoping to salvage some of the histories curated over three decades. The donation itself was a complex task for multiple reasons, including the need to get time off work/away from family, the transportation costs, and the physical labor involved in transporting dozens of boxes via van from Sheffield, hours away, to London. Still, the physical act of moving this collection across England embodied the FWWCP/FED's spirit of material exchange and circulation that would happen each year at the FEDFest in a new location. Ultimately, this donation marked the beginning of the formal FWWCP Collection.

This was a significant event, as the acceptance of the donation also became an acknowledgment of the FWWCP/FED's social and historical worth. Jeff Howarth, Academic Liaison Librarian for TUC Library Collections at LMU, noted at the time that this collection represents "groups of writers on the periphery of society, including ethnic groups, lesbian and gay groups, and members with mental health issues. The archive collection . . . will be of great interest to researchers studying adult education, creative writing, community history, social movements, working class culture, oral history, etc." ("TUC Library"). At the same time, Howarth asserted, "As the material has only just arrived and has not yet been catalogued it is not currently open to the public" ("TUC Library"). A print archive had finally begun to take shape because the *value* "in representing some important aspect from the past" (Caswell par. 16) had finally aligned with the materiality of a space being available and a librarian who appreciated the materials.

What Happens Next? Moving Materials

Once the materials had been deposited and we secured this physical space, we began thinking about how we would get it ready to be used. In other words, we had to think strategically about an audience who might use these materials and how we could make this a living archive. Community conversations tangibly influenced our next steps. For example, in 2014, Jeff Howarth, Steve Parks, Jenny Harding, and I hosted two days of focus groups in London and invited FWWCP/FED members to attend and share their ideas about the network, the archive, and what other possibilities they saw for its use.

One hope that emerged was to collect more documents from other members. But the network had dispersed all over the globe, often without contact information. We worked to gather contact information and reach out to members via email, social media, and word of mouth. In the next months, we learned of more members wanting to donate texts; yet for this to occur, they needed the physical ability to pack, label, and carry materials as well as money to ship them or transport them to London. Working-class conditions often meant transportation money was not readily available. Physical health, for many, also prevented such work. The same difficulties continued for nearly every donation or hopeful deposit.

The physical demands of this work was also something that made my experience unique from the beginning. When I first went to England, I picked up suitcases and carry-on bags full of duplicate books from Nick Pollard in West Yorkshire. I transported them with the help of Pol Nugent via car to the train station and then by myself via two trains to London, tube rides to the airport, and then by plane to Syracuse, New York. In other words, I transported over 75 pounds of books across England and the Atlantic Ocean— an endeavor that, while desired by the FWWCP/FED, still felt worrying to me because I was responsible for rare materials and then tasked with doing something with them in America in order to increase awareness of this network. Interestingly, my ability to accomplish these physically demanding tasks continued to shape my role in new ways—something I hadn't thought of when I began this work. Gathering hundreds of publications into boxes, lifting them into cars and onto trains, and walking suitcases of material between tube stations and FWWCP/FED members' homes was both exhausting and sustaining. This embodied labor is now one

of the proudest pieces of my academic life because it connected me
to people and places that I visited as well as to texts I had only read
about before. It also helped me connect my work to my family in
a new way: not just writing and thinking in the life of the academy
but getting out of university spaces and using my hands in ways that
my family understood and valued. Moving publications was only
possible because of the kitchen-table ethos that the FWWCP/FED
maintained as a transnational organization. The FED expressed
their desire to represent this transnational history, *as long as it
would also be used and circulated*; therefore, we wanted to physically
circulate these texts across geographic borders.

Now I'll describe additional rhetorical choices we made for the
archive to reflect the community relationships and values. My
hope is that this will give readers some insight as to what happens
"behind the curtain" of archival work.

NAMING, PROCESSING, AND DEVELOPING
AN ARCHIVAL COLLECTION

How could decisions about naming and organizing encapsulate
the variety of documents and people involved? Dating back to
1988, the FWWCP members were clear that they wanted to save
"everything relevant to the history of the FWWCP" (Kirkland).
The materials included letters, reports, financial accounts, minutes,
and manuscripts used within and created by members. In this way,
the material partially aligns with the Society of American Archivists'
description of *archives* that includes records "such as letters,
reports, accounts, minute books, draft and final manuscripts, and
photographs—of people, businesses, and government" ("What").
However, these documents (mostly administrative materials)
comprise only a fraction of the full printed collection, with another
2,350-plus publications in the form of poetry, chapbooks, life
histories, cookbooks, autobiographies, and anthologies.

Given their lineage, the naming of the FWWCP's materials
required some reflection and negotiation to think about stakeholders across the project. The group of us leading this project in
2014, including myself and Steve Parks (writing studies), Nick

Pollard (occupational therapy and FWWCP member) and the FED executive committee, Jeff Howarth (librarian), and more were contending with disciplinary/professional and international differences in the rhetoric of preservation as well as the logistical processes. Importantly, the TUC Library at LMU is a *library*, not an archive (even though it does house some archives), in England, which has different naming conventions, standards, and processes than the United States. So, we needed to navigate how various community members, including librarians, humanists, archivists, and students from multiple countries, understood the terminology and might understand the contents. Ultimately, the name ended up officially becoming the FWWCP Collection, with subcategories detailing a difference between "publications" and "administrative documents" or what most might consider more traditional *archives*. The term "collection" falls in line with what Kate Theimer describes as "materials that have been assembled and intentionally brought together" (para 26). This terminology accounts for a wider variety of potential users who might interact with the materials. Yet throughout this project, we use "archive" as the colloquial description of these contents because of the archival history the FWWCP began decades ago. Naming the collection was another rhetorical decision in making these contents usable for multiple stakeholders and a constraint of the location we chose.

Once we moved past the naming, organizing became the priority. This was an immense undertaking. The documents had to undergo multiple valuations to consider what might be included as well as how they would be processed and recorded. While the TUC Library Collections at LMU sponsorship certainly saw *value* (both historic and future) in the FWWCP Collection, they could not provide the immediate labor, funding, and technological tools that would make the collection usable. Dreams of curating a publicly accessible archive were quickly met with the realities of resources (or lack thereof). What emerged in response to these constraints was a flexible methodology that considered varying abilities, resources, and assets among the FWWCP Archival team. We set out to physically move, curate, categorize, organize, box, and shelve an emergent FWWCP/FED collection through constant negotiation of im/mobility, material resources, and emotional, mental, and physical labor.

Sorting

We wanted to sort the boxes of donated materials into identifiable and usable categories. How would someone new to the collection be able to find a publication or specific document? Our discussions about sorting began with the idea of using individual authors, time periods, and themes. My own sense was that a chronological history could be useful or a sorting by writing group might help guide users. Yet during our workshop and focus groups, FWWCP/FED members decided they wanted to illustrate a sense of regional participation. Geographic sorting could show how location impacted working-class people and texts, perhaps through language and dialects, vocational possibilities, food sourcing and production, culture, or regional events. For example, some Yorkshire writing groups included work from coal miners while more coastal areas might highlight docklands work or textiles from the region. Moreover, regional identity could be further nuanced with connections formed within neighborhoods, boroughs, and more. Ultimately, this pushed us to use the following regional categories in England to sort texts: North West, North East, Yorkshire, East Midlands, West Midlands, South East, South West, and London.

Beyond England, the sorting continued by countries in the United Kingdom: Scotland, Wales, and Northern Ireland. Then, we moved toward sorting into a larger European category that consisted of publications from the Republic of Ireland, Germany, Spain, and France; and an international category to include Canada, South Africa, Australia, New Zealand, and the United States. The decision for regional sorting might never have emerged if FWWCP/FED members were not part of these choices. The choice to combine countries under these categories in Europe and International was also a cost-conscious decision made to maximize how many publications we could put into each acid-free archival box, usually costing $25–$30 (or £19–£24) each. For example, to put just four texts from Spain into a box themselves as opposed to within a box with other European materials saved the cost of using extra boxes. We made decisions like this across the collection.

We have been committed to a community-based, reflective, and participatory approach to archival creation for each choice. When we began the physical work of sorting, FWWCP/FED members Dave Chambers, Roger Mills, and Lucy Parker helped this undertaking by moving publications into their regional categories. Of course, having people who lived in the country and knew the groups was particularly useful (e.g., that Prescot Writers were based in Merseyside, which belongs to the North West region; or that

Figure 11: Preliminary sorting of FWWCP documents by regions and writing groups. Photo by Jessica Pauszek.

Figure 12: Sorting of FWWCP documents continued. Photo by Jessica Pauszek.

Pecket Well College was located in Halifax and Hebden Bridge in the Yorkshire region). This process also provided an opportunity for some members to reconnect with each other during the process.

When we didn't know which region a city was in, we had to rely on a map or the internet to help. Sometimes, no location was listed, so we had to do detective work in order to find where a writing group was from or where an author typically attended. Unfortunately, because the groups weren't widely known and were mostly active before the availability of the internet, there wasn't much useful information online. Given that each text is unique and there was no standardized way of publishing in the FWWCP/ FED, we had to learn from and revise our work as we proceeded. The labor necessary to complete such a large and complex task of sorting required more assistance to make substantial progress.

Most sorting and cataloging of the collection has only been possible through extensive labor by me, Vincent Portillo, and university students participating in three study-abroad classes on civic writing and community partnerships (taught in summers 2015 by me, 2016 by Parks and me, and 2018 by Portillo and me). Steve Parks and I developed this course and recruited students each year thanks to his skillful understanding of university structures and willingness to develop an entirely new course to help me be able to do this work as a grad student. The first class ran for four weeks with seven students from across universities in the United States. We would be in the archive a few hours each week in addition to attending writing groups, exploring the city, and reading about civic writing. In my non-teaching time, I would go to the TUC Library Collections at LMU to sort and index the collection for hours. While I absolutely loved this work, it's important to remember that most of our archival progress was reliant on unpaid labor and study-abroad coursework. By June 2015, roughly 1,800 of the publications had been sorted into regions, a task first begun by members and then continued alongside my team of students. Beyond the class, I also used my own time to delve into processing the administrative files, which included over a dozen archival boxes of membership applications, meeting minutes, correspondence, funding requests, applications, and more.

Quite simply, without this study-abroad course, I wouldn't have been able to fund enough trips for me to get to England to do the necessary work. And the collection's work would have taken exponentially longer, if it was accomplished at all. Instead, by teaching, advertising, and recruiting for this course and by applying for grants every year, I have been able to continue building the archive on each of my visits in addition to conducting my own research. On two occasions, I received extra travel grant funding in the amount of $1,000–$2,500 to do research in London. This project has been thrilling, but the reality has also been an extremely time-intensive undertaking. And while many faculty teaching abroad would secure their own apartment in a desirable part of town for four weeks, I would find low-budget options such as dorm rooms that allowed me to stay longer for less. My intent with mentioning these choices and steps is to be transparent: Even though I loved every minute of this travel and work, it required resources, time, labor, and sacrifices that not everyone can or would give. In fact, Portillo and I have personally volunteered weeks of work in London beyond these courses. Ultimately, despite having immense support for the project ideologically, it did not change that the physical work has been enacted with a limited budget and largely voluntary or course-based labor.

Cataloging Texts (Spreadsheets and Metadata Galore)

Beyond sorting, ethical questions arose throughout our curation. By placing FWWCP/FED texts alongside labor histories in the TUC Library Collection at LMU, we were making an ideological argument about the collection, but we also needed to develop a schema to enact this argument through the textual categorization. We had to think rhetorically about how these documents might be used by various audiences and develop a workflow in response. To do so required us to consider the background information or metadata we wanted to create for each document. These choices are easily overlooked by users but are impactful to collections as well the people they represent. This scaffolding is especially important when working with disenfranchised communities that have had to fight for the chance to articulate their identities. As K. J. Rawson describes, there is a "rhetorical power of archival description," because descriptions shape the language used to describe communities as well as the uptake such documents will have with future archive-users (329). Rawson further argues that "there are both policies and politics involved in archival selection" (332). Cataloging or categorizing, though, is necessary to make an archive practically usable. As an ethical response to these concerns, the FWWCP Archival Project relied on insight from members to develop metadata.

Recognizing how crucial naming and description are for an archive of working-class writing/bodies led us to prioritize members' cataloging structures, which we discussed in focus groups, archival meetings, and through group email exchanges. When we began, I didn't know how often I could get to London, and we weren't sure if we could run more than one study-abroad course. This led us to try to do as much work simultaneously as we could. For instance, while sorting documents, we were also cataloging materials. This meant that Jeff Howarth and I developed spreadsheet templates for each region, listing every piece of information that we thought would be useful, such as the author, writing group, title of the publication, date of publication, language it was written in, tags, and more. These initial categorizations revolved around how we hoped users would engage with the materials. FWWCP/FED members suggested that some relevant themes might include gender, race, sexuality, mental health, migration, literacy, community, and activism. Although these categories intersect, the goal was to represent a multifaceted layering of these texts and their emergent networks.

Attention to detail meant that progress was slow. It took me almost an hour to process fifteen publications while accurately filling in this metadata. Involving students in this work certainly enabled us to process more publications, but I still had to look over these for accuracy and to help on unique questions that emerged often. These students did such critical work, and they did it with so much care.[36] Yet as with any project involving multiple people, there were also inconsistencies such as with spelling, errors in sorting or naming, and accidental oversights due to unfamiliarity with some British terminology (such as mislabeling similarly spelled towns in the wrong region or Americanizing the spelling of words like labor/labour).

While we wanted to curate for usability, we also wanted to be reflective about the hierarchical power structures embedded in such cataloging. For example, labeling a text with a tag of "women's writing" or "immigrant writers" already marks this writing and distinguishes it from "working-class writing," or the main goal of the FWWCP/FED. Moreover, these labels mean different things to each person, and we didn't want to make assumptions about the writer: Is writing about empowering women automatically feminist? Is someone who moved countries an immigrant, a refugee,

	Publisher	Creator	Contributor	Title	Date	Type	Format	Genre	Medium	Tags	Description
145	Kensington &	Eddie Adams,		History in Our Bones: Notting Hill lives reme	1993	text	community pub	memoir	book	hotel work, adoption, air t	
146	Hobnail Revie	Ade Dimmick,		Hobnail Review: A Guide to Small Press & Al		text	newsletter	newsletter	booklet	book reviews, comics, ma	
147	Hobnail Revie	Ade Dimmick,		Hobnail Review: A Guide to Small Press & Al	2004	text	newsletter	newsletter	booklet	book reviews, comics, ma	
148	Centerprise	Kay Toms		Home for Tea	1974	text	community pub	poetry	booklet	home, family, poetry, Cent	
149	Tottenham Hi	Tottenham Hi		How Things Were: Growing-Up in Tottenhan	1981	text	community pub	memoir	book	childhood, memory, comm	
150	Centerprise			Howard Mingham 1952-1994: a reading in c	1661	text	community pub	poetry	book	eulogy, Centerprise, Lond	
151	Peckham Publ	Women in Pec	A.J., B.S., Bren	I Want to Write it Down: Writing by Women	1980	text	community pub	prose, photogra	book	education, work, feminism	I Want to Write
152	Peckham Publ	H.J. Bennett		I Was A Walworth boy	1980	text	community pub	autobiography	book	Bermondsey, childhood, c	
153	London Voices	London Voices	Agnes Meadov	I'm Running in the Marathon on Sunday: Poe	1998	text	community pub	poetry, prose	book	London Voices, London, p	
154	The Arts Lab F	Les Milne		I've Been Singing	1977	text	community pub	poetry, prose	booklet	London, The Arts Lab Pre	
155	Working Press	multiple		If Comix No. 2	1989	text	comic book	satire	comic book	war, capitalism, Working	
156	Calvert's Press	Graham Harw		If Comix: Mental	1991	text	comic book	satire	comic book	race, sexuality, capitalism,	Published in 19
157	National Feder	multiple		If it Wasn't for This Second Chance...		text	community pub	informational, c	book, program	National Federation for V	
158	Ethnic Commu	Ethnic Commu	researched, tr	In Exile: Iranian Recollections	1989	text	community pub	biography	book	Iranian, persecution, relig	In Exile is a co
159	Stepney Books	Rosemary Tay		In Letters of Gold: The Story of Sylvia Pankh	1993	text	community pub	memoir, history	book	London, Stepney Books, c	
160	The Basement	Sally Flood		In My World and Other Poems	1989	text	community pub	poetry	booklet	community, class, poverty	Sally Flood's col
161	The Basement	Sally Flood	Front cover ph	In My World and Other Poems	1989	text	community pub	poetry	book	cancer, gender, female, me	Sally Flood's col
162	English Centre	Chelsea Herbe		In the Melting Pot		text	community pub	fiction	booklet	family, English Centre, Lo	
163	Working Press	Richard Turne		In Your Blood: Football Culture In the Late 1	1990	text	community pub	history	booklet	race, conflict, sports histo	
164	Working Press	Micheline Mas		Incurably Human	2000	text	community pub	nonfiction	book	inclusivity, disability, need	
165	The Basement	Alan Gilbey		Ink slinging	1976	text	community pub	poetry	booklet	domestic life, poetry, The	
166	Apples & Snak	multiple		Inside Out poems by women in prison	1995	text	community pub	poetry	booklet	women, gender, family, se	
167	LWT, Schweep	London Weeke		Into Your Past (1914-1939)	1984	text	community pub	guidebook	book	history, local London, Lon	

Figure 13: Example of spreadsheet with metadata from London-based documents.

a migrant? Each of these word choices has connotations attached
to them, so we tried to think rhetorically about the ways we could
describe them broadly. Writing that describes women's experiences,
feminism, masculinity, gendered labor, and more could therefore
be placed in the broader thematic category of "gender." And those
might overlap with other themes of sexuality, race, migration,
etc. As you might expect with such a large network, each theme
also contains material with contrasting viewpoints—sometimes
even problematic ones. However, the FWWCP/FED network
was committed to the role of democratic participation in which
disagreeing viewpoints could be expressed publicly. Therefore,
when we moved to adding more specific phrasing and tagging, we
attempted to use the words and descriptions that came directly
from the writers or their publications when possible.

We have been trying to balance community-based representations
and the potential uses of the materials. Community members were
part of creating the taxonomies and categories that shaped how
their texts would be portrayed and preserved, but some metadata
was also shaped by librarians, archivists, scholars, and students.
For instance, as I met with various professionals, some suggested I
specifically use Dublin Core, a standard for developing metadata, in
order to help with consistency as we build a digital archive, which
would add elements such as "format," "identifier" and "source"
so that we could more fully create a system of identifying each
unique element of this collection. Because a goal for the FWWCP
Collection is to be used in teaching, research, and community-
run projects, I also wanted eventually to visually showcase the
geographic expansiveness of the network. While teaching my first
study-abroad class, it became clear that my American students
were not aware of the regional differences in England and had little
experience with other countries in the UK. This led us to finding
the latitude and longitude coordinates for each publication so that
we could map the publications digitally.

Ultimately, our hope in these moments was to destabilize
traditional power dynamics and gatekeeping mechanisms throughout the process of archival work by focusing on more collaborative,
community-based decisions. We also wanted to create spaces of

reflection so that we could revise our methods when needed. One example of such reflection became the ongoing Archive Presentation at the annual FEDFest. This forum allowed those of us involved in the FWWCP Collection and Digital Collection to come together with FWWCP/FED members to discuss progress as well as to have an open discussion about changes or hopes for the following year. Beyond this, the FED executive committee also had meetings and email chains to discuss ongoing questions or ideas that arose about the archival efforts. These examples represent the transparency and collaboration that were foundational throughout our project—how we developed a methodological approach guided by community values while working to increase the access and useability of the materials. While I didn't know much archival terminology when I started this work, I have since come to see this connecting to what Michelle Caswell describes as "representation" or "the process by which archivists produce descriptive metadata, or data about the data stored in collections" (par. 17). Representation, Caswell argues, includes archivists "creating access points that can aid (or prevent) users from finding collections, bringing certain aspects of collections to the fore (or obscure them through omission), and gaining physical and intellectual control over collections" (par. 17). In the FWWCP Archival Project, members were making choices about what metadata was significant as well as how their collection should be represented and used. The language of critical archival studies allows me to show even more overtly how FWWCP/FED community members have been part of the process of changing their own *provenance*, advocating for the *value* of their histories, and shaping the metadata for their own *representation*. We've made conscious and ethical efforts to prioritize community-based desires while making our conditions and choices transparent.

Creating Reading Guides and Finding Aids

Once we completed a significant portion of the sorting and preliminary metadata, another feature we wanted to develop was a finding aid and set of reading guides. Finding aids, according to the National Archives, are "tools that help a user find information in a specific record group, collection, or series of archival materials.

Examples of finding aids include published and unpublished inventories, container and folder lists, card catalogs, calendars, indexes, registers, and institutional guides" ("Finding Aid Type"). While finding aids take in the whole collection and overview of the contents, we imagined reading guides could function as brief thematic guides specific to the FWWCP/FED publications. While this terminology is used by various archives, libraries, and institutions, the idea for the FWWCP Archival Project was also modeled from an FWWCP genre it produced for decades called publication lists. Publication lists became a chance to share new titles each year with a short description of each text, the date, and where it was published. This often was created in the format of a black-and-white trifold brochure. Building off this model, we had conversations with FWWCP/FED members and created a list of themes that we felt users of the collection might be interested in, including activism; art/design; disability; food; gender; literacy; mental health; migration; publishing; race; and sexuality.

Then, as part of the 2018 study-abroad class, Vincent Portillo and I worked with undergraduate and graduate students to find publications that might fit into these themes (for more course info, see Pauszek and Portillo "Collaborative"; "Social"; "Migration"). Students read the texts, took photos of the covers, wrote summaries, developed keywords, and created a draft of their thematic reading guide. Students also had the opportunity to have conversations with members at the FEDFest to ask questions about their themes. For instance, one student was able to explore the topic of mental health and discuss the creation of the Stevenage Survivors writing group with its organizer, Roy Birch; another talked to Lucia Birch, who had organized FEDFest meals for years, about the key role of food in the FWWCP/FED community. Each reading guide was designed to include an overview of a topic and references to roughly ten publications, including descriptive metadata (such as authors, publishers, writing groups, date published, keywords) and a summary, with the goal being a resource that highlights thematic entry points into the collection. We hoped that by creating these guides, we could increase the circulation and use of the materials.

Given the short span of the summer semester and the workload of reading, writing, and experiential activities for this course, students produced drafts of these reading guides rather than final versions. At the same time, we were also asking FWWCP/FED members via email and in person about publications they would recommend including. Portillo and I then read and helped revise each of these drafts, attempting to cross-reference the guides through tagging with similar keywords (for instance, tagging something in *gender* and *work* or *gender* and *migration*) as well as adding new texts when we found them to the list. This enabled us to show how one text could show up in more than one theme, further illustrating the intersections of class identity with so many other aspects of our lives. Portillo and I continued this work, produced an overview of the FWWCP Collection, a description of contents, directions for navigating the collection, revised and edited reading guides, created new guides based on FED requests (Jewish life, local London, mining, multi/translingual writing, war, work) and co-published them with students, with the end result being eighteen thematic reading guides (Pauszek and Portillo, "The Federation"). We worked closely with a graphic designer who was also a student (not in the course) to consider color, font, page design, paper size, and more. We were able to print a small run of this finding aid and reading guide set, thanks to a small pot of funding I received through another grant. Due to the budget, workload, and labor constraints, finalizing the finding aid/reading guides took over a year and a half.

Three years after the original donation of FWWCP materials, we had sorted all the publications into regions. However, something happened while sorting and indexing simultaneously that we didn't anticipate: if you were looking for a publication in a specific region, you might have to go through anywhere from one to fifteen boxes in a region to find your publication. We had labeled the regions while sorting, but when we began, we didn't know how many publications would be part of each region. For instance, if you wanted to find Sally Flood's *Paper Talk*, we knew it was in the London region; however, London had grown to include over a dozen boxes, and we didn't know which specific box held *Paper Talk*. Asking users or staff to look through multiple boxes seemed problematic or at least unwieldy, so we decided to revise our strategy and re-do some work in order to streamline future research processes. While it might be

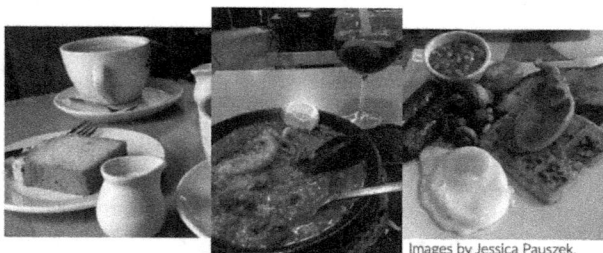

Food

Food is an underlying theme within the texts of the FWWCP. The discussion about food within this collection is often found in texts that also focus on women and migration, as some writing groups used these topics to discuss similarities and difference of food, spices, utensils, and cooking practises between their homeland and a new country. Discussion about food also appears in memoirs about childhood or family, as members reflect on important home recipes, or the availability of various food during their lifetime. For instance, throughout the collection, both World Wars and the Great Slump play a significant role in the acquisition, consumption, and sale of food.

Images by Jessica Pauszek, June 2018

Many food related titles in the collection include traditional recipes from the United Kingdom and abroad, particularly Indian and Caribbean countries. Note that the texts described here incorporate food to different extents. In some titles, food is more prominent, while in others, it is only briefly touched on throughout the writing.

Within the FWWCP more broadly, food has always played an important role in the group. Group meetings and writing groups are always held with tea and biscuits, cakes, and other snacks. Additionally, the annual FED Festival is a time to gather with friends to write and share those writings over lunch and at the pub. Just as these writers explain, food brings us together, allows us to share our varied cultures, and represents the comfort and welcome of being part of a community.

26

Figure 14: Image of the overview page of the Food Reading Guide.

typical for collections to do this from the beginning, the FWWCP Archival Project was impacted by the precarity of its labor, funding, and spatial resources. So, we only realized this problem in the later stages.

Migration

Although the FWWCP began in London, England, the network has included writing/publishing groups from across the globe for multiple decades. Some groups were located throughout the North American, African, and Australian continents. However, FWWCP groups in England often published texts about coming to England as migrants from other places in the world. For instance, within the FWWCP Collection, there are bilingual stories detailing the journey from Poland, Bangladesh, Ireland, Iran, Jamaica, Greece, and more.

Photos by Jessica Pauszek

Each of the texts in this reading guide is concerned with migration, immigration, and emigration in the twentieth century. The publications appear as books, booklets, short stories, poetry, and anthologies.

Often written as a memoir or life history, writers offer reflections on their lives in their home countries, as well as obstacles to meaningful lives in England. Sometimes, writers describe differences between their hometowns and England in regard to housing, culture, food, identity, labour, and stereotypes, while others reflect more on politics and activism.

61

Figure 15: Image of the overview page of the Migration Reading Guide.

Other complexities arose in between our time sorting and cataloging documents. First, the TUC Library Collections at LMU had to move its entire contents over three miles away across London from Holloway Road in Islington to Old Castle Street in Whitechapel. The in-progress FWWCP Collection went with it, thankfully, but the staff decreased, the library's hours diminished, and there were even fewer resources to develop the collection. With over four hundred faculty and staffing cuts and the shrinking of two of London Metropolitan University campuses (Pells), we also worried about the closure of the campus. Quite simply, our project's kitchen-table ethos had created a forceful community, but it had not combated the structural precarity behind this archival effort.

After the relocation of the collection and because of the number of people involved in the accessioning process, we felt it would be necessary to meticulously recheck each publication for accuracy in our master spreadsheet and then relabel each publication and box with an identification number. For the rest of the summer 2018 study-abroad course, Portillo and I, along with three graduate students needing internship hours for their degree program (two from the US and one from the UK), went through each and every box and cataloged its exact contents. Now users can see the exact box in which a publication can be found rather than just the region more broadly. Sally Flood's *Paper Talk* could now be traced to identifier number FWWCP08L02_019 on our spreadsheet, meaning region 08 for London and box number 02 and publication number 19 (out of over 600 in London).[37] With this metadata format, we can also easily add to the collection's contents if we have more donations.

Navigating Finances

I have described many conditions that shaped this project, but two main points have determined its continuation: community support and funding. Community support cannot be quantified—instead, it exists as the kitchen-table ethos, the sense of community values built over time. Without this sense of community—of members inviting me into their homes, feeding, and housing me and without decade-long collaborations—this project would not work. Partnered with this somewhat ephemeral notion of community, there is also the very real matter of finances.

Funding was—and still is—a constant source of precarity for the FWWCP Archival Project. Many people don't want to talk openly about money, but making these factors visible is a key ethical component for this project because we do not want to gloss over material concerns and needs. My own access to funding existed because I was at a research university where I had the opportunity to apply for grants and teach abroad. This application process was also time intensive. To interview members, attend the FEDFest, and transport books, I applied for and obtained various grants between $300–$2,000 each. The FWWCP/FED provided resources in the form of housing, transportation, and food when possible to alleviate expenses for me as a graduate student. Additionally, the Civic Writing London study-abroad course paid most of the transportation and housing costs each summer, but I was only able to maximize this time by being resourceful with where I stayed and how I spent my money. The course was not guaranteed year after year, with Steve Parks, Vincent Portillo, and I taking time to send hundreds of individual emails, visiting classes and events to advertise, and posting flyers across campus to recruit students. We also took decreased stipends for the course in years when the numbers were low. In other words, we were constantly revising what could happen based on the uncertain finances available to us. To be sure, I'm not advocating that anyone can or should make similar choices, but they give context to how this project happened and why.

Grants based on pedagogical and digital work have also been central to allowing this project to expand its circulation. In 2014, we received a CCCC Research Initiative award to develop pedagogical ideas and reflect on using FWWCP materials to teach with at both public and private universities. In 2018, I received a CCCC Emergent Researcher grant to focus on the digital portion of the archive. However, grants often present bureaucratic issues with collaborations across countries. Moreover, while these are major opportunities and successes and a source of pride, I have also applied for at least ten different fellowships and research grants that resulted in rejections. Without financial assets within the FWWCP/ FED, we rely heavily on academic funding, which is inconsistent, time consuming, and dependent upon intellectual/scholarly fashion, and the grant-writing processes are largely invisible labor. Grants also pose a contradiction— a university-sanctioned funding source was the only way this community literacy project could continue. That is, while it is necessary for the community to shape the archive at every stage, they cannot financially sustain it. And these contradictions continue. Unlike organizations with donors or universities with endowments, the FWWCP Collection's budget and resources have been much more inconsistent. And in terms of my own time and labor, I am also acutely aware that I will not be granted tenure based on this archival creation *as scholarly work* unless I publish about it.

Although most of the work I've described here is aimed at the creation of the printed collection in London, the past few years have made us increasingly aware of the importance of digital circulation. Physical space at the TUC Library Collections at LMU laid the foundation for the preservation of working-class histories; yet accessibility and circulation are not maximized with only one print version of each text in London. The COVID-19 pandemic also closed the library for multiple months, preventing most access to the materials. During this time, two masters students (one in Scotland and one in England) were trying to write dissertations using FWWCP/FED materials but could not access the print documents. Digitizing documents is an urgent task, as digital circulation has become a means to catalog information and create free access for global users. The transition from print to digital format offers a means of reinvigorating working-class histories, but, as you might expect, labor and capital do not become less critical in a digital project. It was only through moving jobs and applying for more university-based grants that I was able to secure $40,000 in technology-based funding for the digital components of this project,[38] currently in progress at fwwcpdigitalcollection.org.

CONCLUSION: LEARNING FROM PRECARITY

Collective working-class precarity inspired the need to preserve FWWCP/FED histories, but the collection's sustainability is also dependent on precarious resources. While we didn't solve every issue of precarity (and that wasn't our goal), this learning was critical to shaping an imperfect process in which community members co-curated the archives through stages of shifting provenance and processing. Our methods and methodologies had to account for the realities of people involved—the laboring of bodies, fluctuating finances, physical dis/abilities, technological access, and changing social conditions that affect not only the archive's creation but also its sustainability. These methods challenge hierarchies in archival work by drawing from community expertise and knowledge, and they enabled us to enact a collaborative version that redefines "creatorship" in archives (Caswell par. 15) by engaging the community from which the artifacts emerged.

Ultimately, what we learned from the FWWCP Archival Project that has ramifications for writing studies, working-class studies, and beyond is that our methods have to be malleable enough to account for the literacy practices, agency, and expertise embodied by the communities we engage. One of the greatest assets of the FWWCP Archival Project is the development of a kitchen-table ethos. These practices, grounded in community, shaped my own research methods/methodologies to foreground how community members curate their own histories and acknowledge the material conditions surrounding their lives.

With the rhetorical agency to curate versions of working-class history, the FWWCP/FED (re)shaped the methods of the project. By making visible precarious conditions—including the location, sorting, cataloging, and financing of the archive—we represented the real and embodied experiences of preservation, including the choices and processes that arose. The physical texts represent decades of social histories, but the ethos and methodology of the archive also reveal transnational partnerships, shared resources and struggles, as well as an ongoing commitment to the ethos and value of such history. As we do community-based archival work, attending to the materiality of finances and the labor of physical bodies pushes us to enact methods that are ethically responsive to community members wanting to speak back against their marginalization. Such work manifests not only in how we theorize projects but also through the ideological-turned-material choices of collection, design, finance, naming, and circulation.

Through our partnership, the very people who lived the history framed the vision of the archive. We attempted to enact the FWWCP/FED's collective decision-making as well as destabilize the authority of university partners to suit the needs, requests, and hopes of the community. Each choice was about promoting access and inclusion through preservation. These processes also meant revising choices so that our methods/methodologies considered the precarious realities involved. These intricacies are complex, and the archival processing is ongoing. Yet the history I have told shows how archival work is rhetorical, how our methods can be expanded and must be challenged, and how arguments about methodology must consider not only ideological consequences but also embodied labor and precarity.

Chapter 5

Worker Writer Solidarity

WHAT DOES IT MEAN TO CREATE community through writing? How can communities use writing as an attempt to define not only who they are as a group but also what they value? Can writing be an act of solidarity, of democratic practice, of reflection—even in moments of intense disagreement? To explore these questions, my analysis focuses on documents that are only accessible because the FWWCP Collection now exists at the TUC Library Collections at LMU in England. These archival documents include administrative papers, such as versions of the FWWCP Constitution and its adaptations, meeting minutes, membership applications, correspondence, grant-funding forms, newsletters, and periodicals, including *Federation Magazine*. I also draw from publications housed within the FWWCP Collection and interviews that I personally conducted with FWWCP/FED members. Without the processes detailed in previous chapters—of Sally and others sharing

Figure 16: FWWCP Constitution, 1978.

their stories, of Pecket Well College selling its building that led to our collaborative archival work, of the physical movement of documents to London—this chapter would not exist. My argument in this chapter thus has two key purposes: to analyze the complex material practice of using writing as a means of community-based action, and to showcase the priority of making histories available and archived, enabling these scholarly conversations.

As I've described in previous chapters, there is not one singular story or one defining narrative of either the FWWCP[39] or its archive. In fact, as I'll show, sometimes there were controversial moments, as you might expect from any network involving many people, opinions, and experiences. What stands out across these documents is how FWWCP members navigated contentious moments through deliberative and democratic practices with community solidarity in mind. The FWWCP collectively reworked its identity as an organization both on paper during its revisions of administrative documents and through practices it used to conduct writing groups and workshops, develop publications, and build community. In other words, the FWWCP as a network was able to continually develop in response to the individuals, changing membership groups, political/social events, funding trends, and writing technologies. To be sure, they didn't always get it right, but we can still learn from their efforts, missteps, and successes.

This chapter shows how the FWWCP pushed against deficit-based descriptions and defined themselves in nuanced ways. By composing themselves in self-selected working-class discourses,[40] the FWWCP subverted negative framings and instead presented a new and complex ideological stance about the intricacies of working-class literacy. This network worked to make more inclusive material and actionable changes and to respond to rhetorical contexts across decades, engaging collaboratively against the precariousness of their laboring and class identity. In other words, when both their livelihood as workers and their cultural histories were in jeopardy, the FWWCP used writing and literacy practices to reveal oppressive socioeconomic forces, to expose working conditions, to celebrate working-class identity, to enact new publics for their writing, to explore tensions in working-class communities, and to preserve their own truths about working-class culture.

However, this class-based solidarity also resulted in both intended and unintended consequences for the FWWCP as it found itself addressing identity politics that were splintering the very community being created. Many organizations would disintegrate under these circumstances; the FWWCP, however, became an example for how a community might bend without fully breaking as they continually revised their organizational documents and engaged in participatory discursive practices. One of the most intricate aspects of the FWWCP is how they negotiated coalition politics beyond class-based identities—and how the sponsorship network enabled and constrained these distinctions across decades in both written form and embodied social action. Therefore, throughout this chapter, I explore examples of the nuances of solidarity in the FWWCP Collection—how real working-class communities acknowledged the interwovenness of identities in sometimes problematic and sometimes empowering ways. There are missteps and strengths, growth as well as fracturing. More than any one designation of success and failure, though, the FWWCP archival documents make visible the complex processes of community building, as well as the discursive and material work that solidarity requires.

A CONSTITUTION THAT OPENS
DEBATE THROUGH MULTIPLE GENRES

Many of the previous FWWCP stories I described came from individuals sharing decades-old memories with me. Of course, memories are fallible, so I was particularly curious while sorting through the archival documents: How did the FWWCP members define themselves in those early days? How did they create and sustain a working-class community through their writing as well as their participation? I was interested in how the FWWCP turned their words into action and how these pieces fit together as part of the community's collaborative ethos, beginning with the oldest documents that still exist in the FWWCP materials.

One of the key examples of the FWWCP's belief in collective action emerges in the creation and articulation of their constitution. This document demonstrates literacy practices in which the FWWCP conveys the network's goals, rules, and values. It reads:

> The purpose of the Federation shall be to further the cause of working class writing and community publishing by all means possible, including workshop organisation, local and national publication, live readings and public performance, fund raising and liaison with such persons and bodies may be appropriate. (Federation "Constitution")[41]

The Federation developed during a time when large-scale national politics shifted to include more localized forms of participation, and the FWWCP promoted these community-minded activities as well. Small, local workshops or live readings, fundraisers, and events became the crux of the FWWCP's community building. Bringing people together was a clear intention of the Federation that was open to "groups and organisations in Britain" ("Constitution"). (Today, however, this expansive scope of participation seems narrow compared to its actual membership, which spanned continents.) They even "encourage[d] the development of new writing" rather than standardizing forms, genres, and styles ("Constitution"). From this part of the constitution, we see how the FWWCP developed a collective ethos that would "further the cause of working class writing" through a variety of written and performed genres and modes of circulation. These statements also reflect an explicit push toward making writing public and collaborative, something that continued to challenge individualistic notions of a solitary writer and process.

In addition to the collaborative and active nature of the FWWCP, another distinguishing characteristic was its self-reflexive definition as a working-class organization. As the Federation indicates,

> The term working class is open to various definitions and this is a matter essentially for member organisations to determine, subject to the right of other members and the Federation as a whole to question and debate. ("Constitution")

The FWWCP acknowledged that "various definitions" of the working class were acceptable. The organization promoted the values of challenging as well as refining such definitions through discussion. Such early work of the FWWCP still resonates today, as working-class studies scholar Sherry Lee Linkon explains "we must recognize not only that 'the working class' is not a fixed and bounded entity but that identity itself is not stable" (57). Linkon encourages us to realize that class identity is "multifaceted, complex, and under construction" (57). The FWWCP's constitution embodied this idea by advocating for members to participate in this discussion through questioning and deliberation rather than passive acceptance. Instead of defining one version of any identity, particularly class, for everyone to compare themselves with, the FWWCP was more interested in the active processes that emerge when people negotiate these ideas through written and verbal exchanges. In fact, a key belief in the FWWCP was that class identity was not static and that members themselves should be part of redefining what identity means to them.

While they were open to a variety of interpretations of class identity, the FWWCP also explicitly acknowledged some ideological investments in what working-class writing might entail. For instance, they focused on cooperative writing for a working-class audience and promoted an expansive view of this term: "We favour a *broad definition*. By 'working class writing' we mean writing produced within the working class and socialist movement or in support of the aims of working class activity and self-expression" ("Constitution"). By defining their work as part of "the working class and socialist movement," the FWWCP pointedly marked its stake in many of the national social and political discussions of the time. This leftist alignment was also meant to clearly differentiate the FWWCP from rising far right, even fascist, parties such as the National Front that worked to gain working-class support. Tensions were rising between the government and the working class after nearly 2,000 strikes by industrial workers in 1978 over wages and rights, which would be called "The Winter of Discontent" (Martin). Although the Labour Party held office under Prime Minister James Callaghan from 1976 to 1979 before the election of Margaret Thatcher, these strained social and political climates under both parties permeated the FWWCP's early years.

Similar to the collaboration between striking industrial workers, the FWWCP valued the possibility of collective working-class action for the common good. To make this applicable to writing, they advocated for "community publishing," which they described as "a process of producing and distributing such writing in co-operative and mutual forms (rather than competitive and private), primarily for a working class readership" ("Constitution"). The attention on "co-operative" and "mutual" publishing showcases a communal and democratic sense of knowledge production in which everyone can participate rather than it being a struggle between a select few writers determined to have specific talents, as in the view of the Arts Council.

The constitution's wording represents and encourages an openness toward a multiplicity of people and experiences, but the FWWCP took further steps to respond to the developing, embodied community, which, in turn, became a way of moving between community on the page and in practice. The constitution noted that "[d]ecisions at all levels shall, failing a clear consensus, be by simple majority vote, after open and democratic debate" ("Constitution"). This open and democratic debate also inspired the FWWCP to revise its constitution many times, including in 1978, 1988, 1990, 1991, 1992, 1993, and beyond.[42] In developing bureaucratic genres such as the constitution, the FWWCP members could have created a professional identity that remained fixed; instead, they constantly worked to be representative of living people's experiences.

One major change to the constitution occurred in 1988 when the Federation added that "The Federation is opposed to any form of discrimination" ("Constitution amended at the AGM on 16th April 1988"). They wrote:

The Federation is committed to the policy and practice of equal opportunities and is therefore opposed to any discrimination on the grounds of race, colour, creed, gender, class, sexuality, disability, or age. In implementing this policy, the Federation positively works to provide a forum for the discussion of issues connected with working class writing, racism, sexism, disability, and age. ("Constitution amended at AGM on 16th April 1988")

The rhetoric within the earliest constitutional document acknowledged a wide and inclusive network with expansive possibilities for its membership, but the FWWCP continued to develop and respond to the experiences of its members and social contexts that were impacting working-class people and discussions. These amendments were not perfunctory or performative changes but rather were the result of conscientious forums committed to dialogue and debate. Through the constitution, the FWWCP attempted to develop a rhetoric of collectivity in the purpose, definition, and goals of the organization. The extent to which some members wanted to maintain a working-class ethos rather than develop an understanding of intersectional identities, however, became a topic of interest and tension in the FWWCP.

Conversations in the FWWCP from the late 1970s to 1990s exposed the desire for transparent discussions about who working-class writers were and what explicitly defined working-class writing. This caused subsequent changes in both the rhetoric and the actions of the organization, pushing it to be more attentive to intersecting identity factors. As many writing studies scholars have thoughtfully explored, we know that sponsorship of literacy is often affected by power structures embedded in positions of class, gender, race, sexuality, nationality, language, education, and more (Alvarez; Duffy et al.; Pritchard). The FWWCP was also a sponsorship network for groups and individuals, and while it was meant to focus on working-class identity overall, the community expanded and contracted as individuals and groups pushed against the main sponsorship structure. This involved conversations around the inclusion of working- and middle-class, as well as non-working, members and the different opportunities afforded to each; the role of nationalism and multiculturalism in response to an organization seemingly committed to equal opportunities and working-class

144 / Worker Writer Solidarity

values; the negotiation of gendered identity in a male-dominated network; and much more.

Such discussions sometimes turned into intense and heated debates around what equal opportunities meant in practice. The most vigorous examples from the FWWCP Collection occur in opinion pieces, minutes, and writing workshop descriptions, where some writers/writing groups address groups who specifically name themselves as "women writers," "feminists," "Black writers," "gay writers," and "immigrant writers" rather than using "working-class" to describe themselves to both internal and external audiences. The labeling of these identities without more context is clearly too simplistic and risks essentializing anyone who might identify with these groups as a monolith; however, this use of self-imposed naming prompted complex debates about identity politics and the acknowledgment of identities beyond "working class" within the FWWCP, which were influenced by gender, sexuality, race, religion, nationality, and patterns of experience with work, education, and social life.

The widespread examples connected to equal opportunities within the FWWCP's constitution, "Equal Opportunities Statement," and numerous archival documents make it impossible to describe all the debates, but I will show later how the FWWCP navigated some difficult moments and restructured the network to consider social identities beyond class. Many members took part in debates, meetings, events, workshops, and publications that were focused on parsing out what words such as "working class," "feminism," "sexism," "racism," "antiracism," "socialism," "discrimination," and "opportunities" meant to them and how these understandings shaped (or needed to shape) their groups and the organization. The FWWCP was working with tacit understandings of theory and believed in learning through doing, so these examples represent the complexity of living up to the ideologies of equal opportunities. Community engagement and politics for members required that they get involved through active participation, which meant that working through the theory and language of their transforming policies was organic and lively, muddled and recursive.

These conversations and debates resulted in organizational changes and publications in which the FWWCP used to highlight a more inclusive sense of working-class identity. Even while they debated definitions internally, the FWWCP was savvy about how to advertise working-class writing to the larger outside public. For instance, around 1987–88, groups across the FWWCP were purposefully publishing working-class writing that also engaged discussions of race, ethnicity, age, nationality, disability, gender, etc., and they wanted educators to know about these texts. So, the FWWCP created *Booknews: A Newsletter for People in Education*. In the newsletter's opening, writers noted that an aim of the organization had been to make "writing and publishing accessible to those groups of people ignored or silenced by mainstream publishers" (Federation, *Booknews* 1). To combat this silencing, they created this specific issue to "feature books for the multicultural classroom" (1). While non-white and non-British members were part of the network in the early years, they were in the minority, and this publication provided a means to circulate the ongoing publishing work of members beyond the white, English, male base. The coeditors noted that "in recent years, black writing has become an increasingly dynamic movement within the Federation" (1), and they wanted to specifically promote these books and circulate them to educational communities.

Over twenty-five publications are featured with short descriptions. Here, readers are made aware that the FWWCP group Commonword published "their first anthology of black writers" in 1988 (11); that THAP Publishing launched *"Across Seven Seas and Thirteen Rivers,* a unique collection of ten life stories of Bengali Laska seaman" (11); that *Breaking the Silence*, edited by Manju Mukherjee, provides "an impressive collection of writing about the experience of women within Britain's Asian community" in Punjabi, Gujarati, Hindi, Urdu, Bengali, and English (10); that *Living and Winning,* by Pauline Wiltshire, provides a "life story of a black woman in Jamaica and Hackney" living as a "disabled person" who has "had to face additional prejudice and obstacles in her attempt to live a full and independent life" (10). Beyond these examples, the newsletter describes writing done by "young people," "basic writers" in adult literacy courses, and women with an emphasis on "multiethnic" backgrounds (10–11), all to uplift writing specifically done by working-class people from multiply-marginalized identities.

Here, working-class writing crosses racial, ethnic, gendered, and linguistic boundaries. Indeed, many archival examples demonstrate the FWWCP's priority to make this work visible. I want to be clear, though: while non-white members were involved since the FWWCP's earliest years, the explicit appeals to focus attention on multiethnic, Black, Asian, and women writers often originated from these writers, who still felt underrepresented. Members in the earliest years were often white, male, and English, though there were also Irish members (at a particular time when Irishness was, to many, an additional means of oppression). The FWWCP editors of *The Republic of Letters* described the difficulties of maintaining a collective view when class-based solidarity was sometimes viewed at the expense of other cultural and social positions:

> Even member groups that have started sure of their base and identity have changed. Further, in looking at class *cultural* oppression, we have had to confront its overlaps and entanglements with the oppression of black people. Despite the hard work and self-criticism of people writing now we have had to face the fact that white working class traditions have contributed to these oppressions. (Maguire et al. 20)

The FWWCP began with a collective formation as a distinctly working-class group and then branched out to include individuals and groups that identified with (or as) immigrant writers, women writers, middle-class writers, gay writers, Black writers, Asian writers, adult basic writers, and more. However, this identity-based negotiation of literacy practices was complex—simultaneously affording, complicating, and even prohibiting the agency and mobility of FWWCP members.

Splintering occurred because some FWWCP members believed a focus on identities other than class was an abandonment of working-class values. Others found this to be an empowering and necessary tactic for the inclusion of identities and people within a working-class framework. Many supported this view as well because they personally understood the intertwining of identities. Today, we can talk about this understanding of identity with Kimberlé Crenshaw's 1989 coinage of the term "intersectionality" ("Demarginalizing") or what she described more recently as "a prism, for seeing the way in which various forms of inequality often operate together and exacerbate each other" ("She Coined"). Yet at the time of most FWWCP conversations this term either didn't exist or wasn't accessible to this community outside of the legal and academic discourses where it circulated. While many FWWCP conversations do connect with Crenshaw's description here, I want to focus specifically on the language members used and the ways they were developing an awareness of such interwoven identities without disciplinary terminology at hand.

WRITING COMMUNITIES IN ACTION

Within the FWWCP Collection, many examples illustrate how members used writing to promote their views of community, as the constitution had hoped to support. Letters, performance poetry, newsletters, and opinion pieces written in *Federation Magazine*, for instance, were geared toward open and democratic forms of dialogue. In the 1980 opinion piece "Giving Voices to Worker Writers," FWWCP Chairperson Jane Mace explained how the network functioned as a space where people challenged and supported each other on personal and political fronts. First, she noted the extent of the network's reach with over two hundred titles circulating in the FWWCP and sales that "by now probably total half a million" (Mace). The readership of these publications ranged from local writers, trades unionists, and activists to readers in academic circles, such as oral historians and adult education supporters. Besides the number of publications and scope of circulation, though, Mace reminded members that a key characteristic of the FWWCP community was that it allowed for dissent and debate. Reflecting on a recent event, she noted:

> Debate at the [Annual General Meeting] and the six workshop discussions was often heated. Workshops explored

the importance of people communicating their own history, definitions of socialist writing, and the experience of working-class feminism. (Mace)

FWWCP workshops, as Mace described, functioned as a space for the self-expression of working-class writers, even on contentious political and social topics. Definitional work around socialist terminology was happening alongside workshops committed to exploring the combination of working-class experience and feminism, showing how the FWWCP engaged with topics of political ideology, gender, class, and history simultaneously. While these discussions prompted disagreement, the FWWCP also fostered a community where members would share and celebrate their creative work together: "Controversy raged: but the same people who disagreed round the meeting tables applauded each other's poetry in the evenings" (Mace). Cooperative ethos and democratic debate mentioned in the constitutional documents were part of the community building the FWWCP imagined—community that was not dependent upon agreement.

Living up to the values of cooperative and communal writing in practice naturally took more work than simply defining them in the constitution. As community publishing became an embodied process, it had to account for diverging opinions, life experiences, and ideologies. Sometimes, differences in backgrounds inspired people to identify with each other across experiences and to publish their own story. Take, for instance, the production of Roger Mills's *A Comprehensive Education*, a book about his experiences with the education system while growing up in London. Mills took inspiration from visiting Centerprise, where he found they published "poetry by a young black schoolboy and the autobiography of a middle-aged local taxi driver," which he described as "neither the type of people I had thought of as writers" (qtd. in Maguire et al. 193). Seeing these examples led him to join a workshop and gave him encouragement to continue writing stories that later formed his book. Mills's writing then circulated in schools through what he called "independently-minded teachers" (qtd. in Maguire et al. 195). Examples like this—in which a member gains inspiration or confidence from seeing other working-class people published and then relies on the support of community workshops to share their own writing—were key elements of the FWWCP. This community publishing ethos enabled the FWWCP to counter more traditional (read: institutionalized) forms of literacy that diminished class struggle.[43] Mills's experience expanded the rhetorical spaces and publishing opportunities for him, and this was a common occurrence within FWWCP membership.

While this community-based process was frequent, not every member had the same experience or results. It would be too idealistic to say that the FWWCP always accepted everyone or that it supported all people in the same way. Sometimes, the FWWCP struggled to maintain its democratic and inclusive form of sponsorship. For instance, dialogues about how writing workshops were run and who might be published came up—and conversations about resources (such as funding and printing materials for a publication) sometimes led to the blaming of other groups or group members. Should resources be devoted to a "women's anthology" when this was a *working-class* writing network? Should a group emphasize its distinction as "Black and Asian writers" or "gay and lesbian" or "survivors" in a *working-class* network? Should Southern groups (i.e., including London) have more resources than Northern groups? Questions of representation and equality in community publishing and resources were constant. These moments represent the complexities involved in fostering solidarity in the face of capitalist forces. Sherry Lee Linkon, in her analysis of working-class literature, describes the splintering impacts deindustrialization can have on working-class people in the workforce and beyond, and we can see similar impacts as FWWCP members navigated feelings of anger, resentment, disappointment, and more in their writing. Linkon describes how deindustrialization's effects are often so expansive that they provoke people to "place the blame not on capitalism and its valuing of profit and investor interests but on other workers—immigrants, women, people of color" (3). Capitalism benefits when workers fight each other rather than the system oppressing them. Within the Federation, we see examples of worker solidarity against these forces as well as the fragmenting that happened when worker writers blamed other worker writers for a lack of resources.

Indeed, the FWWCP was impacted by national and international conversations happening at the time around race, multiculturalism, immigration, and women's rights, all of which were recasting (and seemingly eliminating) working-class identity. As previously described, most members of the FWWCP were not considered part of the majority (even if they were citizens in the UK) because their educational backgrounds and socioeconomic classes had often relegated them to marginalized positions. However, conversations around multiculturalism created problems for working-class populations in unexpected ways that pitted race and nationality or ethnicity against economic concerns. As author Owen Jones writes,

> The promotion of multiculturalism in an era when the concept of class was being abandoned meant that inequality became almost exclusively understood through the prism of race and ethnic identity. . . . Most dangerously of all, middle-class people have ended up [according to anthropologist Dr. Gillian Evans] "refusing to acknowledge anything about white working class as legitimately cultural, which leads to a composite loss of respect on all fronts: economic, political, and social." (101–2)

In other words, Jones portrays the problems that emerged under the banner of multiculturalism for working-class people: most significantly, discourses around multiculturalism erased the significance of working-class identity as a unique identity that many working-class people in the FWWCP were attempting to make visible.[44]

Said another way, it seemed as if the working class were simultaneously negotiating contradicting views imposed upon them that both wanted class to be invisible and, if class conversations did exist, wanted to separate white working-class people (usually male) from other working-class members who might also identify through non-class-based means of oppression, including race, gender, sexuality, ethnicity, and more. The problems with these views, of course, are manifold: first, such views render class invisible in ways that further marginalize working-class people; second, strict divisions (such as ethnic or racial or gendered) within the working class can also create false perceptions that those groups are homogeneous when they too are a composite of identities. These middle-class frameworks that devalued class as well as white working-class identity were framings the FWWCP was actively negotiating against in its early years. This type of us/them rhetoric pushes working-class people against each other rather than aligning with, for instance, sociologist Satnam Virdee's description of a "multiethnic coalition of class solidarity" (Virdee), which I believe the FWWCP modeled in many instances.

Not all attempts at community building were positive or inclusive, then. Some FWWCP members were perceived as racist or at least diminishing to non-white working-class members or groups. Or, as described by members in various moments, some structures within the FWWCP became an unintended means of oppression. Simultaneously, though, entire FWWCP groups and individual members were also inviting and building spaces for Black writers' groups, designing ethnic oral history projects from immigrant populations, and creating groups based on mental health awareness, sexual identity, and gendered expression. Opposing actions were occurring in the very same network because of its scale, so it's important to consider the FWWCP as a collective unit with varying (even conflicting) perspectives among its groups and members. An immense value of the FWWCP producing serial documents such as *Voices, Federation Magazine,* and *Fed News* was that they provided space for the representation of numerous opinions together.

One particularly divisive debate about the existence of women's groups appeared in the twenty-fifth issue of *Voices* magazine from 1981. A feminist writing group called Women and Words had joined the FWWCP, much to the distaste of some. While the FWWCP did have a group called Netherley and District Writers' Workshop, which was comprised of many working-class women, it was not exclusively for women and did not use the term feminist in their name. In the *Voices* issue, the discussion of women-only or feminist groups in the Federation was fraught—with some people such as Jimmy McGovern, from the Scotland Road Writers' Workshop, arguing against admitting feminist writing groups that were not explicitly working class. In "A Letter from Jimmy McGovern: Feminist Groups," McGovern quoted a conversation from a few working-class women who felt frustrated after reading a feminist magazine. One woman described how the magazine was "supposed to be about her oppression" yet "written so that she can't understand it" (27). Another woman called the magazine "very middle-class" (26). McGovern believed these few experiences showed "a deep mistrust . . . of the Feminist movement and the apparently middle-class women in it" within the FWWCP (27). Such feminist (read: middle-class feminist) groups diverged from focusing on class-based identity, McGovern argued, and "risk alienating people . . . genuine working-class women, vital to the Federation" (27). Here, too, he quoted a woman as saying she read a feminist article about "lesbianism and [she's] none the wiser" (27). McGovern reminded readers that other journals "committed to feminism" existed already and that the Federation should concern itself with the issues of working-class women and the issues they raised—which he called "issues of sex and class" (27).

At the same time, McGovern appeared to support Netherley women writers, whom he called "working class feminists," rather than "Feminists in general" (27). It isn't clear though what concretely makes other feminists middle class: Is it their job? Their educational background? Self-identification? Instead, feminism is largely entangled with an assumption of middle classness in ways that do not allow a more robust dialogue about possible overlaps between feminism and working-class identity. McGovern unfortunately didn't explain how issues of *sex and class* can be *working-class* while issues of *feminism and class* cannot; moreover, there's an assumption that working-class women in the FWWCP would not be interested in discussing sexuality because one woman didn't appreciate or understand the writing around lesbianism.

A main critique McGovern had about feminists was based on their "exclusive[ness]," and he assumed "feminists would view the Federation as only a second or third string to their bow (excuse sexist metaphors), their primary concern being feminism" (28). Here, McGovern differentiated "genuine working-class women" from the "feminists" he imagined who could not be part of this group due to their middle-class ethos, and he did so, quite unfortunately, by asking readers to overlook what he openly called a "sexist metapho[r]" (28). And the quick but revealing connection made between "lesbianism" and "feminist" suggests there is at least apprehension not only about middle-class feminists but also about lesbian feminists (and a conflation of the two). But why did McGovern believe these groups were in opposition with the mission of the Federation?

McGovern cautioned that even though there was an "irresistible appeal of 'unity,' a unity of oppressed groups everywhere," the FWWCP cannot acquiesce to this at the expense of class-based solidarity (28). For some members, emphasizing other cultural identities as a focus of the network diluted the effectiveness of class identity and the class-based collectivity they spent so long trying to develop. Others advocated that the Federation could be strengthened by amplifying related groups that were not solely focused on class, even increasing Federation membership. In some ways, McGovern attempted to preserve the foundational principle of class identity within the group, but his perspective didn't address why feminist groups would want to join a working-class federation if they weren't interested in actively participating in and cultivating that community. Instead, it seems he had already decided their intentions because, later on, he praised other non-working-class groups and people who had been "invaluable to the Federation" and who understood "the Federation for what it is: a Federation of working class writers and publishers" (28). On the one hand, given the FWWCP's history and dismissal by middle- and upper-class people less than five years earlier, it is understandable for McGovern and others to vehemently advocate for a focus on working-class writers because they had to fight hard to establish this space. Those emotions of dismissal were still raw. However, there seems to be little room in McGovern's argument for someone to be both working class and feminist or middle class but deeply aligned with and in support of working-class values.

Moreover, the term feminist here included lesbians, which seems far beyond the scope McGovern imagined for FWWCP members. (While openly gay and lesbian writers published within FWWCP member groups throughout the 1980s, most publications were post-1981 when McGovern was writing.) Despite others believing in the possibility of solidarity across identities, McGovern's call for unity was at the exclusion of feminist groups, particularly if they seemed to be middle class. His rhetoric became more zealous, advocating for a "ban [on] all non-working class groups":

> So to all comrades who see the Federation as a political weapon I'd say: learn from the feminists, keep the movement exclusive; ban all non-working class groups and so ensure that we have the necessary sense of direction, the necessary common purpose, to use the resultant political clout. (28)

McGovern's rhetoric had multiple issues, but it would be inaccurate to frame him wholly against women. McGovern was wary of feminist groups inside of the FWWCP that were women-only and wary of middle-class takeovers of the FWWCP, but he was supportive of working-class women writers and their participation in the FWWCP. Moreover, his statements were about internal structures and not about the feminist movement at large. In his comments, though, he assumed that feminists would automatically make class identity less important than gendered experience. And he failed to account for experiences across identities. Moreover, by arguing for a ban, McGovern ironically enacted the exclusiveness and alienation that he feared, which was also contradictory to the very nature of the FWWCP that began with accessibility and inclusion. However, McGovern's diminishing view of feminist groups was not, in his writing, the same as dismissing true *working-class women,* who might be feminists, though it is difficult to know how this logic would develop and how such people would automatically adhere to these preconceived ideas of middle- and working-class feminists.

Which is to say, it would be easy to dismiss McGovern, particularly when read through the lenses of today. But that wouldn't allow us to understand the arguments about identity that shaped the FWWCP and how they worked to open forums for discussion. Such work, however, became integral to the FWWCP. In fact, the editorial group of *Voices* write that they

> disagre[e] with many of Jimmy's conclusions. . . . Many women . . . are likely to see themselves in terms other than traditional class ones. . . . Unlike the Royal Family then, VOICES is not afraid of controversy during its silver jubilee. We hold to the old maxim that debate strengthens rather than weakens. (Boyd, "Editorial" 2)

Then, Women and Words followed up with a piece advocating for the FWWCP's ability to sponsor women in positive ways. They interpreted the FWWCP as "helping to give access to writing and publishing to groups in society who are generally barred from those areas, and about breaking down the notion that a writer has to be a solitary genius" (Women and Words 29–30). They noted that the group had attracted interest from thirty to forty women and had begun because they "were sick of hiding [their writing] and feeling stupid and embarrassed about doing it. We believed that other women had the same experience" (Women and Words 29). Even more, they affirmed the impact of the FWWCP's community:

> We feel very strongly that Women and Words has made a difference in our lives—through the confidence that has come from speaking out about our writing, from the pleasure we've got from writing more and having an interested audience for our work, and because it's been a space for us away from the demands of work and family. And we believe that that kind of possibility should be open to everyone who wants it. (30)

These statements were just the beginning of this dialogue.

In true FWWCP spirit, these conversations were encouraged, and the FWWCP created another forum to do so. In a later issue of *Voices 30* from 1983 to 1984, the editors stated, "This is the first in a series of articles in which different members of the Federation put forward their views on the position of 'separatist' groups (i.e., women, black, gay only groups etc.) within the worker writer movement" (*Federation* 24). The debate of feminist/working-class groups from prior years continued to morph and, in the first piece of this forum, the group Scotland Road '83 chimed in. (McGovern was also a member of this group.) Here, Scotland Road '83 expressed their extreme dissatisfaction for FWWCP groups with a separate focus beyond working-class identity, particularly those that may have formed from an "umbrella group" that was admitted as a working-class group but had since split into sub-groups no longer focused on class identity (Scotland Road '83 24). Specifically, they used examples of feminist groups, gay writer groups, and Black writer groups (some having middle-class members)—in which working-class people might have been excluded. This debate required more complexity than calling anyone sexist, homophobic, or racist. Written in a collective voice, Scotland Road '83 argued that the goal of the FWWCP's constitution was to think about how the Federation might "grow and strengthen" (24). They explained that this was a difficult task, often resulting in the dilution and weakening of a community. While acknowledging the importance of broader political movements that drew attention to feminist issues, gay rights, and Black writers, they also rejected the view that these groups should have formally been part of the FWWCP because they saw this as a cost to working-class identity if these groups were exclusive and did not allow other working-class people:

> We in Liverpool support those exclusive groups; we admire what has made them strong; and we follow their example by saying that we do not welcome them as members. Of course in our movement we have individuals who could belong to any of those other movements. . . . We welcome them all as individuals and we value what we can learn of their oppression through their writing. But all these individuals are aware that what unites us is class. (24)

Key to this perspective was that collective class identity should have been at the forefront of each group's identity, even if individuals brought a variety of experiences with them. The problem here was that Scotland Road '83 could not seem to imagine a situation in which groups could prioritize multiple experiences simultaneously or in which class identity could be prioritized at specific moments. They also advocated that no group should be exclusive based on any non-class features. Instead, they used the rhetoric of all or nothing with class identity and the FWWCP.

Scotland Road '83 further framed the logic of rejecting separatist groups around class-based solidarity and described this as an issue of resources. They argued that while other marginalized groups had outlets that "cater exclusively for them outside the Federation," working-class people "only have one outlet: the Federation; and we will jealously guard it" (24). Calling upon the FWWCP's constitution as evidence, Scotland Road '83 defended their view that separatist groups were "unconstitutional" (24). They created what seemed like a slippery slope argument, stating that "umbrella groups" or subgroups within the FWWCP might spread into extremely negative consequences—such as "a subgroup devoted to say fascist verse" (25). The comparison here that allowing a gay writers' group or a women's writing group as part of the FWWCP could then force the FWWCP to admit a fascist group might seem a bit ridiculous to readers today, and the writers admit it would be "nonsense" should such a thing happen against the constitution (25). Still, Scotland Road '83 wanted to make sure that a group wouldn't automatically be allowed to create new subgroups "formed under a criterion other than the working class one enshrined in our constitution" (25). It was true, as well, that the FWWCP wanted to be sure to separate themselves from active right-wing groups. Still, this view overlooks that before any group was admitted, they would have an FWWCP executive committee member attend the group and report back before their provisional member status was accepted or rejected. Fascist verse would contradict the democratic, socialist values of the constitution. Therefore, should a group somehow enter the FWWCP with such political ideology, there would seemingly be mechanisms in place to reject it, or somehow vote them out if a subgroup like this developed along the way.

However, to completely dismiss this concern by Scotland Road '83 would overlook important factors that shaped the FWWCP and its members' intense desire to separate themselves from some nationalistic rhetoric and stereotypes about class identity. These tensions were arising at the same time as implicit and explicit moves toward the erasure of working-class identity. And they were happening simultaneously as some groups felt compelled to respond (with a range of effects, both intentional and unintentional), given the alternatives of the National Front and other far-right movements. Rather than making an argument about the morality or ethics of this debate, I want to think about the effects in order to show representational entanglements within the FWWCP. Dismissing Scotland Road '83 does not provide insight into why some people felt conflicted about how they might safeguard class within a social and political system that was dismissing the working class. It also doesn't allow us to see how the FWWCP as a network did, in fact, include groups with focuses on gender, race, and sexuality (even if some members and member groups disagreed) and how it continued growing and pushing its boundaries each year.

It's important to consider what was at stake if the FWWCP loosened its focus on working-class identity, which had been challenged and discredited since its conception. Scotland Road '83 articulated the importance of the constitution based on class: "[W]e simply need the constitution, for the constitution enables us to stick to our aim—the encouragement of working class writing" (25). Still, it's difficult to understand how a feminist group promoting women's writing or an anthology written by gay writers might be unconstitutional. Even more, the use of such rhetoric, particularly from the standpoint of mostly white, male writers, also pits women writers or gay and lesbian writers as somehow opposed to the goals of the FWWCP. Such debates were happening beyond the FWWCP as well in the broader labor movement, as I'll describe soon with regards to the miners' strike. This is not an agreement of

Scotland Road '83's rhetoric; rather, it shows significant dialogue in the FWWCP about fluctuating social and political values. Given the political context, we must also think about the discourses circulating about white (read: English) working-class people. Some questions emerge from exploring these documents: How do we hold what were real concerns of extremism alongside writing that also felt dismissive of people who were non-white and non-male and non-heteronormative? Does prioritizing class or any other identity always come at the expense of another, and did this happen with the FWWCP more broadly? Can we value both individual identities and collective class ethos? Can there actually be cross-coalitional working-class solidarity?

There are no easy answers, nor do I want to advocate for rhetoric that suggests dismissiveness or worse toward women or other groups based on race, ethnicity, sexuality, or more; rather, this debate in its historical context illustrates that even within the creation of an alternative working-class network such as the FWWCP, there were still more alternatives. There was neither pure working-class identity nor struggle, despite its collective formation and naming as a federation. Constant negotiation enabled hopes for a stronger working-class identity. And because the FWWCP encouraged such dialoguing, there was also room for structural and discursive changes to occur. Sometimes, even a form of elusive cross-coalitional, working-class politics appeared. While some members of the FWWCP couldn't fully imagine this in the moment, hindsight shows us the very real possibilities that emerged.

Support for Striking Miners across Coalitions

Alongside these conversations, there were also larger discussions and actions happening connected to what working-class unity might mean. For instance, I became interested in how working-class people came together during the 1984–85 miners' strike. I hadn't known the miners' history—that they went on strike in response to the threat of pit closures, by the Thatcher government, representing around 20,000 jobs—until Sally Flood and Pol Nugent asked me on separate occasions if I knew about this history.

I didn't, so I watched the fictionalized examples Pol mentioned to me: *Billy Elliot* and *Pride*. These films were useful for me as a viewer who did not have knowledge of these moments, but they soon took on new meanings when I discovered FWWCP archival documents and other community sources that connected FWWCP members and coal miners on strike. Sally and Pol's suggestions nuanced my understanding of FWWCP archival documents and led me to visit Bishopsgate Institute, a notable independent venue in London. Bishopsgate describes how the striking miners gained support from gay and lesbian working-class people and how the miners showed up in solidarity for gay rights as well:

> The alliance . . . was an important factor in turning the tide in the trade union movement in favour of equality measures for lesbians and gay men. At the October 1984 Labour Party Conference, the National Union of Mineworkers sent the following message of solidarity to the Labour Campaign for Lesbian and Gay Rights: "Support civil liberties and the struggle of lesbians and gay people. We welcome the links forged with South Wales and other areas. Our struggle is yours. Victory to the miners." (Jackson)

Archival insights such as these, in essence, brought conversations to life for me in new and unexpected ways, situating me alongside the writing and perspectives of working-class writers impacted by the strikes.

Moreover, though, archival documents illustrate a piece of the materiality involved in attempts at community building. Community and solidarity are words that need action and embodiment for tangible changes, and the FWWCP Collection provides glimpses of the textual traces on the path toward social action. For instance, I found a handmade flyer from 1984 advertising "Miners Poets: a poetry event in the aid of the NUM [National Union of Mineworkers]" (*Federation*, "Minerpoets") with the names of FWWCP writers included. In addition to this, there were artifacts, including a budget report and a diary entry from Roger Mills's time as a paid FWWCP worker, which Roger donated to the TUC in 2022.

Figure 17: Front side of archival flyer about the Miner poets event in aid of the NUM, August 1, 1984.

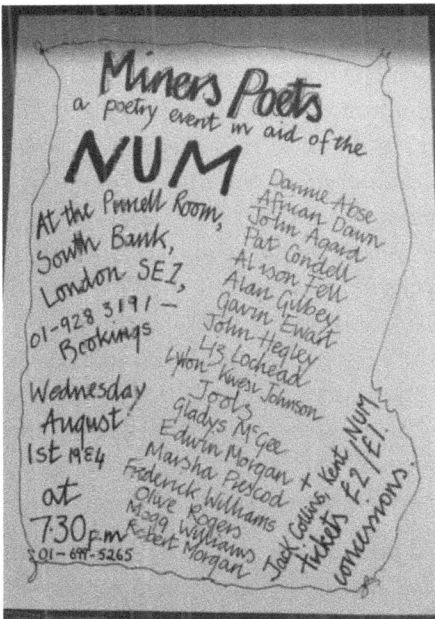

Figure 18: Back side of archival flyer about the Miner poets event in aid of the NUM, August 1, 1984.

The FWWCP Income and Expenditure Report from 1985 indicates that there was £1,140.76 (around $1,580) of income from the "Miners' Benefit" event and that this income was then distributed to the miners (Federation, "Income"). In an entry to his FWWCP diary, Roger Mills noted that he went to

> Blidworth in Nottinghamshire to meet striking miners. . . . The place we went was a communal eating and social centre. It was run by some very strong women who had really discovered their power through the dispute. They told us about the harassment that active trade unionists had been suffering. They also have a quite smart newsletter that they put out to keep morale up. . . . They seemed very pleased to see us and of the opportunity to talk about the things they had been through. ("July 23rd Mon")

These somewhat ephemeral documents showcase the FWWCP's connection to organizing poetry events, fundraising, and purposefully showing up for fellow workers. They worked to support the miners through written and word-of-mouth testimony, as well as to assist the financial precarity striking miners and their families were facing. Moreover, the FWWCP showed up—literally driving to communities and metaphorically through creating rhetorical spaces to showcase these issues—for striking miners.

Additional examples of community building (in this case, specifically around the strikes) emerged as I sorted through the FWWCP Collection. I found a community publication from 1987 entitled *We Struggled to Laugh*, written by The Barnsley Miners Wives Action Group. This publication includes stories from women who describe the personal effects of the strike, as well as how their roles in their communities changed through creating and managing soup kitchens, demonstrating and picketing, fundraising, and more. In the foreword to the book, Arthur Scargill, president of the National Union of Mineworkers (NUM) during the strikes, wrote:

> This book is a testament to the strength of women in struggle, women whose energy is vital to the progress of not only the British working class, but humanity itself. I accept that it

has become all too easy for trade union officials to sing the praises of women who, during the miners' strike of 1984/85, mobilised and sustained a level of popular support never surpassed in our history. . . . Today, the energy and talents of these women are at work in a multitude of campaigns—against nuclear power, for peace, for women's rights and socialism. . . . I argued that Women Against Pit Closures should be working in close alliance, side by side, with the Branches and Areas of the NUM. Today, I argue that more fiercely than ever. (Barnsley Miners Wives Action Group 4)

Here, Scargill commended the role that women had in the miners' strike and admitted how women continued to have tangible impacts on the world around them. Many women in this publication also realized their agency in the strike and beyond, and they wrote how the working class needed a coalitional effort to make change. For instance, Linda from Park Mill wrote:

So let's muster our forces, the whole working class,
They've done it before on our kind,
Let's stand up and tell them enough is enough,
If we all stick together we'll find
That there's plenty of people who are willing to fight,
They'll support us and help us along,
They've been waiting for years for a cause such as ours,
To fight for our rights can't be wrong. (Barnsley Miners
Wives Action Group 8)

In Linda's call to the "whole working class" (8) and in Scargill's acknowledgment of the necessary "close alliance" between women and the NUM (4), they indicated the strengths and possibilities of a working-class group that united across experiences. Here, we get a sense of how working-class women's active involvement profoundly impacted what was traditionally a male-dominated sphere.

The active and collaborative creation of *We Struggled to Laugh* also exemplifies how the FWWCP used writing to build community amid dividing moments. As Nick Pollard remembers, this publication came about through the negotiation of FWWCP member Beth Edge (of Heeley Writers), who was a teacher in Barnsley. The Heeley Writers were committed to transcribing meetings of the women's support group during the strike, but this work turned into the anthology of poetry and prose featuring the poem above (Pollard, Personal Correspondence). This project eventually involved the Heeley Writers, the women in Barnsley, as well as the National Union for the Mineworkers, who partly funded this project, and provides an example of how the FWWCP was not only about producing writing but also focused on the community-based process of writing, collaborating, and publishing.

By convening together, writing and publishing, fundraising and protesting, the FWWCP collectively pushed against individualistic rhetoric from Thatcher's tenure and worked toward preventing widespread pit closures. Unfortunately, the strike ended almost a year later in March 1985 with the miners defeated. The result was not the large-scale social and economic change that many working-class people fought for, but there are tangible pieces of community building visible through these archival documents that showcase the support working-class people gave to each other. These examples show the real ways that working-class people both within and beyond the FWWCP enacted solidarity as they found commonalities across their diverse experiences. Still, though, the actions of the FWWCP didn't quite meet the full needs and realities of the political moment, as these solutions of fundraising and publishing did not integrate working-class identity into more widespread public discussions. Such moments of solidarity reveal how the FWWCP—influenced by working-class women writers—made small, meaningful social changes within working-class communities. In some ways, this validated the point some FWWCP members made about prioritizing class identity: The key point of organizing was working-class action rather than women's rights. Working-class women impacted these moments in tangible ways, but it was in collaboration with other working-class people. Yet the results were also largely inadequate in the strike. While members of the FWWCP were arguing in writing about what role non-working-class identities should play in the network, larger socioeconomic and political forces necessitated action across communities. The publications, fundraising, and events represented some hopeful coalitional moments, but they also made apparent that any widespread working-class success emerged with the support of groups that identify across and are marginalized because of gender, race, sexuality, ethnicity and more.

When Policies and Organizations Change for People

While the miners' strike provided a tangible national example of the need for solidarity across marginalized groups, the FWWCP was still trying to understand what it needed to do internally as an organization still hoping to "further the cause of working class writing" (Federation, "Constitution"). The FWWCP did this through continuously creating and revising written forms such as newsletters, magazines, and constitutional and policy statements to embody democratic participation and consider questions of equality (of who gets published and is privileged or silenced) in response to a changing membership. To put it simply, the FWWCP was having a bit of an identity crisis, with some advocates wanting to expand working-class identity to explicitly represent additional positionalities and others wanting to maintain a status quo focused on the working class only. Creating an understanding of working-class identity that accounted for intersections across social groups was challenging, but it was something that the FWWCP pursued across their tenure in both community-based genres of writing and processes of publishing.

One form of this internal review and identity discussion revolved around the creation and revision of policy documents throughout the 1980s and 1990s. Unlike the miners' strike that was rooted in the exigence and threat of closures, FWWCP discussions and changes were less time-bound and the group could be deliberate (though perhaps too slow at times) in their attempts toward change. In the 1980s, the FWWCP executive committee created an "Equal Opportunities Statement" to supplement the group's constitution, stating: "We welcome all people irrespective of their race, gender, disability, age, sexuality, educational attainment or class" (Federation, "Equal Opportunities Statement"). This document, and its many iterations, prompted dialogue about how working-class identity might intersect with other identities in competing and allied ways. In effect, the Equal Opportunities Statement was an official acknowledgment from the executive committee that the embodied experience of individual FWWCP members was not equal and needed to be more explicitly acknowledged. In 1986, the FWWCP executive committee issued an "Anti-Racist and Sexism Statement," which prompted increased attention to Black and women writers specifically through the creation of a women's anthology, *Move Over Adam,* and a "Black Writers Day." They also had a "Women in the Federation" event on March 1, 1986, for which their goal was to "talk about how we see ourselves: as women, as working class, as black etc.—do we have conflicts about which is our primary identity" (Federation, "Minutes of Executive Meeting No. 8").

Such projects increased dialogue about the possibilities of working-class solidarity. One executive member described how differences "give strength to [the] common cause" of the FWWCP:

> We meet under a common banner of "Working Class Writers," but . . . all members have different backgrounds, different problems and consequently different priorities, within the overall aims of a working class organization. These differences must be acknowledged, respected and enjoyed, because they give strength to our common cause. We welcome writers from all racial and ethnic backgrounds and believe that the Federation must reflect the strength and diversity of the working class in Britain. (T. J., "Letter")[45]

This rhetoric of "reflect[ing] the strength and diversity of the working class in Britain" suggests that coalition building can happen across differences. Indeed, other members also felt that working-class people could identify with each other without being a homogeneous group. *FedNews* Issue 3 featured an interview with poet Benjamin Zephaniah, who stated how he felt "part of an International working class" community through his poetry: "I write the way I speak . . . and even if I write a rasta poem, white working class people identify with it because of the slang, it's down to earth, straight to the point" (1).

Multiple members supported a more expansive vision of working-class people, particularly at the intersection of race and gender. This ultimately led to the full creation and revision of the "Anti-Racist and Sexist Statement" and an explicit addition of workshops and publications devoted to working-class writing from women, Black writers, gay writers, disabled writers, and more. While some were still concerned about groups that might be seen as "separatist" in that they were not *only* working class, one member articulated her ideas about inclusive class-identity as such:

> The Federation exists for working class people and working class writing and there are black working class people and there are gay working class people who write . . . they should be encouraged along with the traditional white working class. . . . All groups must satisfy the Exec[utive Committee] . . . and a separatist group would have to prove as much as any other that they fulfilled the criteria, that is, to show they are furthering workers culture. (T. J., "Letter")

In this way, the framing of separatist groups is not either working class or non-working class; rather, it follows that a group could be both promoting working-class culture and writing from other positionalities.

Rebecca O'Rourke, chair of the FWWCP at this time, also described her support for groups that expanded working-class identity. She reflected on being part of the Women's Day where over fifty women attended workshops and shared their stories:

> Being working class doesn't account for all our experiences. All of us in the Fed are there because we define ourselves as working class people committed to developing a distinctly working-class identity in writing. But those of us who bring other life experiences and identities with us can't leave them at the door. . . The working class has its ignorance and

prejudices, it also has a generous solidarity that works against this. Those of us who have the power that comes from being men, heterosexual or white have to recognize that women, blacks, and gays, have the right to meet as WORKING CLASS PEOPLE with those who share their particular experience. It's not an either/or situation: it's being both and all at the same time [sic]. ("Response")

These examples underscore working-class women attempting to navigate positions of both privilege and marginalization within the FWWCP, particularly while external sociopolitical forces were working to fracture working-class solidarity.

Yet while many members acknowledged the humanity of working-class people across backgrounds, the network more broadly needed to grapple with how the Federation would represent and understand itself as a unit. On the one hand, the previous "Equal Opportunities Statement" and the "Anti-Racist and Sexism Statement" helped create a rhetorical space for people, particularly those identifying as women and Black writers, to express their concerns about marginalization occurring even within the distinction of working-class writers. Special events and publishing projects such as these marked more concrete attempts toward inclusion, and writers who identified in these ways had more opportunities to speak up to the larger organization. On the other hand, the distinctive labeling of women and Black writers could be limiting to populations who identified differently with another community (e.g., male, white, Irish, gay, etc.) or entered the FWWCP with the intention of finding commonalities in working-class writers. Still, the goal behind naming such distinctions, beyond class identity, emerged because many members felt they were *simultaneously* discriminated against because of their racial or gendered identities. Within these endeavors, there were attempts to talk across experiences of race and gender, sexuality, and more. These documents and their revisions caused somewhat conflicting paths in the FWWCP, a theoretical framework that sought to open up discussions of identity separate from class; and workshops that struggled to tangibly find connections within the binary thinking of working-class/other identities framework. Such examples sometimes led to conflated ideas of identity in the writing and actions of the FWWCP.

We see the results of such discursive conflation in the "Minutes of Plenary Session" document from January 24, 1987, collaboratively written by some executive committee members. This document includes brief report paragraphs with one entitled "Black and Women Writers in the Fed." This document drew attention to the benefits of discussions around race and gender and the difficulties of enacting ideas that were ethically responsive to the needs of the FWWCP. For instance, some conversations noted suggestions of implementing quotas of "black people on the executive [committee]" and a "workshop on black writers at the [Annual General Meeting]" to promote the work and representation of black writers (Federation, "Minutes of Plenary Session"). Additionally, this document emphasized the need for all groups to "examine ways of positively encouraging black people to join, not just talk about it" ("Minutes of Plenary Session"). In this way, the executive committee took steps to openly reflect on the racial breakdown of the organization's leadership and groups. The FWWCP attempted to be inclusive and to prioritize the experiences of Black and women writers through these discussions, but simply adding these labels to a workshop did not provide a governing vision of an intersectional working class.

Within these discussions, there were also honest critiques noted by some that "black people and women were lumped together as a subject and that some people felt as if they might not be welcomed to attend such specific events" ("Minutes of Plenary Session"). Here, we have another instance in which the language of inclusivity fails to account for the lived experiences of the stakeholders involved. Naming groups of people on a document and hoping the discussion appeals to everyone is clearly not the same as actively making the FWWCP accessible and inclusive for all who want to be involved. But such discussions did actually produce changes over time with the revision of constitutional documents and policy statements; the inclusion of non-class-focused writing groups; the increase of more women, Black, and immigrant executive committee members and group members; the addition of writing groups across various continents; transnational community-building in the form of sharing publications, creating multi- and translingual publications, and international events; and the production of thematic anthologies beyond working-class-only experiences.

We see some of this action at the 1987 Annual General Meeting and within subsequent publications. FWWCP member group Cultureword held three sessions on "Black writing" throughout the weekend that were meant to be about "what is different, and special, about Black writing" ("A.G.M. 1987" 2). Nick Pollard held an "Anti-Racism in the FWWCP" workshop to consider what the Federation "could and should . . . be doing" about racism ("A.G.M. 1987" 3). And Lemn Sissay held an additional workshop called "Black Writers in the FWWCP" to "develop and review issues around Black writers [sic] participation in the Federation" ("A.G.M. 1987" 4). Multiple workshops were hosted by women, but only one was explicitly about women's writing, where Laureen Hickey discussed the "successful women's day" and the "possibility of a Federation women's anthology" ("A.G.M. 1987" 3). Still, events such as these marked attempts to "change deeply ingrained attitudes and prejudices to build trust and respect" (O'Rourke, "Chair's Report 1986–1987" 1). Raising awareness about these perspectives, for some, created a sense of solidarity and empowerment to negotiate new ways of being in the FWWCP.

The FWWCP members continued, however, to realize feelings of commonality and policy documents only go so far without a truly coalitional framework that produces solidarity. Such cohesion had to be enacted through actions as well as language, and they had to address questions of equality and access: which ideas and members were represented on the executive committee, in publications, and in workshops? One idea emerged to publish a newsletter open to participation from all members. In 1987, Laureen Hickey noted that the impetus was that some workshops "fe[lt] isolated from the executive [committee]" (Federation, "Newsletter" 1). The newsletters, then, became a conversation starter where groups could participate in more public discussions about the connection between the executive committee and membership, how to encourage participation when relying on volunteers to lead the organization, and follow up with discussions on the Black Writers Day and other events. The newsletter genre morphed into *FedNews*, another public forum for members to openly discuss their thoughts. Conversations continued around the affordances and constraints of a working-class network. Indeed, in *FedNews* Issue 3, the coeditors asked readers to reflect on how "Women and Black people [are] perceived through the language we use" (1), and they suggested that it is often in a way "that excludes them from the solidarity of a working-class position" (1). Taking issue with this, they discussed "strategies for implementing" their Equal Opportunities Policy, noting the success of their Women Writers' Day that later spurred a women's anthology, women-led workshops, and women on the executive committee. They made clear that "The Fed must continue to develop this area, allowing open discussion on how women are portrayed in our work—exploitation as well as positive aspects" (1). In addition to changing how women participated in the FWWCP, the coeditors acknowledged that "as a predominately white organization" they could "widen our understanding and encourage black writers to become active and black groups to affiliate" (1). Some suggestions for doing this, they noted, required building on two recently successful events such as Black Writers Day in London and Liverpool. Multiple events around this time took place focusing on Black writers, including workshops, writing days, and publication events; these changes were meant to move past discussion and into demonstrable action.

In fact, almost all *FedNews* issues between 1988 and 1993 focused on how the FWWCP could grow as a community with different voices. In *FedNews* Issue 1, the editors wrote that the Federation

> acts as an umbrella for a whole spectrum of people. . . . There is common ground, yes, but that does not mean we all share *identical* objectives and ideals. Nor that we all face the same oppressions. . . . We can grow and learn from disagreements

if we bring them out in the open and *use them* rather than sitting on them with a 'we're all the same' smile. (1)

To endorse this idea of dialoguing, each *FedNews* issue included a section called "Fedback," so writers could share feedback about a recent debate or ask each other questions. Additional sections often included interviews, book reviews, members' poetry and prose, as well as announcements about member groups. But the rhetoric of inclusivity—of mutual and community publishing—did not always manifest in inclusive practices for everyone. Rather, developing solidarity was often tension filled and messy. In each phase of the FWWCP, solidarity and community were not just obscure ideals; they were rooted in the real process of creating change through concretized actions, revised writing, open dialogue, and publishing.

Tensions continued to play out through discussions of gender and class, particularly about the extent to which new groups needed to emphasize class identity. A rhetoric of understanding and respect circulated through documents such as the "Anti-Racist and Sexism Statement" and the "Equal Opportunities Statement," falling in line with many openly democratic facets of the FWWCP. However, major problems existed within these documents and the discussions surrounding them. For instance, naming racism and sexism (as well as sexuality, religion, age, nationality, etc.) under the same statement without any discussion about them individually risked conflating the experiences and therefore became so broad that the documents often failed to adequately represent complex identity issues. By combining "sexism" with "anti-racism," there is an implied statement that discrimination based on sex and race can be handled interchangeably. To be sure, some FWWCP members wanted to bring race and gender discussions together in ways that created a sense of solidarity and commonality among members. But how about racism that occurs against women? Where does racism against men of color fall into these categories? What about sexism that occurs in connection to sexual preferences and gendered identity? In other words, putting the sweeping terminology "sexism" and "anti-racism" in a single policy fails to acknowledge complex identities, the interplay of these terms, and the embodiment that manifests beyond the rhetoric through the lived actions of members. These discussions continued to move away from class identity, however, which also caused ongoing tensions within the organization.

This debate folded into others about the core struggles of class-based identity that would continue to define the FWWCP. Increased attention to race and gender also prompted questions for some of the white (read: English, male) working-class FWWCP members and put them in a difficult but necessary rhetorical space to respond. While some debates emerged specifically around racism and sexism, others drew attention to issues of class privilege, social standing, and persecution based on national identity. The FWWCP, in many ways, was trying to save class identity as its foundational tenet while separating itself from the fascist extreme of the National Front (1970s) and later the far-right British National Party (1980s) that were trying to gain white working-class voters. Moreover, during the 1970s and 1980s, a series of right-wing attacks on Black community bookshops and leftist bookshops occurred, including bookshops where FWWCP publications circulated ("We Won't"), so members had to consider these threats and the reality of people trying to bring far-right views into working-class groups (see also Federation, *Voices no. 29*). The original goal of supporting writing in the working-class and socialist movements continued to be a complex endeavor as members grappled with external sociopolitical forces and internal group dynamics.

Inclusivity was explicitly addressed on a bureaucratic level through a revision of the FWWCP constitution, which stated:

By "working class writing" we mean writing produced within the working class and socialist movement or in support of the aims of working class activity and self-expression. . . . The Federation is committed to the policy and practice of equal opportunities and is therefore opposed to any form of discrimination on the grounds of race, colour, creed, gender, class, sexuality, disability, or age. In implementing this policy the Federation positively works to provide a forum for the discussion of issues connected with working class writing, racism, sexuality, disability and age. ("Constitution 1991")

Although there are distinct and explicit connections between the "Equal Opportunities Statement" from the early '80s and the 1991 constitution, the process that enabled these changes created tension for years—tension that contributed to both the growth of the organization's scope and the departure from a (seemingly) stable sense of working-class identity. While the FWWCP didn't necessarily thrive on these frictions, its commitment and ability to keep evolving in response represents how strongly they felt about the promises of working-class unity.

Importantly, acknowledgment of prejudices across the organization and the belief in widespread improvement didn't mean that every single person struggled with these concepts. Here again, the complexity of a federation with hundreds of individuals arises. Many members saw connections across working-class identity without overlooking other backgrounds. Member Laureen Hickey wrote in 1992 that "[t]he beauty of the Federation has been the coming together of people of many different age groups and regional backgrounds" and admitted that such space would, of course, then "reflect the contradictions of the working class, sexism being one such issue" ("Gender and Class Workshop"). These rich understandings of working-class experiences continued throughout the FWWCP's tenure. As we read beyond constitutional documents and policy statements, there are many examples in the FWWCP Collection—in letters, op-ed pieces, publications, workshop descriptions, and more—that represent the difficult and embodied work of actively shaping the community. The FWWCP Collection makes visible how a community tried to heal and unify itself even while they were unclear how to do so—and, yet, they kept working and revising their community through debate and dialogue, workshops, public events, and publications.

CHALLENGING THE MARGINS AGAIN

One result from discussions of working-class identity and intersectional understandings for FWWCP members centered on alignment against a middle-class takeover of the organization. For instance, as a response to the "Equal Opportunities Statement" and subsequent discussions, the executive committee organized a writing festival event in 1993 called "Writing From the Margins." The phrasing of this title was meant to evoke a sense of solidarity and empowerment through writing that emerges "from the margins" or from those in the working class rather than from a position of privilege. And, in fact, the very members themselves soon challenged "margin" and "privilege." Some members felt as if even the naming of this festival proved contradictory to what was happening within the organization—most notably, what one member, Alan Scanlan, suggested was the rise of a middle-class hierarchy.

In an open letter to the FWWCP executive committee, Scanlan described how class distinctions within the FWWCP have become a mechanism to reify the marginalization many working-class people already felt—the marginalization the FWWCP originally intended to combat. Throughout his letter, Scanlan drew attention to distinctions of class, access to education, national identity, and social stigma, and, by doing so, he illustrated how the "Equal Opportunities Statement" was not always beneficial for all members when put into practice. Scanlan wrote:

> I see it as necessary for me to have to remind the FWWCP hierarchy of exactly who "the marginalized" are. . . . What is the criteria for being Marginalized? Call me old fashioned, but how about "poverty" for starters? Too radical? Ok how about being educationally disadvantaged? How about being disabled? Mentally ill? How about being one of the above and also being Irish, black, Asian? And a gay woman into the bargain? . . . I am talking about the fundamentals of deprivation, vulnerability to exploitation. A genuine-real life underclass minority, majority call it what you like, but IT IS THERE, and yeah it is "writing from the margins." (2)

Throughout, Scanlan argued that the original intentions of the FWWCP to provide access to writing and publishing opportunities for *all* working-class people had been co-opted by middle-class members taking needed resources from truly "marginalized" or "disadvantaged" working-class participants (2). This language and sentiment echoed the complaints of some members years earlier about middle-class feminist groups that did not accurately portray working-class women.

To support his claim that the "Equal Opportunities Statement" contradicted many of the practices of the FWWCP, Scanlan described two people who would seem to have "equal" access and publishing opportunities from attending the same writing group. As Scanlan tracked the two people and the process through which they might publish, he explained significant differences that emerged. First, he noted that "Person A" was an Oxbridge [i.e., from Oxford or Cambridge] graduate who could use "DTP" or desktop publishing and computers, arguing that these factors gave this person social capital and resources. In this way, Person A had educational resources (coming from a university background), technological competency, and resources for publishing and writing assistance, as well as social standing that could impact the access they had to succeed. On the other hand, Person B, Scanlan noted, did not have the same technological, social, or educational resources. Instead, this person was a part-time, "semi-skilled worker," who left school at age fourteen. He was also unable to use computers and was "a politically persecuted minority" in England at this time (4–6). Scanlan noted that while Person A's publication idea in the FWWCP writing group was indeed realized through its successful publication, Person B's was not, due to the combination of these factors and various difficulties. Later, Scanlan self-identified as Person B, an Irish immigrant who did not have desktop publishing capabilities, the needed cultural capital, or the resources that allowed Person A to succeed.

While both people might have had "equal opportunities" as part of the FWWCP, Scanlan argued that their positions were clearly unequal and favored Person A in ways that took resources away from the members who needed them most. He questioned the executive committee: "What constitutes equality in opportunity for access to publication? What do you really mean or understand by 'access for all' and 'writing from the margins'?" (8). Scanlan distinguished between the original working-class ethos that formed the FWWCP's foundation as a collectively marginalized population with the more current group, who accepted members with university degrees, from various social standings, and who had many technological capabilities. While some might view this letter, which Scanlan wanted circulated, as divisive or creating a binary between working- and middle-class people, Scanlan showed the nuances within groups of working-class members (such as their capacity for technology, national background, social standing, type of education, and job status). In effect, Scanlan advocated for a continued focus on the marginalized working class and increased transparency regarding resources for writing and publishing, especially before the FWWCP branched out to include groups of people beyond Britain (something the executive committee was beginning to pursue through global connections). Similar to Scotland Road '83 and McGovern, Scanlan was extremely worried about losing the working-class ethos of the organization. His understanding of groups interacting across identities differed, though, from these perspectives over a decade earlier: Scanlan recognized the intersections of identity positions among marginalized people.

So, how might we read Scanlan's letter in its context? First, he drew attention to what he considered the "fundamentals of deprivation, [and] vulnerability to exploitation" (2). He named such vulnerable people as those who might be viewed as "educationally disadvantaged," "disabled," or "mentally ill," while also considering how these experiences may also be compounded through other identities, such as "being Irish, black, Asian" (2). All of these identities contributed to a further marginalization of a working-class person, Scanlan argued. To add more nuance, Scanlan asked what it would mean to think about sexuality and gender by being "a gay woman" as well? This question acknowledged the multiple forms of discrimination that occurred simultaneously within the working class and how these were compounding positions, each needing consideration. Scanlan articulated that working-class oppression could be felt across boundaries. Importantly, though, class provided the lens for these questions. Even while acknowledging each of these positions and their relation to the "margins," Scanlan's main purpose was to make a statement about class identity by juxtaposing how working-class and middle-class differences manifested. Ultimately, Scanlan argued that opportunities between classes were not equal, offering a scathing critique of some of the executive committee's practices. He concluded, "It is very easy (and hip) to talk equal opportunities and draft 'lovely' policy but implementation (especially if it interferes with your own ambitions) is another thing altogether" (10). Through this example, debates emerged about how the FWWCP should use their resources. Scanlan's attention to class, in some ways, corresponded with the argument Scotland Road '83 made, in that class identity was the main factor of marginalization and should be a unifying principle for the FWWCP; conversely, though, Scanlan saw himself as part of an enterprise for combating multiple oppressions felt by the working class within the complex framework of identities. He more accurately described the positionalities (gendered, raced, educational, mental and physical ability, sexuality, national origin, etc.) that played a role within class oppression, thereby prompting a generous reading of his ethos and goals.

Onward! Continuing through Disagreement

Ultimately, the FWWCP developed a model that allowed the group to continue amid debates and tensions. For example, across the decades, many women writers encouraged conversations about the inclusion of multiple identities. By focusing on women writers here, I am not conflating all women's experience to be the same; rather, I am attempting to show how some women responded to these occurrences and identified a need to change how working-class women fit into this environment. At a complex time when multiculturalism was impacting public debate, and the politics of Thatcherism and the Conservative party limited the working class, many women in the FWWCP navigated this terrain by using literacy to position themselves rhetorically as writers. They were also advocates of institutional change, engaging in and expanding their own writing groups as well as the FWWCP more broadly, sometimes in conditions that might have been hostile or indifferent to their literary production.

Such work was done understanding working-class oppression through compound lenses. For example, in 1986, Laureen Hickey wrote,

> There should be space for women and black members to get together within the Federation and that this will strengthen the Federation's working class base if done correctly. I hope you don't mind but I am attempting to weave together my personal experience with my political views as I don't think the two can be separated. . . . At the age of sixteen I was very aware of three specific oppressions. The first oppression was my class, the second was my sex, and the third was of ethnic oppression. ("Different Backgrounds")

This statement accentuated what was missing from the Scotland Road '83 argument. That is, she explained the interwoven nature of personal and political events through the intersectionality of class, sex, and ethnicity. Hickey's statement was combined with stories of other members and presented to the executive committee as part of the push for an "Equal Opportunities Statement." This encouraged ongoing revisions of their constitutional documents. That is, statements such as these productively reframed the goals of the FWWCP and impacted future structures of the organization. Beyond these structural changes, which included the production of women's anthologies and workshops and the inclusion of writing groups focused on racial, gendered, sexual identity, there were also attempts to promote more inclusive ideologies as well.

One way the FWWCP built on their views of accessibility and opportunities for all was through themed workshops, festivals, and publications, and with the explicit goal of expanding writing groups beyond England. These discussions emerge throughout the meeting minutes. In 1986, the executive committee wrote,

> If any members of the Federation wanted to get together they should be allowed to and even helped to do so by the Federation. Bringing interest groups together would actually

give women and black people inspiration/confidence to go back into mainstream groups. . . . Black people, gays, and women [sic] were part of the working class but often the most oppressed sections and it was naïve to assume that all are equal within the one workshop and can function on same basis. ("Agenda and Minutes")

Here, there is an admission of the multiple oppressions felt by working-class people, similar to Hickey's description. These admissions are followed with the idea that there must be a separate rhetorical space permitted for working-class people who are also marginalized beyond their class.

It is difficult to prove a cause-and-effect relationship here, but I want to describe how confidence often led to increased participation. Throughout her thirty-plus year tenure, Sally Flood was an advocate for women's writing as both a personal and collaborative enterprise. Indeed, her work functioned in ways that she describes as personally empowering but also structurally important. After Sally was part of the 1976 founding group, she became a constant in several writing groups and the executive committee and a leader for many events and workshops. After feeling the FWWCP's support firsthand, Sally wrote "Working Together Alone," a piece in which she noted the importance for working-class women writers to "tak[e] history back where it belongs" (31). She described the cultural significance of the FWWCP "stick[ing] to the material they know and understand" and thereby creating a "working-class structure" (31). Sally explained how "established literary groups" dismissed that writing "coming from the lower classes could be relevant to 'Literature'" (31). As a response, she noted that "[i]t has since become clear that working class writing is not only relevant to the times we live in, but is culture at its very roots" (31). Further, she wrote that her own participation with the FWWCP has influenced her identity as a woman: "Since becoming part of the Federation I have enjoyed a freedom I never had before. . . . I know several other women who feel the same" (31). Sally described a new sense of agency and women's participation, which pushes her to acknowledge that "[w]e hope that women's participation will become even stronger in the future. This is not detrimental to men, as we plan an even balance" (31), perhaps due to the tensions throughout these discussions. Still, Sally built on this framework over four decades to continue her writing, recruit new members, and change the structure of the FWWCP to be more inclusive of working-class women and members who identified from other marginalized backgrounds.

Sally has been an agent of change through her personal publications as well as through many group efforts. During the early 1980s, a short description of the FWWCP was written up for the magazine *Woman & Home,* and an FWWCP paid worker at the time had an overwhelming response from over ninety women asking for more information. The feelings of confidence and empowerment Sally gained from the FWWCP community were clearly appealing to many others. An internal example of this was when Sally took a lead role in the creation of *Move Over Adam: A Women's Anthology,* published in 1990. This was a significant publication that received positive responses and circulated widely. As part of the "About the Federation" section within the book, they wrote "The Federation is our collective, national voice. . . . All the groups are committed to new kinds of writing based on working class experience and creativity, which include a strong combination from women, Black, and Gay writers" (Women of the Federation of Worker Writers and Community Publishers 68). Here, we get a sense of how some FWWCP members were purposeful in their desire to build community and to put forth a unified and supportive voice while recognizing that unity does not mean homogeneity. The editors note,

> This anthology is the result of a project embarked upon by a collective of women in the Federation of Worker Writers and Community Publishers. The idea arose from a successful women's day on women's writing. . . . Women were asked to submit scripts. The response was good and the final selection, published here, we hope reflects the rich variety of the Federation's membership. (Women of the Federation of Worker Writers and Community Publishers 4)

Move Over Adam was a collaborative effort that only existed because members participated in a variety of stages (from Sally and others wanting to create the anthology to the FWWCP executive committee organizing a women's day, all the participants attending workshops, and then women submitting their work and organizing the publication). Ultimately, through these steps, we can grasp how women's involvement and the support of this participation impacted the FWWCP. This legacy slowly changed the FWWCP's ethos to be more welcoming to women writers and writers across identities, but the work of inclusion was an ongoing process.

HOW DO WE MEASURE SUCCESS?

In the years after the "separatist" debate, the FWWCP took steps to ensure new rhetorical opportunities for all its members. But what other examples are there of how the FWWCP tangibly changed as a network to be more inclusive, to align more in solidarity across working-class populations? Throughout, I've tried to show that there are no simple ways to explain the FWWCP's evolving ideas about class identity in connection to the whole range of identities. What we do see from the FWWCP's history though is how people navigated moments of tension with understanding and compassion, and then they decided as a group to repeatedly make changes in response in their organization.

A few examples of these changes include: a Black Writers Day; Women in the Federation events; an anthology for women; themed booklists that featured Black writers and women writers and Asian writers; many individual publications about working-class writers from diverse backgrounds that explore how they bring working-class identity in conversation about mental health, ethnicity, racial identity, disability, sexuality, and more. There were also thoughtful conversations spurred from deep listening when FWWCP worker Al Thompson and two other white members attending a meeting led by Black writers. Here, the Black writers proposed ideas and suggested that "Black writers should not be seen in a direct or identical relationship with working class writers" because "black writers have distinctive identities, interests, and needs based on race" (Thompson 1). From the original debates almost a decade earlier, the FWWCP continued pushing its boundaries and values, and its membership and members' ideas also changed sometimes as a result.

Moreover, in the FWWCP, people sometimes even changed their minds based on open discussions. In 1989, Jimmy McGovern reflected on his own changes in mindset in *FedNews* Issue 1:

> I am conscious of an enormous debt which I'll never fully repay. Quite simply, the Worker Writer movement, Scottie '83 in particular changed my life. It changed by a gradual process of education. I sat and listened to people describing what it was like to be a woman, or gay, or black, and I learned from this and was able to face up to, to examine, the sexism and racism instilled in me from birth. . . . that, surely, is our strength: we educate and change our members . . . our strength lies in our ability to educate each other. The workshop is the place for this—the place for people to make mistakes and learn from them. (11)

To read this reaction alongside the earlier quotations from McGovern and Scotland Road '83 highlights what multiple FWWCP members express about the ability to learn and even understand different values and experiences when you can come together in conversation.

The original 1976 FWWCP and its narrow focus on working-class identity is much different if we compare it to what the organization looked like after sixteen years at the 1992 "Writing and Equal Opportunities" event. There were workshops that expanded ideas of working-class writing in extensive ways across race, gender, ethnicity, sexuality, disability, and more. These workshops included "Black Writing in Britain Today" by Lemn Sissay; "Asian Women's Writing in Britain" by Shelley Khair; "Writing, Gender, and Class" by Laureen Hickey; "Counteracting Negative Stereotypes" by Linda McGowan; "Writing About Sex & Sexuality" by Rebecca O'Rourke; "Stimulating Writing in ABE [Adult Basic Education]" by Pecket Well College, and more ("Writing and Equal Opportunities" 1).

The inclusion of new member groups over these years also expanded the scope of the FWWCP internationally. By 1990, the FWWCP had contacts in France, Australia, Ireland, and the United States. Another group, Buchu Books, joined the FWWCP in 1991 from South Africa with associate membership, which was created so non-UK groups could participate in the community. Additionally, a group from 1992 called the Ethnic Communities Oral History Project, located in London, was devoted to telling the history of immigrants to England through multiple languages. By 1993, there were forty-four groups of FWWCP members in England and one in Ireland, in addition to three provisional members, and associate member groups in Liverpool (1), South Africa (1), Spain (1), Australia (2), New Zealand (1), and West Virginia, USA (1) (Federation, "Full Membership 1993–1994"). The geographic spread of the FWWCP was also complemented through a transformation in publications, now with varying themes, such as the creation of a special Women's Issue for *Federation Magazine* in 1996. There was an explicit move in each of these moments to expand the FWWCP's understanding of working-class identity. In the 1995–96 FWWCP Strategy Report, it listed that the executive committee "consists of 50% women and 50% men, of which 30% are Afro-Caribbean and 10% Asian. During the past three years, there are Executive members who are retired, have physical disabilities, and reading and writing difficulties" (2).

To be sure, there isn't a singular measurement for understanding success in the FWWCP in percentages or numbers of members, languages used, or geographic locations. But as I consider these conversations and developments, they clearly represent an intentional and reflective attempt at inclusion and class experiences. They underscore how the FWWCP never settled or stagnated its desire to be responsive to working-class people. And they call attention to the possibilities of listening and learning and even allowing each other the chance to change our minds.

LEARNING FROM THE FWWCP'S WRITING AND ACTION
As I explore these materials in the FWWCP Collection, I often think about the archival silences that the FWWCP histories might

fill. Jacqueline Jones Royster and Gesa E. Kirsch pose thoughtful
questions about recovery work that I feel embody the spirit and
ethos of uncovering working-class voices in the FWWCP. They ask,
"How do we include—and value—ordinary women's rhetorical
activities, activities that have often been called mundane, not
noteworthy, or extracurricular?" (36). While Royster and Kirsch
focus on women writers, the FWWCP represents such a site where
"ordinary" people—working-class people—have taken part in
rhetorical activities and literate acts in important ways, especially
considering theorist Raymond Williams's argument that "culture
is ordinary," as it is constructed through the "ordinary processes
of human societies and human minds" (93). Royster and Kirsch
also suggest the power of understanding archival work through
the framings of the writers themselves: "How do we render their
work and lives meaningfully? . . . How did *they* frame (rather than
we frame) the questions by which they navigated their own lives?"
(20). I think about how Sally Flood, Roy and Lucia Birch, and
so many community members opened their homes to me to share
their writing, about how archiving alongside members allowed me
to see their history from their own perspectives. As such, I've tried
to show the FWWCP on their own terms, from their own framings,
in their own words.

As I reflect on the FWWCP Collection, I feel compelled
to emphasize how forward-thinking they seemed, wanting to
archive themselves, framing questions about their own group, and
foregrounding deliberative dialogue through publishing. While few
people have seen these documents before, I believe the FWWCP
Collection allows us to see how the FWWCP "rendered their [own]
work and lives meaningfully" and how they "frame[d] the questions
by which they navigated their own lives" (Royster and Kirsch 20).
The same ideas of community, confidence building, and solidarity
that Sally shared with me at her kitchen table are echoed across
FWWCP documents by countless members. Even more, through
their own archival attempts, written history, and their engagement
with my archival work, FWWCP members have actively performed
vital work in reanimating their own histories for contemporary
readers.

As I look at these rarely seen or studied texts, I notice many possibilities for them. The FWWCP archival documents allow us to track how the Federation developed as a working-class collective within an unstable political environment and then adapted to a changing membership base from a predominantly English, white, male group of writers to a transnational and multicultural group that highlighted diverse languages, nationalities, genders, sexualities, and cultures. This process involved plenty of conflict, invoked through power relations between identity politics, rhetorics of multiculturalism, and the enactment of equal opportunities. Revisions and new publications represent tensions of how to negotiate working-class identity from a variety of racial, cultural, gendered, and educational backgrounds. In other instances, the FWWCP had to think about how groups dedicated to women's rights, Black writers' identity, gay writers, or mental health awareness would fit in without altering the founding mission of the group. But they continued this process through open publications in newsletters, letters, group reports, workshops, and more. With the inclusion of each group, the FWWCP both gained examples about working-class narratives and widened the scope of its reach in meaningful but complicating ways. From this context, questions emerged from both pragmatically and ideologically driven perspectives, having to do with what it means to be working class and how this framing might change when we consider embodied experiences of members.

We learn that the FWWCP was complex, diverse, and expansive. It was a network of community writers that evolved across geopolitical spaces, from within working-class identities, and among decades of social change in ways that complicate notions of literacy, community histories, and community work. And it was a working-class organization that had problems negotiating its own identity. But when the political landscape favored others, the FWWCP created avenues to self-sponsor their writing, furthering an evolving sense of working-class communities. Within the collective, which was itself an alternative structure, we also see how subgroups arise, challenge, and change this structure. The FWWCP created spaces for people to share their stories with confidence and develop a public voice through their own life histories and poetry.

When many people and institutions discounted the working class, the FWWCP composed themselves in a way that challenged traditional forms of bureaucracy and intellectualism by negotiating working-class discourses, ideologies, and social activity for themselves. The FWWCP shows us how a community attempted to create rhetorical space and build solidarity in the wake of deindustrialization and how fracturing and healing happen along that path. The FWWCP left us not only with remnants but with thousands of documents to consider what community building looks like in action and how working-class people write their way through life. Most importantly, the FWWCP gives us real examples of how people form communities that allow for disagreement and tension, confidence and compassion, imperfection and growth, forgiveness and solidarity.

Conclusion

If Worker Writers Ran the Dartmouth Seminar

MANY WOULD AGREE THAT THE 1966 Dartmouth Seminar, or the "Anglo-American Conference on the Teaching and Learning of English at Dartmouth College" (Harris x), contributed significantly to the creation of the field of writing studies. It was a moment of transatlantic collaboration by scholars interested in exploring the question "What is English?" as part of a multi-week seminar held in Hanover, New Hampshire. The seminar relied on prominent organizations such as the British National Association of Teachers of English, the Modern Language Association, and the National Council of Teachers of English—sponsors that continue to influence writing studies today—bringing together scholars to discuss their theories of teaching and writing. The scholars invited to Dartmouth were overwhelmingly representative of a particular group: white, male, middle-class and upper-class, Anglo scholars. The work of this seminar or conference spurred the creation of the International Federation of Teachers of English (IFTE), and its participants have remained widely cited figures in the field. For many, this history represents some of the established origins of writing studies, and details from this history are preserved in archives across institutions and through numerous retellings in scholarship. The seminar's centrality even spurred a fiftieth-anniversary conference and ongoing annual research seminars.

Stay with me for a moment, as I wonder: What writers did Dartmouth imagine, and which writing, writers, and histories may have been rendered invisible in that process? For example, did the Dartmouth Seminar leave room in the Writing Studies Universe[46] for worker writers like Sally Flood, Roger Mills, Florence Agbah,

Alan Scanlan, and others? For worker writers who were composing at their factory machines, in their homes, and in community spaces with others, whether working or unemployed? The Dartmouth Seminar plays a central part in the history that many learn on our way into the discipline and one that impacted organizations that still exist today as key institutions in conversations about writing and English studies. I want to reflect a bit here on the stories and writers that it privileged and imagine an alternative as well, thinking about the FWWCP/FED. What I'm really interested in is power and preservation—the factors that allow Dartmouth's history to continue to live on but that present a constant struggle for many communities, including the FWWCP/FED. The Dartmouth Seminar's legacy has been preserved through archival documents in multiple collections from the Carnegie Corporation (held at Columbia), NCTE (University of Illinois Urbana-Champaign), through a photograph at Dartmouth College, and through the personal collections of James Nimmo Britton (University College London), Wallace W. Douglas (Northwestern University), James Porter Moffett (University of California Santa Barbara), and Merron Chorny (University of Calgary), allowing for yet another layer of material sustainability in maintaining these histories. The number of archives that house documents connected to the Dartmouth Seminar—and the support that represents at numerous levels—illustrates structural preservation that was impossible with the FWWCP Collection for decades. Therefore, I offer an interpretation of these two histories (the Dartmouth Seminar and the FWWCP/FED) using material resources we now have access to.

Throughout this book, I've described the material conditions shaping how working-class writers in the FWWCP/FED and Pecket created and sustained community writing and publishing groups for decades. I offered some possibilities with a historization of this network by telling a story of the creation of a physical archive—as a value statement that their histories and literacies are indeed worthy of preservation. But I also want to make visible some of the disparities that enabled the preservation of the Dartmouth Seminar on one hand and prevented the FWWCP/FED's progress on the other. Class solidarity inspired FWWCP/FED members to write and publish publicly for the first time, and bringing their stories into writing studies reveals some hidden or lesser-known histories of working-class writers today. In *A Rhetoric of Remnants,* Zosha Stuckey asks, "How do we complicate a one-sided historical record? How do we give presence to participation that has no written record? How do we historicize what seems to be silent and absent?" (97).[47] While working-class writers do have a demonstrable written record, as we can witness from the FWWCP/FED, this record has largely remained "silent and absent" from academic conversations, within the readings we teach, and as part of the stories we tell about our discipline. Using Stuckey's premise, I'd like to imagine what further inclusion and acknowledgment of working-class writing and histories might contribute to disciplinary conversations.

Unlike the Dartmouth Seminar's stable nearly month-long atmosphere in which intellectuals were able to thoughtfully explore what writing might mean for others, particularly students, the FWWCP Archival Project represents more unexpected writing happening in the factories and in the communities of working-class people who had no place at the Dartmouth table or in classrooms imagined and presumed to be upper- and middle-class spaces. Unlike the Dartmouth Seminar, which brought together a group of American, Canadian, and British scholars with institutional affiliations, the Federation of Worker Writers and Community Publishers was a transnational self-organized group of worker writers. They published community writing from over 120 groups across England, Wales, Northern Ireland, the Republic of Ireland, Scotland, Spain, France, Germany, Australia, New Zealand, South Africa, the United States, Canada, and more. The FWWCP also included writing about the migration and work experiences by individuals and communities from Bangladesh, Greece, Jamaica, Iran, Ghana, Poland and more—not casting these writings as deficient in any way but as representative of the FWWCP community. These were people who remained outside of the imagined focus of Dartmouth; instead, they might fall under the category of "disadvantaged" students who Dartmouth attendees focused on (Squire, "Proposal" 4). Yet while Dartmouth inspired scholarship about trans*atlantic* collaboration and the creation of a teaching federation, the FWWCP/FED produced an extensive trans*national* community, creating a writing and publishing federation run by and for the working class. The FWWCP/FED was not known or valued by most academics during its time, but an explicitly working-class history offers new understandings of writing, literacy, and community collaborations.

In effect, there are disjunctions in these stories: one group (Dartmouth Seminar participants) was brought together, authorized by national institutions, heavily funded, and supported to shape an entire discipline through writing across the decades; the other group (FWWCP/FED) was made up of people who struggled to even be recognized for their writing, knowledge, and skills (which later involved teaching and collaborative publishing). If you comb through the histories of writing studies, working-class writing by working-class writers more specifically is a blip rather than the dominant record. I juxtapose these stories to show how resources have shaped the possibilities and limitations of both. To be sure, there are limits to this comparison, as the Dartmouth Seminar was rooted in pedagogical goals and therefore has many reasons to be archived by institutions. Moreover, participants were asked to come to Dartmouth because of their expertise. But I'm also interested in thinking about representation: Why couldn't this seminar have heard from students themselves, or the very people considered "disadvantaged" in their use of language (Squire, "Proposal" 4)— those with firsthand knowledge that might impact the Seminar's curriculum reform agenda? But my main point in linking these conversations is to think about the role of archives in connection to writing, specifically reflecting on the labor, finances, and other resources required for such preservation. In addition, I want to consider what writing and literacy in the field might look like when it is inclusive of multiple communities' histories and experiences, including the precarious circumstances that shape them. Let me be clear: no single event or group can stand for the whole history of a field or community, but I begin here because the time period of the Dartmouth Seminar corresponds closely with the emergence of working-class community writing networks and provides a useful exercise for rethinking how we might bring in community voices from the past and contend with the deindustrial impacts that continue to shape class identity today.

What if our Dartmouth moment instead featured the solidarity and community of the FWWCP/FED: the start of not only a worker writer movement but of the process of including working-class voices within our understandings of literacy, archives, and community partnership work? What could such literacy look like, rooted in the voices of working-class people, with rich and complex class-based histories narrating their stories of education, labor, migration? What could a field look like that valued transnational understandings of writing across linguistic, ethnic, geographic, gendered, and classed borders? We cannot go back in time, and the answers to these questions are not as simple as including transnational working-class voices and literacies in the present day. Rather, they involve identifying historical, material, ideological, and methodological ways that class has often been neglected or elided from our disciplinary narratives and archival work. Looking at the materiality of the Dartmouth Seminar, we can consider what it would mean to reenvision the people, writings, and resources overlooked in the process, and what it could mean moving forward. Ultimately, this chapter considers where we locate these various moments in the field and argues that focusing on materiality and precarity allow us to expand our origin stories and what counts as knowledge and literacy in this work.

THE MATERIALITY OF THE DARTMOUTH SEMINAR

The complex legacy of the Dartmouth Seminar and its impact on writing studies extends far beyond the seminar, which can be attributed to the material support it had along the way. Indeed, the fact that multiple archives already exist connected to this is important because it represents how people valued its history and sponsored its preservation. From the earliest planning ideas of the seminar, the goal was to have an "important and lasting effect on the teaching of English" (Caws 2). To do this required resources: financial, institutional, labor based, publishing, and more. Some of the implications and affordances of these extensive resources are apparent throughout the publications and pedagogical shifts in the field; other implications are more elusive, left for us to reimagine what the field might look like had the seminar gone other directions. To consider some of these questions, we must look at the resources the Dartmouth Seminar had and its materiality (where it was, how it came to be, who paid for it, and so forth). Then, I will provide a more speculative reading focused on class, considering how, as Tim Cresswell notes, place (Dartmouth) is an assemblage or "gathering of materialities, meanings, and practices" (6). Indeed, the spaces we gather to write and meet matter, and institutional spaces have many forms of social, political, and even economic power. I want to consider what "materialities, meanings and practices" (6) were included or not at Dartmouth and who was excluded. Looking at Dartmouth's materiality allows us to see the implicit and explicit ways that class and power manifested before, during, and after the event. Class, of course, is not only about money but also about what we have access to and what resources we have. The Dartmouth Seminar had plenty of all of these.

While multiple collections hold documents about the Dartmouth Seminar, my analysis here uses two main sources: first, the digital Dartmouth '66 Seminar Exhibit curated by Annette E. Vee with contributor Megan McIntyre (Dartmouth '66), and second, James Nimmo Britton's (a Dartmouth attendee) personal papers held at University College London. These collections exist because multiple scholars, institutions, archivists, and librarians made valuations and deemed them important enough to be preserved in print or digital forms. Still, as Amy Wan reminds us regarding the Dartmouth Seminar's digital exhibit, preservation isn't always equivalent to access: "[T]his digital exhibit provides open access to historical documents that once were only available if you had the means to travel. . . . Who can speak and tell the histories of our field relies on who has access to these kinds of documents" ("Access and the Dartmouth Seminar").

Indeed, I was never able to travel to see these documents in person, but I can now see them online. Thanks to the fantastic curatorial work of Annette E. Vee and Megan McIntyre, this collection provides crucial context about the attendees, the funding, the goals, and more. The other collection (James Nimmo Britton's) that I rely on here was one that I'll later describe finding only through a serendipitous connection made during a trip to London while working on the FWWCP Collection. As I described in Chapter 4, my own ability to travel for the FWWCP Collection was dependent upon time-consuming work and the unpaid labor of grant applications, course development, and more—only possible through my graduate institution and later internal funding through my new university faculty positions. What we find across these collections is clear: the tangible material resources for the Dartmouth Seminar were extensive, including financial support, institutional space, transportation costs, housing needs for weeks, and ways to print, publish, and circulate writing.

To start, the financial investment in Dartmouth was significant, as documented on the title page of the "Proposal for an International Seminar on the Teaching and Learning of English" submitted by James R. Squire (executive secretary of NCTE). The submission was made "on behalf of: [the] National Association for Teaching English, [the] Modern Language Association of America, [and the] National Council of Teachers of English," and the budget request was to the Carnegie Corporation for $174,560 to run the conference ("Proposal"). (A calculation from the US Bureau of Labor Statistics based on inflation suggests that this would be over $1.6 million today.) In the end, the Carnegie Corporation funded the seminar for $150,000, a budget that, even without adjustment for inflation, would be enviable today in most scholarly endeavors. Simply put, the Carnegie Corporation funding enabled myriad possibilities. Importantly, the funding allowed the conference organizers and participants to think about sustainability beyond a one-time event—something not possible when you're worried about where the money will come from next.

Beyond the financial investment, though, many other resources were needed. The physical location of where the seminar would take place was also a key concern. Early on, discussion revolved around what locations might be suitable based on what college institutions would support the seminar. Having access to a variety of elite and mostly private educational spaces was another way that class manifested in the Dartmouth Seminar. Squire describes that the choice of possibilities for the seminar, before they landed on a location, included "Dartmouth College (Hanover, NH), Middlebury College (Middlebury, Vermont), Cornell University (Ithaca, NY) and facilities at the University of California, Berkeley, or Stanford University in Palo Alto, California" ("Proposal" 8). These proposed sites centered on Ivy League or elite and private universities, and one public land-grant and highly regarded school in UC Berkeley. Because the seminar was granted a large sum of money for this event, the geography of the universities was not much of a factor. Unlike community members and scholars today who face costly registration fees, transportation needs, and housing, the Carnegie Corporation grant took care of expenses for invited scholars. Seed money for future projects was also available.

Another key piece for the Dartmouth Seminar was who would do the intellectual labor—that is, who would attend. The planning committee (with sponsors such as *College English* and *The English Journal*) were in agreement about the "essential need for such an international seminar and on the potential impact of its results on schools in all English-speaking countries over the next decade or two" (Squire, "Proposal" 2). Interestingly, despite the possibility of impact on "all English-speaking countries," representatives from only Canada, the United States, and Great Britain were involved ("Proposal" 2). Here, we see how English-speaking countries had narrowed to Anglo-American and British countries rather than an expansion of stakeholders. Admittedly, one archival document summarizing a 1964 phone call between Peter Caws (Carnegie Corporation) and Albert Kitzhaber (president of NCTE at the time) indicates that, during the planning stages, Kitzhaber thought it necessary to bring in "even representatives from Africa and other parts of the Commonwealth" as part of the discussion (Kitzhaber and Caws 2). In this document, Caws also states that Kitzhaber felt "[t]he field is too important and the time too crucial to permit the profession the luxury of ignoring what is going on in other parts of the world" (2). The result, though, did not reflect these hopes of a more expansive and global conference.

To be sure, no single conference or event can be everything for everybody; however, when the stakes of such an event might very well influence schools across English-speaking countries, I wonder what it would mean to have included other voices, nationalities, classes, speakers, and more, like the FWWCP/FED attempted. The funding for the Dartmouth Seminar could have provided a space to be inclusive of people who might not otherwise be able to afford events like conferences, but ultimately the invitees list within the proposal was exclusive and distinctly academic. What was clear from the proposed attendees list was that the goal was to invite scholars from notable institutions (examples include Princeton, Harvard, University of York, University of Oxford, UC Berkeley, etc.) as well as some practitioners in high schools—but seemingly no one from non-traditional schooling or community education or other backgrounds that might have additional insight on the types of students and concerns that interested the participants. Even more, while the proposal indicates that scholars would be from Great Britain, there was a privileging (purposeful or not) of scholars from universities in England rather than the whole of the UK. Canadian universities had two delegates on the proposal, with one delegate attending. Only one "alternate delegate" was listed from a university in Scotland and another was from the Welsh Department of Education, but no first-round invitees came from these locations or Northern Ireland and none from parts of the Commonwealth[48] (Squire, "Proposal" 25). Quite simply, this was not a representative or inclusive set of delegates when the goal was meant to be internationally reaching. The exclusivity of the seminar in terms of who was invited and who they imagined writers to be matters because this event had a strong influence on shaping how we understand English and writing from a disciplinary mindset as well as how these values played out in curriculums and language policies emerging from government powers and archives.

Finally, beyond the materiality of the seminar itself, there were publishing resources and distribution networks built into the structure and proposal that are quite different from working-class, self-publishing outlets that non-academics such as the FWWCP/ FED would need to rely on. Squire notes that at the end of the seminar, the expectation was that reports would emerge by two writers (who would be supported by a "releas[e] from other academic and writing responsibilities during the semester immediately following the seminar" ("Proposal" 10). One report would be for the general public and one for the profession. Moreover, the intention was that one report would be "published jointly in Britain and North America by the NATE, MLA, and NCTE" ("Proposal" 30). The results were *Growth through English* by John Dixon and *The Uses of English* by Herbert J. Muller. For what eventually became Muller's book, the proposal notes that "[t]his book would be published commercially in Britain and the United States. . . . Half of the royalties would revert to the author; half to the development fund" (31), which included additional activities in other countries involved. Moreover, a year after the seminar, James Squire requested the allocation of funds specifically for the distribution of Dixon's book: "[W]e would like to use these for printing and distributing 5,000 copies of the book by John Dixon to influential educational leaders throughout the three countries" ("Letter and Report from Squire to Caws" 2). Beyond the two published reports, funded and distributed widely, at least ten other pamphlets, papers, or articles from the seminar were supported by the likes of *College English*, NCTE, *PMLA*, *The English Journal*, and more. Of course, these were smart decisions on the part of the attendees, but they present publishing and distribution possibilities not afforded to those outside of well-resourced university settings.

At every stage of this process, resources were shared by elite, sustaining, and wide-reaching organizations. Moreover, the seminar is known about today in part because of these resources through funding of publications—built into the proposal—with the goal to circulate the work of the Dartmouth Seminar. Some attendees became figureheads of writing studies, education, and English for years to come, while others' work extended beyond disciplinary interests. James Britton, for instance, was called on to later participate on the Bullock Report, an educational report in

England for the "Committee of Enquiry appointed by the Secretary
of State for Education and Science" who was then Margaret
Thatcher (Britton, *A Language*). Britton worked on this report,
eventually subtitled *A Language for Life*, with a committee that
researched reading, writing, and language use across the curriculum
within British primary and secondary schools. His extensive work
on language and learning have led to Britton being described as
"the father of expressive writing" (Honeychurch 329) as well
as being "one of the twenty most cited authors in *CCC* between
1980–1993" (Durst 385). In effect, the legacy of the Dartmouth
Seminar and its attendees prevailed for decades within the field and
beyond, as well as in the theoretical and pedagogical practices of
teaching English and writing, for years to come.

Within these archival examples, we see a widespread network
of sponsorship with substantial resources in the form of money,
institutional backing, intellectual capital, working space, lodging,
and distribution networks. The resources that existed for the
Dartmouth Seminar are not shared by many scholars, even today.
Still, my point is not to critique the Dartmouth Seminar in its
entirety or any of these elements individually, as there have been
many positive impacts from the seminar and its attendees' work,
particularly represented through collaboration across countries and
a turn toward personal and expressive writing rather than current-
traditional approaches. However, I do want to pinpoint some of
the more specific class-based impacts we can understand within this
history because these resources were part of promoting an ideology
about writing and English that largely failed to acknowledge the
precarity and diversity other students, scholars, and writers were
facing in everyday contexts.

Class Assumptions

So far, I've written about the Dartmouth Seminar focusing on
concrete examples of what resources existed; however, some of
the ways class manifests in discussions are less about specific items
and more connected to presumed characteristics, ways of being,
or ideologies. Therefore, I'd next like to discuss the ideologies or
beliefs that shaped the seminar by situating the FWWCP alongside

it. How might FWWCP writing have been interpreted by scholars at the Dartmouth Seminar and beyond with the frameworks established there? Would Stepney children and East End adults fit into Dartmouth's conversations? While the Dartmouth Seminar and some of its participants enhanced a field that allowed for personal narrative to enter the classrooms, I suggest it did so in a way that molded students into a middle-class sensibility, largely failing to acknowledge working-class students and their experiences—let alone providing an entry point to bring in working-class writing from beyond the university. In many ways, this created a limited vision of writing as a middle-class activity with middle-class values.

The prevalence of middle-class values within composition classrooms has deep roots in the connection between correctness and morality (Bloom). But what class assumptions were circulating at the Dartmouth Seminar? Considering its participants, Joe Harris explains, "Most were males, and, as far as I can tell, all were white" (x). Referencing a photo of the seminar participants, Harris notes, "Everyone is white, and I count only three women. Almost everyone appears to be middle-aged and middle class" (xiii). Further, he notes,

> It's hard to imagine taking a similar photo today. The com-position of the group in the room would be different. The students we work with identify with a range of ethnicities, cultures, classes, and nations—and we now better understand the need to reflect that diversity in our professional meetings and journals. (xiii–xiv)

While I'm unsure what Harris means exactly by "appear . . . middle class" (xiii) in a photo (I suspect it's the professional attire with collared shirts with ties, slacks, and dress shoes), these markings are reminders of the presumption that composition is a "middle class enterprise" (Bloom). Indeed, ideas regarding composition's middle classness have been forwarded through rendering non-middle-class students and writing as deficient or even invisible at various moments throughout the field's history, so I was certainly curious to see the embodied presence of Dartmouth attendees alongside their ideological values.

But the composition of the Dartmouth group is just one aspect that interests me; alongside this, I'm interested in how assumptions of class have rendered everyday literacies of the working class largely invisible. My goal in writing about the FWWCP Archival Project has been to bring us back to these everyday literacies and the people who have been dismissed. But when I read archival documents connected to the Dartmouth Seminar, it appears that working-class students and participants were largely absent from the conversations. When they were a part, they were looked at as nonstandard. For instance, within the proposal for the Dartmouth Seminar, there is a definition of what English is and a description about the values of English and literature that center on their ability to help us "develop as human beings" (Squire, "Proposal" 14). Perhaps many teachers and writers would have a similar view on the potential for writing (or English) to connect and develop us as humans. However, the proposal further states,

> Through English we communicate and understand other people, come to terms with the world around us, develop as human beings. Language makes possible the intellectual and emotional growth that distinguishes us as human beings. Ct [sic]. the plight of the disadvantaged child; his potential not realized. This negative aspect is rightly noted; the positive side—what English can do—needs exploring and exploiting just as much. (Squire, "Proposal" 14)

Here, we see that Dartmouth is concerned with the possibilities of language and its potential to help us develop as human beings—as well as the concerns over English usage. Interestingly, Dartmouth's participants seemed most concerned with school-age students (eight to eighteen years old), although there are connections made to college-level impacts through the archival materials. In the proposal, another goal was articulated as addressing "the problem of *disadvantaged children* who have not been able to develop the *command of language which they need for normal social and educational motivation*" ("Proposal" 4, emphasis added). The projections were lofty for the seminar, which was expected to have impacts on future curriculum across countries, so I think that focusing on these nuances is relevant. Here, we see a disconnect between "disadvantaged children" clearly labeled in a deficit-based way, as experiencing a "plight" of unrealized potential, and those who can participate in "normal" situations. But who did the seminar participants imagine were these "disadvantaged children"? To consider this requires thinking about the assumptions, values, or ideas that circulated through these statements.

The proposal focuses specifically on the immense power that English holds rather than on the possibilities of multiple languages. Further, it emphasizes the issues that arise when one does not have a proper command of English and the ways "language deficiencies" become connected to widespread problems: "Failure in English, however, means more than failure in one school subject; failure in English implies personal, social, intellectual, and economic failure" (Squire, "Proposal" 16). Here, the proposal suggests that knowing English is connected to morality, as well as social status, and can impact future success economically, personally, and intellectually. I wonder: What might the Dartmouth Seminar have said about this English writing from East London published in *Stepney Words*?

> I am just a boy
> with a lot of dreams
> but what's the point
> I won't get nowhere
> I'm just ordinary
> nothing special just
> . . . ordinary
> got no chance in this
> world unless you're
> . . . clever
> which I'm not.
> (Searle 1)

In the poem, the anonymous writer notes that they are "just ordinary" and that he is a boy who has "got no chance" because he's not clever. From a grammatical standpoint focused on standardization, the double negatives in "won't get nowhere" and "got no" show incorrect usage. Yet the writing is full of expressive detail about how this working-class boy feels about his life and future. And what if he is strategically writing in this way to capture his own language for the audience he anticipates—that is, people like him? Is the anonymous poet representative of a "disadvantaged" child that the Dartmouth Proposal worries about? The rhetoric of "command" (Squire, "Proposal" 4) is reminiscent of the pushback Chris Searle and his students received from administrators calling the working-class Stepney students "fallen children" (qtd. in Wells). This view also shows signs of middle-class assumptions about moralistic views of correctness, properness, respectability, and more (Bloom).

In the Dartmouth Seminar, so-called disadvantaged children appear to fit into at least two specific frameworks: children with nonstandard English dialects and children from lower socioeconomic backgrounds. To the first: The framing of students within Dartmouth is troubling, invoking, for instance, the issue of students with "deviant dialects" that vary from "standard English," deemed to be a problem "because they will need such skill in our society" (Squire, "Letter from Squire to Caws" 3). Deviance in this example appears to include students who are nonstandard English-producing students, a label often placed on multilingual students and students perhaps born outside of England and the US. Critiques of the Dartmouth Seminar have been offered by scholars regarding its nationalism, its Anglo-American stance, and its lack of engagement with other languages and dialects, as well as the way native English speakers are folded into its assumptions (Harris; Trimbur, "The Dartmouth"). In these critiques, we see multiple ways in which the Dartmouth Seminar missed opportunities that could have expanded the field's emphasis specifically in terms of the globality of English. As Harris writes in "Updating Dartmouth":

> The 1966 conference also failed to confront the growing use of English as a global language. . . . And although everyone wanted to help students claim a stronger voice in their culture—indeed, there is a quiet class animus to much

of the talk at Dartmouth that I find bracing—that culture was imagined in traditional and nationalistic terms as, well, "Anglo-American." (xiv–xv)

While Harris focuses most specifically on language differences and nationality here, I would like to follow up on the idea of "class animus" (xv), particularly thinking about socioeconomic backgrounds.

Secondly, the proposal also places emphasis on the view that "disadvantaged children" are those with lower socioeconomic backgrounds. James Squire further indicates in a letter that "a sizeable group" of participants "supported the conventional view that the school provide young people with sufficient skill to make possible economic and social mobility" ("Letter from Squire to Peter Caws" 3). Under these ideas, it follows that without economic or social mobility, these students will be read as deficient in some way. These statements perpetuate the views that economic and social mobility is something sought by all and that it must come from Standardized English, something "disadvantaged" and "deviant" students lack. The privileging of standardized learning in school highlights a hierarchy that pits school-based education and language against learning that happens in homes and communities. For instance, it is clear within Dartmouth's framework that a sufficient remedy for these deficits would not come from within the community itself, as "many [Dartmouth attendees] expressed doubts about current inner-city language programs" (Squire, "Letter from Squire to Caws" 3). While it is not defined what or who "inner-city" references here, I read this as a euphemism for students from often poorer, immigrant, and/or largely non-white public programs (read: not from middle-class Anglo spaces). Interestingly, though, alongside this view of the inadequacies of inner-city programs, there is also a documented attitude between the Dartmouth participants that "dialects should be respected and that one obligation of the English teacher was to help all young people learn to understand and respond to dialects other than their own" ("Letter from Squire to Caws" 3). It further states "that efforts should not be made to change their patterns of speech and writing" (3). Devaluing inner-city programs and "deviant" dialects is juxtaposed with seemingly performative statements about valuing and respecting variations of language use, creating tensions between the emphasis on standardization and the respect for diversity.

Throughout the Dartmouth Seminar documents, there are conversations about how "[l]iterature stands for humanity" (Squire, "Proposal" 14). But I am left wondering: what literature specifically? We know from the above that it is connected to Standardized English. Here again, I recall the Arts Council's vehement judgment of the lack of "solid literary merit" in FWWCP writing (qtd. in Maguire 149) and the dehumanizing way they berated members for believing they might take part in literary conversations as writers. While the Dartmouth proposal emphasizes that the goal should be to underscore the positive aspects of language, it appears that only certain (read: Standard-English-speaking, white, middle-class) experiences are those that are marked as positive. It's clear though: deviant, disadvantaged, fallen, working-class writers don't fit into the Dartmouth framework. Instead, it portrays an extremely limited view of working-class communities, framing them in terms of what they lack. The examples of writing that we see from the Basement Writers and the FWWCP as evidenced by Sally Flood and the Stepney students' strike in previous chapters is that writing can be done by working-class people, be it in workshops or at home or at school, and that writing can impact people personally and economically, and it can inspire social change. But there isn't a belief in these examples that anyone *needs changing*. Their experiences are already enough and worthy of representation. Even in disagreements, the FWWCP members often expressed support for the community and openly valued differing opinions and means of expression. Writing, in these examples, can build confidence and create community. Writing can emerge from children and in octogenarians alike; from immigrants and native-born community members; in English or in a variety of dialects and languages. The image of writing produced at the Dartmouth Seminar, however, was something different; writing was for intellectuals and experts at elite institutions, who directed instruction sometimes at children who need developing.

Who Gets Archived? "Selective Clientele" at Dartmouth and the "Community" They Missed

Because this book has centered on the materiality of archives and the precarity of working-class writing and writers, I want to conclude with some material differences evinced by the archival trajectories of the Dartmouth Seminar and the FWWCP/FED. I've already mentioned that Dartmouth's history has been archived in no fewer than seven institutional archives (and I suspect there are many more) staffed with professional archivists to secure this history. This is alongside the numerous forms of preservation and widespread circulation of ideas through scholarship, conferences, exhibits and more. The FWWCP Collection on the other hand has, for a decade, stitched together pieces of collaboration among community members, students, faculty, and staff to hopefully secure these materials in one location without consistent resources.

While working to preserve the stories from the FWWCP/FED, searching for archival space, boxes, and resources to establish an archive, I found out that University College London's (UCL) Institute of Education held the personal archives of Dartmouth Seminar attendee James Britton. This felt a bit like the serendipity of archival work that Gesa E. Kirsch and Liz Rohan describe in *Beyond the Archives,* because I was staying around the corner at the time. I decided to explore Britton's files. I had known some of Britton's work within writing studies but hadn't made any explicit connections between him or Dartmouth and the FWWCP until I saw a one-sentence footnote in Chris Searle's book where he notes that Britton described the students' language in *Stepney Words* as "'unliterary' but full of honesty and conviction" (17). Unliterary. The parallel here between "unliterary" and the Arts Council's critique immediately came to my mind. The definition of "unliterary" reads, "Not literary; lacking literary character; (also) unlearned" (*Oxford English Dictionary*). As I reflected on this and on Dartmouth's deficit framing, I wanted to dig deeper. So, I reached out to Chris Searle to see if Britton said anything else. In a personal correspondence with me, Searle noted that Britton seemed to support the publication of *Stepney Words* and suggested that the phrasing of "unliterary" was likely meant to signal "how close the poems were to written speech" (personal communication). I was glad to hear Searle's interpretation and context. It seemed to fit the characterizations of Britton as a champion for expressive writing. However, the context that Searle gave me still made me consider the ways writing from the FWWCP/ FED might be characterized by Dartmouth's ideologies as a whole: unliterary. Read in the context of the FWWCP's history, this phrasing too closely resembled the deficit-framings FWWCP/FED writers constantly experienced. Why couldn't everyday language be connected to our humanness and representative of our multiple forms of knowledge? Whereas Dartmouth's organizers questioned if students would "develop as whole human being[s] . . . " or "will his thinking in words have depth. . . . or will he be inarticulate in his daily life" (Squire, "Proposal" 1), Chris Searle and the FWWCP believed in the depth that comes from each of our experiences. And many in the FWWCP believed that everyday language could be literary as well.

Still thinking of this, I went to UCL to see what, if anything, Britton himself might have said about Dartmouth, working-class writing, or community writing in his personal papers. Much of this archive had yet to be processed. After hours of exploring interesting but mostly unrelated materials, I found a folder of archival documents that provided a glimpse at the personal letters and correspondence Britton exchanged with numerous writing studies scholars, well-known publishers, editors, and educators. Here, I also came across a short piece, typewritten and seemingly unpublished elsewhere, from 1986 entitled "The Dartmouth Seminar—Elegy or Eulogy?" This piece provides a few of Britton's reflections on the event and the twenty years since. It immediately seemed like an exciting find.

In this two-page piece, Britton writes toward the end: "Probably the most surprising and puzzling finding is the fact that five years after the Dartmou[t]h Seminar, at the International Conference on Teaching and Learning English at York University, there was widespread rejection of one aspect of the seminar—its selective clientele" ("The Dartmouth Seminar"). Reading this, I was not surprised by the comment about "selective clientele." After all, the seminar—similar to the field's history—appeared to be largely decided, shaped, and molded by white, middle-aged, middle-class, English-speaking men with elite educational backgrounds. And as Britton himself illustrates, a critique of this is often found by those same people to be "puzzling." In addition to this note about clientele, Britton suggests another missed opportunity at Dartmouth: community impact. He concludes the document noting that "[t]he final outcome is still to seek: I shall suggest that the growth model needs somehow amending to take account of the fact that education is an effect of community" ("The Dartmouth Seminar"). Here, Britton acknowledges that the growth model of writing needs to account for education "as an effect of community" ("The Dartmouth Seminar"). When I read this statement, I thought of all the moments in the FWWCP/FED that showcase how writing, literacy, and education were wholeheartedly impacted by community. About the *effect of community* the Stepney Strike had on East Enders. About the *effect of community* that gave Sally Flood confidence to write, publish, and switch jobs. About the *effect of community* that was the main reason the FWWCP Collection could even exist decades after its origins. The *effect of community* of the kitchen-table ethos that brought me into this project and sustained it. Without community, without the FWWCP/FED, so many members expressed that they would never be published, would never be writers, and would have extremely different lives. Many members went as far as saying that their writing group changed their lives. While Dartmouth may have missed that "education is an effect of community," as Britton noted, these words embody everything about the FWWCP's mission ("The Dartmouth Seminar").

This statement by Britton helped me understand what I have learned through FWWCP/FED but that I needed to keep reminding myself about within my hope for writing studies: We must examine who we include in our discussions and the community impacts of education to understand the literacies of writers continually marginalized or overlooked. The precarity of worker writers and their communities deeply impacts educational experiences and should be taken into account within community partnerships. In particular, these commitments can push us to think about how our literacies are impacted by our class identity and communities. Unlike Dartmouth, there was no expected continuation of the FWWCP, but the *effect of community* formed a federation and sustained it for decades. As a consequence of Dartmouth's "selective clientele," the seminar missed an opportunity to explore how working-class communities are distinct, often defined by their solidarity and collectivity—and this impacts them differently than other classes.

Ironically, while Britton's response suggesting the potentially negative impacts of the Dartmouth Seminar's exclusivity has found its home in an archive, and Dartmouth's often negative views of disadvantaged students have been archived in multiple places, it took decades for the FWWCP to *even be considered* archivable. The FWWCP and later FED fought to get external validation of the value of artifacts that described the powers of writing and community for working-class people. And when enough support for this project had finally coalesced, the possibility of creating an actual archive was still precarious at every moment.

CONCLUSION: THE "UNLITERARY" AUTHORIZING THEMSELVES

What can we learn from the FWWCP/FED about the "effect of community" on writing, about including a multiplicity of identities and challenging "selective clientele[s]" when we think about writers and readers? In their story, the FWWCP emerges because of working-class precarity—but their history also details how Sally, Florence, Roger, and the FWWCP/FED found ways to authorize and value themselves through their community network. Members became precarious archivists as they fought for others to recognize the value of their work. The work of the FWWCP/FED crossed political and discursive boundaries by focusing on those who felt stigmatized by their working-class status, those who spoke multiple dialects of British English and other languages completely, and those who were locals or immigrants making their literacy known through writing. These narratives, built through a working-class ethos of collectivity and solidarity, contribute to an expansive vision of literacy across countries, languages, and generations.

Through the development of writing groups, the production of texts, the circulation of writing, and now the archiving of this writing, the FWWCP/FED and the FWWCP Archival Project have preserved a working-class writing network. This archive shows us how community groups responded in ways that made sense to them and challenged what didn't; they did this through linguistic and cultural differences, across geopolitical spaces, and within diverse educational contexts. Over and over, the FWWCP/FED challenged the structures and discourses that excluded them and renegotiated their practices to reflect expansive approaches to class.

On an ethical level, I hope that centering class, focusing on precarity, and highlighting a transnational network of working-class people through partnership work pushes the field to value working-class voices and problematize deficit narratives. Doing so allows us to see the valuable ways worker writers use literacy to meaningfully engage in rhetorical acts that can produce social change and to embody multiple forms of expertise. As these stories illustrate, laboring can instill varied senses—of pride, shame, hope, despair—in working-class communities and form the focus of how they articulate their identity in the spaces around them. More than that, though, I hope that we also continue to make visible the material conditions and ideological views that shape how and why some stories are preserved while others are not.

Ultimately, the FWWCP Collection provides examples of working-class solidarity through writing and publishing—not only as an end point but as a process of community. The work of these writers shows how working-class communities generate new literacy practices and perform rhetorical acts in response to their own needs. Through the FWWCP Collection, we have a model of what grassroots community organizing looks like, how community-led writing, teaching, and publishing function, and what self-generated community work can teach us about the process of writing together and building solidarity. It is this belief in solidarity that I believe can motivate others to continue telling their stories and reading beyond the text for the humanity of each writer.

Preface: Factory Foundations and Rust-Belt Beginnings

1. *Busia, busha,* and *babcia* are the most common Polish spellings for *grandma,* but we've always spelled it *bushia,* so I have stuck to this personal albeit technically incorrect, spelling here.
2. See terminology and abbreviations page.

1. Becoming a Worker Writer

3. The FWWCP had different levels of membership, based on whether groups could attend the Annual General Meeting.
4. Between 2013 and the present, the members of the executive committee have changed a little, but those listed here have been the main motivators of the FWWCP Archival Project.
5. For instance, valuable labor-based collections such as the International Workers of the World (IWW) or *Arab Americans and the Automobile—Voices from the Factory Collection* and others are not specifically focused on the creation of working-class writing.
6. I heard about the FWWCP first from Parks and Pollard's article "The Extra-Curricular of Composition: A Dialogue on Community Publishing," which sparked my interest in studying community partnership work. Then, taking my first course with Steve Parks in 2012, I saw even more connections between my personal life and academia.
7. This is a Liverpool phrase meaning "delighted" or "very pleased."
8. This represents the universities currently involved through the organizational labor of Steve Parks, Jenny Harding, Nick Pollard, and me. However, as people changed jobs, more universities and scholars have lent support along the way.
9. Individual donations have been made to the Working-Class Movement Library in Manchester, England, and Bishopsgate Institute in London, which are both phenomenal sites to explore working-class histories. In terms of scope, however, neither site provides an extensive overview nor houses a comparable and large-scale representation of

FWWCP/FED publications and administrative documents as the TUC.

10. Beyond the printed FWWCP Collection, we have worked to reanimate the FWWCP/FED histories through the FWWCP Digital Collection beginning to make these documents accessible worldwide (see Pauszek "Preserving Hope"). This site now exists at fwwcpdigitalcollection.org.

11. Michelle Caswell and other archival scholars understandably critique those who overlook that archives are tangible and that critical archival studies (a whole discipline) centers around this labor.

12. While FWWCP/FED members describe themselves as "working class" and use the term for purposes of class solidarity, many fall into the category of "working poor" or fluctuate between working and looking for work. As Penney and Lovejoy note, further designations of class such as the "welfare class" might better describe some people's experiences ("Navigating"). Here, I use "working class" most prevalently because that comes from the community I'm collaborating with; however, I will also describe moments of class negotiation, discrepancies, and naming distinctions.

13. Trimbur wrote this in a 1993 review of Richard Ohmann's *English in America*. Interestingly, Ohmann's book was published the same year the FWWCP began.

2. Building a Federation

14. While traditionally we refer to scholars by their last name, I struggled with this question throughout this project. I have chosen to use first names as an indication of the deeply personal relationships created through this project and the community-based values of the FWWCP/FED. I want to foreground those principles in first-name references to members as we would in person. However, as this book argues, FWWCP/FED members should be taken seriously as intellectuals.

15. As I write, Sally is ninety-nine. Sally continued writing into her nineties.

16. I have transcribed this moment to showcase Sally's accent and speech patterns as I heard them. The politics of transcription are complex, and I've tried to highlight the nuance of Sally's language, dropping letters and contracting words. However, in the remaining transcriptions I have chosen to keep the letter *h* for readability.

17. Yiddish word for *temple*.

18. I am grateful to Emma for making me aware of this Lorde work.

19. While there are different ways to refer to this conflict, the naming here comes from the National Archives in the UK.
20. Risa Applegarth notes the rarity of scholarship on "children exercising rhetorical agency" (52), and in many ways, this framing fits not only the children of Stepney but also the working-class adults. While it's beyond the scope of this chapter, the students' organizing and poetry highlight their rhetorical prowess.
21. Jennifer Harding, Steve Parks, Nick Pollard, and I have written about the importance of this moment for various FWWCP writers (see "Alliances").
22. The strike also resonated deeply with the students. As one of Searle's students recounted years later, *Stepney Words* provided a new means of agency for those involved to make their voices publicly known: "It was one of the proudest days of my life, it taught me that you can make a stand. It was about dignified mutual respect [. . . Searle] believed everyone could produce work of value" (qtd. in The gentle author, "The Stepney").

3. Biscit Politics

23. The use of "Pecket" illustrates how members choose to name and represent themselves as a collective. In most examples that I use, Pecket has decided to write in a collective voice rather than be acknowledged individually.
24. Most members dislike the term *literacy* because they were often framed negatively as being "illiterate," as I indicate here. However, I use these terms in order to describe the affordances of the group's work, their capabilities, and to show how Pecket breaks this binary of il/literacy.
25. The SNCC Digital Gateway is an exciting new resource with primary and secondary history about Highlander, the Citizenship Schools, Freedom Schools, and more, including key figures like Septima Clark (see "Septima Clark").
26. Spelling and dialect choices made by Pecket Wellians are kept throughout this chapter.
27. This tension with language was also represented in the United States' college education policies and the need to create the "Students' Right to Their Own Language" resolution that encouraged teachers to seek to understand linguistic disparities and to make these differences a useful part of learning rather than a means of deficit or exclusion. See Conference on College Composition and Communication.

28. In *Literacy, Economy, and Power*, scholars have complicated Brandt's work to explore "how the concept of sponsorship has been appropriated and used" (Duffy et al. 3). This work touches on the need for universities to undergo ideological shifts, but Pecket pushes on these examples, thinking about self-directed community sponsorship.

29. See Ross for additional Pecket members.

30. Some individual FWWCP groups were able to receive regional funding such as Yorkshire Arts funding and North West Arts funding, etc.

31. Although the physical structure of Pecket Well College was sold in 2011, the money from the building went on to preserve the legacy of Pecket through an oral history and archival project that continued through 2014.

32. Scholars have written about the intersections between university and community structures via the *public turn* and community engagement projects, particularly thinking through the ethical and logistical questions of working with communities (Deans et al.; Goldblatt; Mathieu; Parks, "Strategic"; Restaino and Cella). These projects show multiple models for conceptualizing community work, but they provide a vision of literacy and sponsorship that relies on institutional support more so than self-directed work like Pecket's.

4. Archival Labor

33. In recent years, I have been able to rely on exciting work done by Ellen Cushman ("Language"), Janice W. Fernheimer et al. ("Sustainable Stewardship"), K. J. Rawson ("The Rhetorical"), and Jim Ridolfo et al., to discuss the implications of creating *digital* archives connected to various marginalized communities. Still, though, I was navigating material concerns with developing a physical archive in London (as well as a digital one) while my own location and institutional affiliations shifted.

34. *Co-opted* is a common FWWCP/FED term that signals support. Co-opting someone in this context means appointing or inviting them into a group or committee, which illustrated an important moment of acceptance and trust.

35. Pollard began collecting FWWCP materials in 1982 and was an executive member from 1985 to 1989, 1991 to 2007, and editor of *Federation Magazine* from 1991 to 2007. This work gave him access to many publications and minutes and gave him the ability collect more with travel to executive meetings across the country.

36. For each study-abroad class, we developed a collaborative publication, reflecting on attending writing groups, meeting members, and processing archival materials. See Barlow et al.; Pauszek, *Preserving Hidden Histories;* Pauszek and Portillo, "The Federation."

37. We are currently revising naming conventions as the metadata is moved into a new system at the TUC at LMU. An alternative code for this publication will be TUC/FWWCP/H/02/009.

38. See Pauszek, "Preserving Hope" for a further digital archival discussion.

5. Worker Writer Solidarity

39. Because this chapter focuses on documents from the original 1976 to 2007 time frame of the network, I am distinctly using "FWWCP" in most moments to indicate this specific chronology.

40. Here, I'm reminded of Andrea Lunsford's argument that we must pay attention to "composing ourselves" (72) as a field.

41. See Federation of Worker Writers and Community Publishers in the bibliography for all subsequent "Federation" citations.

42. It is almost certain that additional constitutional revisions were made, but I've only indicated the documents we have evidence of in the archive.

43. Nick Pollard remembers that in the 1980s, some FWWCP publications circulated in schools through the Inner London Education Authority Booklist as well as through the National Association for the Teaching of English (NATE). NATE also became a reciprocal FWWCP member years later.

44. A racialized split of the working class meant that political parties could draw loyalties from each of those groups, arguing for a nationalistic rhetoric and effectively diminishing the solidarity of class-based groups. Such rhetoric conflates nationalism with white, English identity. Jones describes this strategy for those in the far-right British National Party, arguing that it "cynically manipulated mainstream multiculturalism," having the effect of "recasting white working-class people as an oppressed ethnic minority, allowing [the BNP] to appropriate anti-racist language" for white working-class British people (234).

45. I have chosen not to use the full member's name here because this correspondence was meant to circulate to the executive committee.

Conclusion

46. Chris M. Anson describes the Dartmouth Seminar's impact on the "Universe of Writing Studies" in terms of graduate programs, journal

development, and expansion of research methods in "After the Big Bang: The Expanding Universe of Writing Studies."

47. Stuckey's focus on bringing attention to perspectives of pupils and family members of a Syracuse asylum school differs from my focus on working-class writers, but Stuckey's methodological framework is a valuable tool that asks us to listen ethically and openly to what and who has been silenced.

48. On Vee and McIntyre's list of participants, Frederic Cassidy is listed as being Jamaican/American nationality but coming from a university in America. In the proposal, he was one of the alternative delegates, but he did attend.

WORKS CITED

Agbah, Florence. 'The Hole in the Wall." *Beyond the Green Door*, 10 Jan. 2015, https://web.archive.org/web/20181211032131/http://pecket.org/green-door/the-hole-in-the-wall/.

Agbah, Florence, et al. "Hudds Interview." Interview by Jessica Pauszek. 2015.

Al Tech Update: Cleanup Action to Begin at Superfund Site. New York State Department of Environmental Conservation, Mar. 2014, https://www.dec.ny.gov/docs/remediation_hudson_pdf/atsscfs.pdf.

Alvarez, Steven. *Brokering Tareas: Mexican Immigrant Families Translanguaging Homework Literacies*. State U of New York P, 2017.

Anson, Chris M. "After the Big Bang: The Expanding Universe of Writing Studies." *The Expanding Universe of Writing Studies: Higher Education Writing Research*, edited by Kelly Blewett, et al., Peter Lang, 2021, pp. 5–26.

Applegarth, Risa. "Children Speaking: Agency and Public Memory in the Children's Peace Statue Project." *Rhetoric Society Quarterly*, vol. 47, no. 1, 2017, pp. 49–73.

Barlow, Zachary, et al., editors. *Crossroads: The Writing of the Trans-Atlantic Worker Writer Federation*. Parlor Press, 2016.

Barnsley Miners Wives Action Group. *We Struggled to Laugh*. 1987. FWWCP Collection. TUC/FWWCP/TUC Teaching Collection. TUC Library Collections at London Metropolitan University, London, England.

Barton, David, and Mary Hamilton. *Local Literacies: Reading and Writing in One Community*. Routledge, 1998.

Billington, Michael. "Margaret Thatcher Casts a Long Shadow over Theatre and the Arts." *The Guardian*, 8 Apr. 2013, www.theguardian.com/stage/2013/apr/08/margaret-thatcher-long-shadow-theatre.

Bloom, Lynn Z. "Freshman Composition as a Middle-Class Enterprise." *College English*, vol. 58, no. 6, 1996, pp. 654–75.

Boyd, Phil. "Editorial." *Voices 25,* 1981, pp. 1–2. FWWCP Collection. TUC/FWWCP/A/08. TUC Library Collections at London Metropolitan University, London, England.

Branch, Kirk. *"Eyes on the Ought to Be": What We Teach When We Teach about Literacy.* Hampton Press, 2007.

Brandt, Deborah. "Sponsors of Literacy." *College Composition & Communication,* vol. 49, no. 2, 1998, pp. 165–85.

Britton, James. *A Language for Life (Report of the Committee of Inquiry Appointed by the Secretary of State for Education and Science under the Chairmanship of Sir Alan Bullock F. B. A.).* Her Majesty's Stationery Office, 1975.

———. "The Dartmouth Seminar—Elegy or Eulogy?" Institute of Education Archive, 1986. James Nimmo Britton Collection. UCL Special Collections, IOE Archives. London.

Carter, Genesea, and William Thelin, editors. *Class in the Composition Classroom: Pedagogy and the Working Class.* UP of Colorado, 2017.

Carter, Shannon, and James Conrad. "In Possession of Community: Toward a More Sustainable Local." *College Composition & Communication,* vol. 64, no. 1, 2012, pp. 82–106.

Caswell, Michelle. "'The Archive' Is Not an Archives: Acknowledging the Intellectual Contributions of Archival Studies." *Reconstruction: Studies in Contemporary Culture,* vol. 16, no. 1, 2016, http://reconstruction.digitalodu.com/Issues/161/Caswell.shtml.

Caws, Peter. Memorandum from Peter Caws as preface to the proposal (1966). 16 Nov. 1965. Carnegie Corporation Archives, 716.1. Anglo-American Seminar on the Teaching of English, 1964–1977. Columbia University. *Dartmouth '66 Seminar Exhibit,* https://wac.colostate.edu/repository/exhibits/dartmouth/selection-of-13-documents/6-memorandum/.

Cedillo, Christina V., and Phil Bratta. "Relating Our Experiences: The Practice of Positionality Stories in Student-Centered Pedagogy." *College Composition & Communication,* vol. 71, no. 2, 2019, pp. 215–40.

Community Archives and Heritage Group. "Home." www.communityarchives.org.uk/index.php. Accessed 10 Aug. 2024.

Conference on College Composition & Communication. "Students' Right to Their Own Language." *College Composition & Communication,* vol. 25, 1974.

Crenshaw, Kimberlé. "Demarginalizing the Intersection of Race and Sex: A Black Feminist Critique of Antidiscrimination Doctrine, Feminist Theory and Antiracist Politics." *University of Chicago Legal Forum,* vol. 1989, no. 1, pp. 139–67.

————. "She Coined the Term 'Intersectionality' Over 30 Years Ago. Here's What It Means to Her Today." Interview by Katy Steinmetz. *Inequality Now*, special issue of *TIME*, 20 Feb. 2020, https://time.com/5786710/kimberle-crenshaw-intersectionality/.

Cresswell, Tim. "Place." *The SAGE Handbook of Human Geography*, edited by Roger Lee, et al. SAGE, 2014, pp. 3–21.

Cushman, Ellen. "Language Perseverance and Translation of Cherokee Documents." *College English*, vol. 82, no. 1, 2019, pp. 115–34.

————. "Wampum, Sequoyan, and Story: Decolonizing the Digital Archive." *College English*, vol. 76, no. 2, 2013, pp. 115–35.

Daniel, James Rushing. "Freshman Composition as a Precariat Enterprise." *College English*, vol. 80, no. 1, 2017, pp. 63–85.

————. *Toward an Anti-Capitalist Composition*. Utah State UP, 2022.

Deans, Thomas, et al., editors. *Writing and Community Engagement: A Critical Sourcebook*. Bedford/St. Martin's, 2010.

DeGenaro, William. "'The New Deal': Burkean Identification and Working-Class Poetics." *Rhetoric Review*, vol. 26, no. 4, 2007, pp. 385–404.

DeGenaro, William, editor. *Who Says? Working-Class Rhetoric, Class Consciousness, and Community*. U of Pittsburgh P, 2007.

DePalma, Michael-John. "Archives as Resources for Ethical In(ter)vention in Community-Based Writing." *Teaching through the Archives: Text, Collaboration, and Activism*, edited by Tarez Samra Graban and Wendy Hayden, Southern Illinois UP, 2022, pp. 212–26.

Desser, Daphne. "Reading and Writing the Family: Ethos, Identification, and Identity in My Great-Grandfather's Letters." *Rhetoric Review*, vol. 20, no. 3–4, 2001, pp. 314–28.

Douglas, Whitney. "Looking Outward: Archival Research as Community Engagement." *Community Literacy Journal*, vol. 11, no. 2, 2017, pp. 30–42.

Duffy, John, et al., editors. *Literacy, Economy, and Power: Writing and Research after Literacy in American Lives*. Southern Illinois UP, 2013.

Dunbar-Odom, Donna. *Defying the Odds: Class and the Pursuit of Higher Literacy*. State U of New York P, 2007.

Durst, Russel K. "British Invasion: James Britton, Composition Studies, and Anti-Disciplinarity." *College Composition & Communication*, vol. 66, no. 3, 2015, pp. 384–401.

Eck, Susan J. "Brooks Locomotive." *Western New York History*, https://wnyhistory.org/portfolios/businessindustry/RAILROADS/brooks_locomotive/brooks_locomotive.html.

Enoch, Jessica. "Coalition Talk: Feminist Historiography: What's the Digital Humanities Got to Do with It?" *Peitho Journal*, vol. 15, no. 2, 2013, pp. 40–45.

———. *Domestic Occupations: Spatial Rhetorics and Women's Work.* Southern Illinois UP, 2019.

———. *Refiguring Rhetorical Education: Women Teaching African American, Native American, and Chicano/a Students, 1865–1911.* Southern Illinois UP, 2008.

Enoch, Jessica, and David Gold. "Seizing the Methodological Moment: The Digital Humanities and Historiography in Rhetoric and Composition." *College English*, vol. 76, no. 2, 2013, pp. 105–14.

Epps-Robertson, Candace. *Resisting Brown: Race, Literacy, and Citizenship in the Heart of Virginia.* U of Pittsburgh P, 2018.

Federation of Worker Writers and Community Publishers. "Agenda and Minutes." 1986. FWWCP Collection. TUC/FWWCP. TUC Library Collections at London Metropolitan University, London, England.

———. "A.G.M. 1987." FWWCP Collection. TUC/FWWCP/O/05 Minutes. TUC Library Collections at London Metropolitan University, London, England.

———. "Anti-Racist and Sexism Statement." 1986. FWWCP Collection. TUC/FWWCP/O. TUC Library Collections at London Metropolitan University, London, England.

———. *Booknews: A Newsletter for People in Education,* no. 1. 1988. FWWCP Collection. TUC/FWWCP/H/12. TUC Library Collections at London Metropolitan University, London, England.

———. "Constitution."1978. FWWCP Collection. TUC/FWWCP/ O/04 Constitutional. TUC Library Collections at London Metropolitan University, London, England.

———. "Constitution Amended at the AGM on 16th April 1988." FWWCP Collection. TUC/FWWCP/O/04 Constitutional. TUC Library Collections at London Metropolitan University, London, England.

———. "Constitution 1991." 1991. FWWCP Collection. TUC/FWW CP/O/04 Constitutional. TUC Library Collections at London Metropolitan University, London, England.

———. "Development Report November 1989." 1989. FWWCP Collection. TUC/FWWCP/O/09 Development Reports. TUC Library Collections at London Metropolitan University, London, England.

———. "Equal Opportunities Statement." 1980. FWWCP Collection.

TUC/FWWCP/O/04 Constitutional. TUC Library Collections at London Metropolitan University, London, England.

———. *FedNews Issue 1*. 1989. FWWCP Collection. TUC/FWWCP/O/01 Federation Magazines. TUC Library Collections at London Metropolitan University, London, England.

———. *FedNews Issue 3*. 1990. FWWCP Collection. TUC/FWWCP/O/01 Federation Magazines. TUC Library Collections at London Metro-politan University, London, England.

———. "Full Membership 1993/1994." 1994. FWWCP Collection. TUC/FWWCP/O/09. Development Reports. TUC Library Collections at London Metropolitan University, London, England.

———. "Income and Expenditure." 1985. FWWCP Collection. TUC/FWWCP/O/09 Development Reports. TUC Library Collections at London Metropolitan University, London, England.

———. "Minerpoets." 1984. FWWCP Collection. TUC/FWWCP/Roger Mills. TUC Library Collections at London Metropolitan University, London, England.

———. "Minutes from Executive Meeting No. 8." 1986. FWWCP Collection. TUC/FWWCP/O/09 Development Reports. TUC Library Collections at London Metropolitan University, London, England.

———. "Minutes of Plenary Session." January 24, 1987. FWWCP Collection. TUC/FWWCP/O/09 Development Reports. TUC Library Collections at London Metropolitan University, London, England.

———. Newsletter. 1987. FWWCP Collection. TUC/FWWCP/Roger Mills. TUC Library Collections at London Metropolitan University, London, England.

———. *Once I Was a Washing Machine*. 1989. FWWCP Collection. TUC/FWWCP/C/02 Anthologies and Publications. TUC Library Collections at London Metropolitan University, London, England.

———. "Strategy Report: The Federation and Its Membership." 1995–1996. TUC/FWWCP/O/09 Development Reports. TUC Library Collections at London Metro-politan University, London, England.

———. *Voices no. 30*. 1983/1984. FWWCP Collection. TUC/FWWCP/A/08. TUC Library Collections at London Metropolitan University, London, England.

———. *Writing*. 1978. FWWCP Collection. TUC/FWWCP/O/02 Anthologies and Publications. TUC Library Collections at London Metropolitan University, London, England.

———. "Writing and Equal Opportunities." 1992. FWWCP Collection. TUC/FWWCP/O. TUC Library Collections at London Metropolitan University, London, England.

Fernheimer, Janice W., et al. "Learning to (Re)Compose Identities: Creating and Indexing the JHFE Jewish Kentucky Oral History Repository with Undergraduate Researchers and Jewish Rhetorical Practices." *Teaching through the Archives: Text, Collaboration, and Activism*, edited by Tarez Samra Graban and Wendy Hayden, Southern Illinois UP, 2022, pp. 227–47.

Fernheimer, Janice W., et al. "Sustainable Stewardship: A Collaborative Model for Engaged Oral History Pedagogy, Community Partnership, and Archival Growth." *The Oral History Review*, vol. 45, no. 2, 2018, pp. 321–41.

"Finding Aid Type." *National Archives and Records Administration*, www.archives.gov/research/catalog/lcdrg/elements/findingtype.html.

Flinn, Andrew, et al. "Whose Memories, Whose Archives? Independent Community Archives, Autonomy and the Mainstream." *Archival Science*, vol. 9, 2009, pp. 71–86.

Flood, Sally. "FED Festival Interview." Interview by Jessica Pauszek, 20 Nov. 2013.

———. "Mount Terrace Interview." Interview by Jessica Pauszek, 15 June 2015.

———. *Paper Talk.* 1979. FWWCP Collection. TUC/FWWCP/H/02/009. TUC Library Collections at London Metropolitan University, London, England.

———. *Window on Brick Lane.* 1980. FWWCP Collection. TUC/FWWCP/TUC Teaching Collection. TUC Library Collections at London Metropolitan University, London, England.

———. "Working Together Alone." *Women's Review*, no. 4, 1980, p. 31. TUC/FWWCP/O/05 Minutes. TUC Library Collections at London Metropolitan University, London, England.

Freire, Paulo. *Pedagogy of Freedom: Ethics, Democracy, and Civic Courage.* Translated by Patrick Clarke, Rowman & Littlefield, 1998.

FWWCP Digital Collection. The Federation of Worker Writers and Community Publishers, https://fwwcpdigitalcollection.org.

Gere, Anne Ruggles. "Kitchen Tables and Rented Rooms: The Extracurriculum of Composition." *College Composition & Communication*, vol. 45, no. 1, 1994, pp. 75–92.

Glenn, Cheryl, and Jessica Enoch. "Invigorating Historiographic Practices in Rhetoric and Composition Studies." *Working in the Archives: Practical Research Methods for Rhetoric and Composition*, edited by Alexis E. Ramsey, et al., Southern Illinois UP, 2009, pp. 11–27.

Glynn, Sarah. "The Spirit of '71: How the Bangladeshi War of Independence Has Haunted Tower Hamlets." *Socialist History Journal*, no. 29, 2006, pp. 56–75.

Gold, David. "Remapping Revisionist Historiography." *Research Methodologies*, special issue of *College Composition & Communication*, vol. 64, no. 1, 2012, pp. 15–34.

Gold, David, and Jessica Enoch, editors. *Women at Work: Rhetorics of Gender and Labor*. U of Pittsburgh P, 2019.

Goldblatt, Eli. "Alinsky's Reveille: A Community-Organizing Model for Neighborhood-Based Literacy Projects." *College English*, vol. 67, no. 3, 2005, pp. 274–95.

Graban, Tarez Samra, and Wendy Hayden, editors. *Teaching through the Archives: Text, Collaboration, and Activism*. Southern Illinois UP, 2022.

Gramsci, Antonio. *Selections from the Prison Notebooks*. Edited and translated by Quintin Hoare and Geoffrey Nowell Smith, International Publishers, 1971.

"GROW Constitution." *Grass Roots Open Writers*, https://www.hugofox .com/community/grass-roots-open-writers-grow-19770/constitution/.

Gruwell, Leigh. *Making Matters: Craft, Ethics, and New Materialist Rhetorics*. Utah State UP, 2022.

Hamilton, Mary, et al. "Learner Voices at Pecket: Past and Present." *Fine Print*, vol. 37, no. 1, 2014, pp. 15–20.

Harding, Jennifer, et al. "Alliances, Assemblages, and Affects: Three Moments of Building Collective Working-Class Literacies." *College Composition & Communication*, vol. 70, no. 1, 2018, pp. 6–29.

Harris, Joseph. "Updating Dartmouth." *The Power of Writing: Dartmouth '66 in the Twenty-First Century*, edited by Christiane Donahue and Kelly Blewett, Dartmouth College Press, 2015, pp. ix–xix.

Hesford, Wendy S., et al. *Precarious Rhetorics*. The Ohio State UP, 2018.

Hickey, Laureen. "Different Backgrounds." 1986. FWWCP Collection. TUC/FWWCP/O/07-09. TUC Library Collections at London Metropolitan University. London, England.

———. "Gender and Class Workshop." 1992. FWWCP Collection. TUC/FWWCP/C/07-09. FWWCP Collection. TUC Library Collections at London Metropolitan University, London, England.

Honeychurch, Joyce. "Language, Cognition, and Learning: Expressive Writing in the Classroom." *Journal of Curriculum and Supervision*, vol. 5, no. 4, 1990, pp. 328–57.

Howarth, Jeff. "TUC Library Acquires Federation of Worker Writers and Community Publishers Archive Deposit." *Trades Union Congress Library Collections Blog*, 1 Aug. 2014.

Jackson, Mike. "Lesbians and Gays Support the Miners (Bishopsgate Archive)." *Bishopsgate Institute*, n.d., https://www.bishopsgate.org.uk/ collections/lesbians-and-gays-support-the-miners-bishopsgate-archive.

Jackson, Rachel C., and Dorothy Whitehorse DeLaune. "Decolonizing Community Writing with Community Listening: Story, Transrhetorical Resistance, and Indigenous Cultural Literacy Activism." *Community Literacy Journal*, vol. 13, no. 1, 2018, pp. 37–54.

Jacobs, Dale, editor. *The Myles Horton Reader: Education for Social Change.* U of Tennessee P, 2003.

Jarratt, Susan C. "Speaking to the Past: Feminist Historiography in Rhetoric." *Walking and Talking Feminist Rhetorics: Landmark Essays and Controversies*, edited by Lindal Buchanan and Kathleen J. Ryan, Parlor Press, 2010, pp. 19–34.

John, Corrine. "Interview with Corrine John." Interview by Pol Nugent. *Beyond the Green Door*, 1 Dec. 2014, https://web.archive.org/web/20170421104041/http://pecket.org/green-door/interview-with-corinne-john/.

Jones, Owen. *Chavs: The Demonization of the Working Class.* Verso, 2012.

Kahn, Seth, et al., editors. *Contingency, Exploitation, and Solidarity: Labor and Action in English Composition.* WAC Clearinghouse/UP of Colorado, 2017.

Kannan, Vani, et al. "Performing Horizontal Activism: Expanding Academic Labor Advocacy throughout and beyond a Three-Step Process." *Literacy in Composition Studies*, vol. 3, no. 1, Mar. 2015, pp. 131–42.

Kates, Susan. "Literacy, Voting Rights, and the Citizenship Schools in the South, 1957–1970." *College Composition & Communication*, vol. 57, no. 3, 2006, pp. 479–502.

Kirk, John. *Twentieth-Century Writing and the British Working Class.* U of Wales P, 2003.

Kirkland, Michael. "Archivist." FWWCP Collection. TUC/FWWCP/O/05 Minutes. TUC Library Collections at London Metropolitan University, London, England.

Kirsch, Gesa E., et al. "Unsettling the Archives." Special issue of *Across the Disciplines*, vol. 18, no. 1/2, 2021, https://wac.colostate.edu/atd/special/archives/.

Kirsch, Gesa E., et al., editors. *Unsettling Archival Research: Engaging Critical, Communal, and Digital Archives.* Southern Illinois UP, 2023.

Kirsch, Gesa E., and Liz Rohan, editors. *Beyond the Archives: Research as a Lived Process.* Southern Illinois UP, 2008.

Kitzhaber, Albert, and Peter Caws. Record of telephone conversation between Albert Kitzhaber and Caws, 1964. Carnegie Corporation Archives, 716.1. Anglo-American Seminar on the Teaching of English,

1964-1977. Columbia University. *Dartmouth '66 Seminar Exhibit*, https://wac.colostate.edu/repository/exhibits/dartmouth/selection-of-13-documents/1-telephone-record/.

Lathan, Rhea Estelle. "Testimony as a Sponsor of Literacy: Bernice Robinson and the South Carolina Sea Island Citizenship Program's Literacy Activism." *Literacy, Economy, and Power: Writing and Research after Literacy in American Lives*, edited by John Duffy et al., Southern Illinois UP, 2014, pp. 30–44.

Ławicki II, James L., and Andrzej D. Gołębiowski. "Kosciuszko Polish Home Association." *Polonia Trail Western New York*, 3 June 2016, https://poloniatrail.com/location/kosciuszko-polish-home-association.

L'Eplattenier, Barbara E. "An Argument for Archival Research Methods: Thinking beyond Methodology." *College English*, vol. 72, no. 1, 2009, pp. 67–79.

Lindquist, Julie. *A Place to Stand: Politics and Persuasion in a Working-Class Bar*. Oxford UP, 2002.

Linkon, Sherry Lee. *The Half-Life of Deindustrialization: Working-Class Writing about Economic Restructuring*. U of Michigan P, 2018.

Linkon, Sherry Lee, and John Russo. "Twenty Years of Working-Class Studies: Tensions, Values, and Core Questions." *Journal of Working-Class Studies*, vol. 1, no. 1, 2016, pp. 4–13.

Liverpool 8 Writers' Workshop. "Socialist or Working Class? A Position Paper." 1980. FWWCP Collection. TUC/FWWCP/Roger Mills. TUC Library Collections at London Metropolitan University, London, England.

Lorde, Audre. *Sister Outsider: Essays and Speeches*. Crossing Press, 1984.

Lunsford, Andrea A. "Composing Ourselves: Politics, Commitment, and the Teaching of Writing." *College Composition & Communication*, vol. 41, no. 1, 1990, pp. 71–82.

Luther, Jason. "More than Paper Islands: The Pandemic Circuitry of Quaranzines." *Reflections: A Journal of Community-Engaged Writing and Rhetoric*, vol. 21, no. 1, 2022.

Mace, Jane. "Giving Voices to Worker Writers." *Arts Alert*, 1980. FWWCP Collection. TUC/FWWCP/O/13 Newpaper Articles, Pamphlets, and Ephemera. TUC Library Collections at London Metropolitan University, London, England.

Maguire, Paddy, et al. *The Republic of Letters: Working Class Writing and Local Publishing*, edited by Dave Morley and Ken Worpole. New City Community Press, 2009.

Marko, Tamera, et al. "Proyecto Carrito—When the Student Receives an 'A' and the Worker Gets Fired: Disrupting the Unequal Political Economy of Translingual Rhetorical Mobility". *Literacy in Composition Studies*, vol. 3, no. 1, 2015, pp. 21–43.

Martin, Tara. "The Beginning of Labor's End? Britain's 'Winter of Discontent' and Working-Class Women's Activism." *International Labor and Working-Class History*, no. 75, 2009, pp. 49–67.

Martinez, Aja Y. *Counterstory: The Rhetoric and Writing of Critical Race Theory*. National Council of Teachers of English, 2020.

Mathieu, Paula. *Tactics of Hope: The Public Turn in English Composition*. Boynton/Cook Publishers, 2005.

McGovern, Jimmy. "A Letter from Jimmy McGovern: Feminist Groups." *Voices no. 25*, 1981, pp. 26–28. FWWCP Collection. TUC/FWWCP/A/08. TUC Library Collections at London Metropolitan University, London, England.

Mills, Roger. *Everything Happens in Cable Street*. Five Leaves Publications, 2011.

———. "July 23 Mon." 1984. FWWCP Collection. TUC/FWWCP/Roger Mills. TUC Library Collections at London Metropolitan University, London, England.

Monberg, Terese Guinsatao. "Ownership, Access, and Authority: Publishing and Circulating Histories to (Re)Member Community." *Community Literacy Journal*, vol. 12, no. 1, 2017, pp. 30–47.

Mutnick, Deborah. "Pathways to Freedom: From the Archives to the Street." *College Composition & Communication*, vol. 69, no. 3, 2018, pp. 374–401.

Nowak, Mark. *Social Poetics*. Coffee House Press, 2020.

Nugent, Pol. "Pecket Interview." Interview by Jessica Pauszek. 23 June 2015.

"Origins and History." *Sir John Cass's Foundation*, 2004, https://sirjohn cassfoundation.com/about/originshistory/ (site inactive).

O'Rourke, Rebecca. "Chair's Report 1986–1987." 1987. FWWCP Collection. TUC/FWWCP/Roger Mills. TUC Library Collections at London Metropolitan University, London, England.

———. Response to Women's Day. 1986. FWWCP Collection. TUC/FWWCP/O. TUC Library Collections at London Metropolitan University, London, England.

Parks, Stephen. *Class Politics: The Movement for the Students' Right to Their Own Language*. 2nd ed., Parlor Press, 2013.

———. "Strategic Speculations on the Question of Value: The Role of Community Publishing in English Studies." *Unsustainable: Re-*

Imagining Community Literacy, Public Writing, Service-Learning, and the University, edited by Jessica Restaino and Laurie JC Cella, Lexington Books, 2013, pp. 55–78.

Parks, Steve, and Nick Pollard. "The Extra-Curricular of Composition: A Dialogue on Community-Publishing." *Community Literacy Journal*, vol. 3, no. 2, 2009, pp. 53–78.

Pauszek, Jessica, editor. *Preserving Hidden Histories*. New City Community Press, 2016.

Pauszek, Jessica. "Preserving Hope: Reanimating Working-Class Writing through (Digital) Archival Co-Creation." "Unsettling the Archives," special issue of *Across the Disciplines*, vol. 18, no. 1/2, 2021, pp. 145–61.

Pauszek, Jessica, and Vincent Portillo. "Collaborative Preservation of Working-Class Histories: The FWWCP Collection (Part 1)." *Trade Union Congress Library Collections Blog*, 16 July 2018, https://tuclibrary.blogs.londonmet.ac.uk/2018/07/16/collaborative-preservation-of-working-class-histories-the-fwwcp-collection-part-1/.

———. "Collaborative Preservation of Working-Class Histories: Social Concerns in the FWWCP Collection (Part 2)." *Trade Union Congress Library Collections Blog*, 6 Aug. 2018, https://tuclibrary.blogs.londonmet.ac.uk/2018/08/06/collaborative-preservation-of-working-class-histories-social-concerns-in-the-fwwcp-collection-part-2/.

———. "Collaborative Preservation of Working-Class Histories: Migration, Food, and Cultural Heritage in the FWWCP Collection (Part 3)." *Trade Union Congress Library Collections Blog*, 30 Aug. 2018, https://tuclibrary.blogs.londonmet.ac.uk/2018/08/30/collaborative-preservation-of-working-class-histories-migration-food-and-cultural-heritage-in-the-fwwcp-collection-part-3-by-jessica-pauszek-and-vincent-portillo/.

Pauszek, Jessica, and Vincent Portillo, editors. "The Federation of Worker Writers and Community Publishers Collection: An Introduction to the Trades Union Congress Library Holdings Including the FWWCP Publications and Administrative Documents." Finding Aids, 2019.

Pecket Learning Community. "Pecket!", 10 Jan. 2015, https://web.archive.org/web/20170521042257/http://pecket.org/.

———. "What We Mean by 'Access'." n.d. FWWCP Collection. TUC/FWWCP/C. TUC Library Collections at London Metropolitan University, London, England.

Pecket Well College. "Forging a Common Language, Sharing the Power." *Worlds of Literacy*, edited by Mary Hamilton, et al., Multilingual Matters, 1994, pp. 227–36.

————. *Opening Day Book.* Pecket Well College, 1992. FWWCP Collection. TUC/FWWCP/C/11. TUC Library Collections at London Metropolitan University, London, England.

————. *Sharing Dreams.* Pecket Well College, 1987.

Pells, Rachael. "London Metropolitan University cuts 400 jobs and closes two campuses." *The Independent,* 1 June 2016, https://www.independent.co.uk/news/education/education-news/london-metropolitan-university-cuts-400-jobs-and-closes-two-campuses-a7059231.html.

Penney, Emma. 2022. Unpublished manuscript.

Penney, Emma, and Laura Lovejoy. "Navigating Academia in the 'Welfare-Class.'" *Journal of Working-Class Studies,* vol. 2, no. 2, 2017, pp. 54–65.

Penney, Emma, and Sophie Meehan. "About." *Working Class Writing Archive.* http://workingclasswritingarchive.ie/.

Pollard, Nick. Personal correspondence. 20 Apr. 2024.

Powell, Katrina. "Hidden Archives: Revealing Untold Stories." *Journal of American Studies,* vol. 52, no. 1, 2018, pp. 26–44.

Powell, Malea. "2012 CCCC Chair's Address: Stories Take Place: A Performance in One Act." *College Composition & Communication,* vol. 64, no. 2, 2012, pp. 383–406.

————. "Dreaming Charles Eastman: Cultural Memory, Autobiography, and Geography in Indigenous Rhetorical Histories." *Beyond the Archives: Research as a Lived Process,* edited by Gesa E. Kirsch and Liz Rohan, Southern Illinois UP, 2008, pp. 115–27.

Pritchard, Eric Darnell. *Fashioning Lives: Black Queers and the Politics of Literacy.* Southern Illinois UP, 2016.

Ramsey, Alexis E., et al., editors. *Working in the Archives: Practical Research Methods for Rhetoric and Composition.* Southern Illinois UP, 2009.

Rawson, K. J. "Queering Feminist Rhetorical Canonization." *Rhetorica in Motion: Feminist Rhetorical Methods & Methodologies,* edited by Eileen E. Schell and K. J. Rawson, U of Pittsburgh P, 2010, pp. 39–52.

————. "The Rhetorical Power of Archival Description: Classifying Images of Gender Transgression." *Rhetoric Society Quarterly,* vol. 48, no. 4, 2018, pp. 327–51.

Restaino, Jessica. *Surrender: Feminist Rhetoric and Ethics in Love and Illness.* Southern Illinois UP, 2019.

Restaino, Jessica, and Laurie Cella, editors. *Unsustainable: Re-Imagining Community Literacy, Public Writing, Service-Learning and the University.* Lexington Books, 2013.

Ridolfo, Jim, et al. "Balancing Stakeholder Needs: Archive 2.0 as Community-Centered Design." *Ariadne,* vol. 63, 2010.

Riedner, Rachel. "Where Are the Women? Rhetoric of Gendered Labor in University Communities." *Literacy in Composition Studies*, vol. 3, no. 1, 2015, pp. 122–30.

Rose, Mike. *The Mind at Work: Valuing the Intelligence of the American Worker*. 2nd ed., Penguin, 2014.

Ross, Cilla. *Telling It! Our Oral History of Pecket Well College (1985–2014)*. Pecket Learning Community, 2014.

Royster, Jacqueline Jones. *Traces of a Stream: Literacy and Social Change among African American Women*. U of Pittsburgh P, 2000.

Royster, Jacqueline Jones, and Gesa E. Kirsch. *Feminist Rhetorical Practices: New Horizons for Rhetoric, Composition, and Literacy Studies*. Southern Illinois UP, 2012.

Russo, John, and Sherry Lee Linkon, editors. *New Working-Class Studies*. ILR Press, 2005.

———. "The Social Costs of Deindustrialization." *Manufacturing a Better Future for America*, edited by Richard McCormack, Alliance for American Manufacturing, 2009, pp. 183–215.

Scanlan, Alan. "Writing from the Margins: A Letter to the FWWCP Executive Committee." 1993. FWWCP Collection. TUC/FWWCP/O/06-09. TUC Library Collections at London Metropolitan University, London, England.

Schell, Eileen. *Gypsy Academics and Mother-Teachers: Gender, Contingent Labor, and Writing Instruction*. Heinemann, 1997.

Schneider, Stephen A. *You Can't Padlock an Idea: Rhetorical Education at the Highlander Folk School, 1932–1961*. U of South Carolina P, 2014.

Scotland Road '83. "Separatist Groups: The Great Debate." *Voices*, no. 30, 1983/1984, pp. 24–25. FWWCP Collection. TUC/FWWCP/A/08. TUC Library Collections at London Metropolitan University, London, England.

Searle, Chris. *Classrooms of Resistance*. Writers and Readers Publishing Cooperative, 1975.

———. *None but Our Words: Critical Literacy in Classroom and Community*. Open UP, 1998.

———. Personal communication. 2015.

Searle, Chris, editor. *Stepney Words*. Reality Press, 1971. FWWCP Collection. TUC/FWWCP/Roger Mills/ 02. TUC Library Collections at London Metropolitan University, London, England.

"Septima Clark." *SNCC Digital Gateway*, 26 Apr. 2018, https://snccdigital.org/people/septima-clark/.

Shipka, Jody. *Toward a Composition Made Whole*. U of Pittsburgh P, 2011.

Squire, James. Proposal for an International Seminar on the Teaching and Learning of English. 3 Nov. 1965. Carnegie Corporation Archives, 716.1. Anglo-American Seminar on the Teaching of English, 1964-1977. Columbia University. *Dartmouth '66 Seminar Exhibit*, https://wac.colostate.edu/repository/exhibits/dartmouth/selection-of-13-documents/4-proposal/.

———. Letter and Report from Squire to Caws. 20 Feb 1967. Carnegie Corporation Archives, 716.1. Anglo-American Seminar on the Teaching of English, 1964-1977. Columbia University. *Dartmouth '66 Seminar Exhibit*, https://wac.colostate.edu/repository/exhibits/dartmouth/selection-of-13-documents/11-letter-and-report/.

———. Letter from Squire to Caws. 23 Sept. Carnegie Corporation Archives, 716.1. Anglo-American Seminar on the Teaching of English, 1964-1977. Columbia University. *Dartmouth '66 Seminar Exhibit*, https://wac.colostate.edu/repository/exhibits/dartmouth/selection-of-13-documents/10-letter-from-squire-to-caws/.

Standing, Guy. *The Precariat: The New Dangerous Class*. Bloomsbury, 2011.

———. "The Precariat and Class Struggle." *RCCS Annual Review*, vol. 7, 2015, pp. 3–16. http://journals.openedition.org/rccsar/585.

Stuckey, Zosha. *A Rhetoric of Remnants: Idiots, Half-Wits, and Other State-Sponsored Inventions*. State U of New York P, 2014.

Tett, Lyn, et al., editors. *More Powerful Literacies*. NIACE, 2012.

TheFED. "Home." *TheFED—A Network of Writing and Community Publishers*, http://www.thefed.btck.co.uk/.

The gentle author. "The Stepney School Strike of 1971." *Spitalfields Life*, 16 Aug. 2011, https://spitalfieldslife.com/2011/08/16/the-stepney-school-strike-of-1971/.

Theimer, Kate. "Archives in Context and as Context." *Journal of Digital Humanities*, vol. 1, no. 2, 2012, pp. 1–2.

Thompson, Al. "Black and Asian Writers . . . and the FWWCP: A Report by Al Thompson to the FWWCP Executive & AGM." 10 Apr. 1990. FWWCP Collection. TUC/FWWCP/O/09-10 Development Reports. TUC Library Collections at London Metropolitan University, London, England.

T. J. "Letter to Executive Community." 1986. FWWCP Collection. TUC/FWWCP/O/06-09. TUC Library Collections at London Metropolitan University, London, England.

Trimbur, John. "Review of *English in America: A Radical View of the Profession*; *The Politics of Letters*, by Richard Ohmann." *College Composition & Communication*, vol. 44, no. 3, 1993, pp. 389–92.

————. "The Dartmouth Conference and the Geohistory of the Native Speaker." *College English*, vol. 71, no. 2, 2008, pp. 142–65.

"Unliterary." *Oxford English Dictionary,* https://www.oed.com/search/dictionary/?q=unliterary.

VanHaitsma, Pamela. "New Pedagogical Engagements with Archives: Student Inquiry and Composing in Digital Spaces." *College English*, vol. 78, no. 1, 2015, pp. 34–55.

Virdee, Satnam. "On Race, Class and the Politics of Solidarity." *Labor History Today* from Union City Radio, 2020, https://soundcloud.com/chrisgarlock/satnam-virdee-m4a.

Vee, Annette E. (curator) and Megan McIntyre (contributor). *Dartmouth '66 Seminar Exhibit.* WAC Clearinghouse, 2021, https://doi.org/10.37514/TWR-J.2021.1.1.01.

Wan, Amy. "Access and the Dartmouth Seminar." WAC Clearinghouse, 2022, https://wac.colostate.edu/repository/exhibits/dartmouth/critical-reflections/access-and-the-dartmouth-seminar/.

Warnick, Chris. "Locating the Archives: Finding Aids and Archival Scholarship in Composition and Rhetoric." *Working in the Archives: Practical Research Methods for Rhetoric and Composition*, edited by Alexis E. Ramsey, et al., Southern Illinois UP, 2009, pp. 91–101.

Welch, Nancy. *Living Room: Teaching Public Writing in a Privatized World.* Boynton/Cook Publishers, Inc., 2008.

Wells, Tim. "Stepney Words, Poetry and a Schoolkid's Strike." *Stand Up and Spit*, 14 Jan. 2016

"We Won't Be Terrorised out of Existence: Black Bookstores in England Resist Fascist Attacks." *The Black Scholar*, vol. 9, no. 10, 1978, pp. 45–47.

"What Are Archives?" *Society of American Archivists*, 12 Sept. 2016, https://www2.archivists.org/about-archives.

Williams, Raymond. "Culture Is Ordinary." *The Everyday Life Reader,* edited by Ben Highmore, Taylor & Francis, 2002, pp. 91–100.

Willis, Paul. *Learning to Labor: How Working Class Kids Get Working Class Jobs.* Columbia UP, 1977.

Women and Words. "Women and Words." *Voices no. 25*, 1982, pp. 29–30. 1981. FWWCP Collection. TUC/FWWCP/A/08. TUC Library Collections at London Metropolitan University, London, England.

Woodin, Tom. "'A Beginner Reader Is Not a Beginner Thinker': Student Publishing in Britain since the 1970s." *Paedagogica Historica: International Journal of the History of Education*, vol. 44, no. 1–2, 2008, pp. 219–32.

———. "Building Culture from the Bottom Up: The Educational Origins of the Federation of Worker Writers and Community Publishers." *History of Education*, vol. 34, no. 4, 2005, pp. 345–63.

———. *Working-Class Writing and Publishing in the Late Twentieth Century: Literature, Culture and Community.* Manchester UP, 2018.

Women of the Federation of Worker Writers and Community Publishers. *Move Over Adam: An Anthology of Short Stories.* Prescot, 1990. FWWCP Collection. TUC/FWWCP/O/02 Anthologies and Publications. TUC Library Collections at London Metropolitan University, London, England.

Zandy, Janet. *Hands: Physical Labor, Class, and Cultural Work.* Rutgers UP, 2004.

Zavala, Jimmy, et al. "'A Process Where We're All at the Table': Community Archives Challenging Dominant Modes of Archival Practice." *Archives and Manuscripts*, vol. 45, no. 3, 2017, pp. 202–15.

Zweig, Michael. *The Working Class Majority: America's Best Kept Secret.* 2nd ed., Cornell UP, 2012.

Works Referenced from the FWWCP Collection

Agbah, Florence. *The Survivor.* 1987. FWWCP Collection. No box. TUC Library Collections at London Metropolitan University, London, England.

———. *Ways of Learning.* 1987. FWWCP Collection. TUC/FWWCP/C/11. TUC Library Collections at London Metropolitan University, London, England.

Federation of Worker Writers and Community Publishers. *Federation News* and *Federation Magazine.* TUC/FWWCP/O/01 Federation News and Magazines. TUC Library Collections at London Metropolitan University, London, England.

———. *It's Our World as Well: Poetry and Prose by Children of the Federation of Worker Writers and Community Publishers.* 1990. TUC/FWWCP/O/02 Anthologies and Publications. TUC Library Collections at London Metropolitan University, London, England.

———. *Stories for Children.* 1989. TUC/FWWCP/O/02 Anthologies and Publications. TUC Library. Collections at London Metropolitan University, London, England.

———. *Voices no. 29.* 1983. FWWCP Collection. TUC/FWWCP/A/08. TUC Library Collections at London Metropolitan University, London, England.

Mills, Roger. *A Comprehensive Education.* 1978. FWWCP Collection. TUC/FWWCP/H/03. TUC Library. Collections at London Metropolitan University, London, England.

INDEX

AUTHOR

Jessica Pauszek is an assistant professor of English and director of first-year writing at Boston College. Her work brings together community literacy, working-class studies, archival methods, and digital humanities. Growing up in a predominantly Polish, working-class community in western New York shaped her interest in writing about labor, deindustrialization, immigration, and how we preserve these histories. Alongside community members in England, she has co-curated a print archive of thousands of working-class publications and administrative documents from the Federation of Worker Writers and Community Publishers at London Metropolitan University's Trades Union Congress Library. She has led the development of the digital collection at fwwcpdigitalcollection.org. Pauszek was awarded a CCCC Emergent Researcher Grant for this work and Honorable Mention for the 2018 CCCC James Berlin Outstanding Dissertation Award. She is coeditor of *The Best of the Journals in Rhetoric and Composition* and the *Working and Writing for Change Series* of Parlor Press. Her work has appeared in *Across the Disciplines, College Composition and Communication, Community Literacy Journal, Literacy in Composition Studies,* and *Reflections: A Journal of Community-Engaged Writing and Rhetoric.*

BOOKS IN THE CCCC STUDIES IN WRITING & RHETORIC SERIES

This book was typeset in Adobe Garamond and Myriad Pro by
Barbara Frazier.
Typefaces used on the cover include Garamond and News Gothic Std.